House of the Tiger King

House of the Tiger King

A Jungle Obsession

TAHIR SHAH

LARGE PRINT
Oxford

First published in Great Britain 2004
by
John Murray (Publishers)
a division of Hodder Headline

Published in Large Print 2006 by ISIS Publishing Ltd.,
7 Centremead, Osney Mead, Oxford OX2 0ES
by arrangement with
John Murray (Publishers)
a division of Hodder Headline

British Library Cataloguing in Publication Data
Shah, Tahir
House of the Tiger King. – Large print ed.
1. Shah, Tahir – Travel – Peru
2. Geographical myths
3. Incas – Peru – History
4. Large type books
5. Description and travel
I. Title
918.5'0465

ISBN 0–7531–5659–8 (hb)
ISBN 0–7531–5660–1 (pb)

Printed and bound in Great Britain by
T. J. International Ltd., Padstow, Cornwall

A Tomás, un gran viajero y un gran amigo

A journey is a fragment of Hell

Arab proverb

Contents

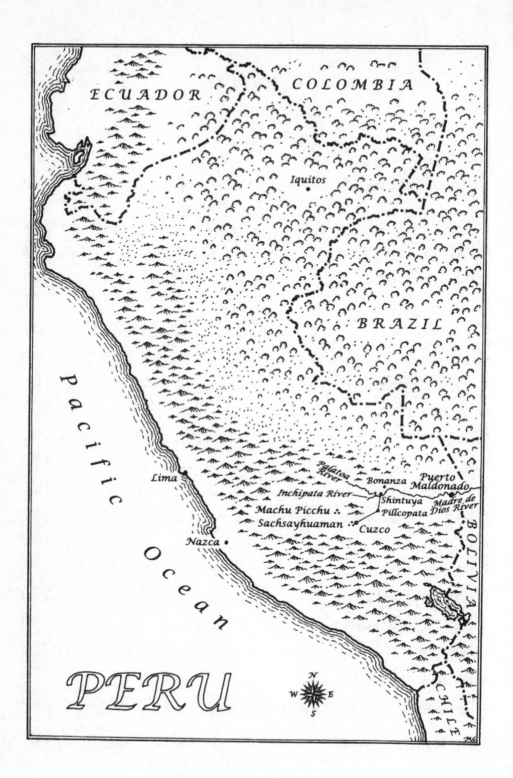

ECUADOR

COLOMBIA

Iquitos

BRAZIL

Pacific

Palatoa
River

Bonanza

Puerto
Maldonado

Lima

Inchipata River

Shintuya

Machu Picchu

Pillcopata

Madre de
Dios River

Sachsayhuaman

Cuzco

Nazca

Ocean

BOLIVIA

PERU

N
W   E
S

CHILE

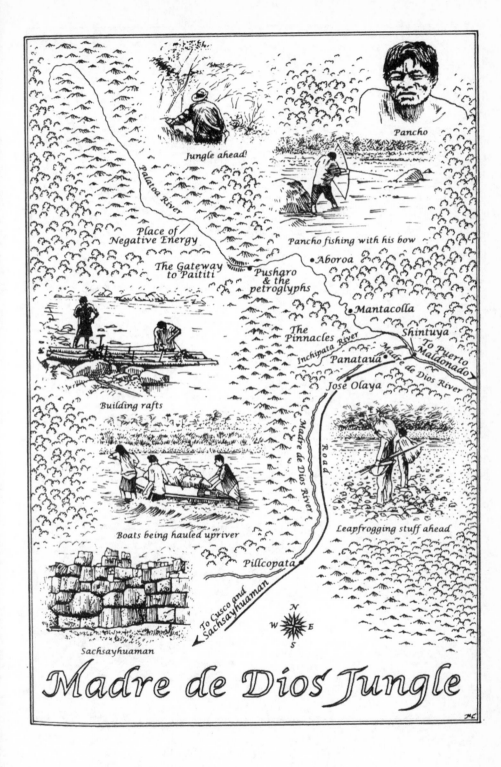

Jungle ahead!

Pancho

Pancho fishing with his bow

Palatoa River

Place of Negative Energy

The Gateway to Paititi

Pusharo & the petroglyphs

• Aboroa

• Mantacolla

The Pinnacles

Shintuya

Inchipata River

Madre de Dios River

To Puerto Maldonado

Panataua •

José Olaya

Building rafts

Madre de Dios River

Road

Leapfrogging stuff ahead

Boats being hauled upriver

Pillcopata

To Cusco and Sachsayhuaman

N
W   E
S

Sachsayhuaman

Madre de Dios Jungle

CHAPTER
ONE

Blistered Feet
To prevent the feet from blistering, it is a good plan to soap the inside of the stocking before setting out, making a thick lather all over it. A raw egg broken into the boot, before putting it on, greatly softens the leather.

The Art of Travel, Francis Galton, 1872

The men had lost their smiles and their cheap grins. Their cheeks were gaunt and unshaven, their eyes ringed with dark circles. I felt their hatred, their judgement. They would have killed me if they had thought they could get away with it. But their fatigue was so extreme that none of them could devise a plan by which to end my life.

We crouched on the shore, cold, crunching pebbles beneath our boots. No one had the energy to speak. We had progressed, or regressed, to a state of dumbness. Conversation merely reminded us of the suffering. With a fleeting telepathic glance I could now quiz the porters about their loads, tell them to rest, or give the detested order to move on.

The canopy of jungle hung like a tremendous barricade, concealing us from our world. There was an energy about it, a despicable power, a sense of consciousness. It watched you, scanning your movements, observing minutely as you stumbled ahead through the river. Thank God for the river. It was the only blessed thing for a thousand miles. The slick ribbon of water had allowed us to traverse the densest cloud-forest on earth, Madre de Dios, the Mother of God.

Morale was low, and with every mile it waned a little more. We had all lost the skin on our feet, eroded by the sand in the strong current, and each man had succumbed to the fits of dengue fever that savaged us in the long, insect-ridden nights. There was diarrhoea too, but the most accursed affliction was the guinea worms. They bored out from the soft tissue of our inner thighs mocking our feebleness.

The team of twelve porters had been chosen for their brute strength. It seemed like a lifetime ago that I had hired them, down at their village where the river was wide. They had been all smiles then, boasting of their muscles, their courage, their love of adversity. It had been I with the doubt, the fear, the dread. But after sixteen weeks in the jungle our roles had reversed. I had lost all fear and all doubt. I knew now that the ruins were up there, waiting for us. I was certain of it. It was a simple matter of perseverance, pushing ahead behind Pancho, our guide. Endure the unendurable a little longer, and the greatest lost city in history, Paititi, the El Dorado of the Incas, would be mine.

As we crouched there on our haunches, pack straps biting into our shoulders, Pancho straightened his left index finger, then directed it slowly towards the top of a

2

mountainous ridge. The men took a sudden breath. No one dared say a word.

"*Arriba*, up," he said, in a whisper. "Up there."

Following the course of the river was arduous, but at least it was possible. We all knew that hacking up into the undergrowth would be tantamount to suicide. As leader of the expedition, it fell to me to drag the others forward. But men stripped of health and enthusiasm are dead weight. They had no interest in the instant glory that is showered on the man who finds the ultimate goal of exploration: a Lost City.

The porters were only half the problem. Also in tow was a small knot of Europeans: two Swedes, one Russian and a listless Bulgarian. The Swedes were diehard film-makers — a father and his son. They were making a documentary of my quest. The Bulgarian was making a film of them making a film about me. As for the Russian, he was a millionaire banker who was paying his own way. I had agreed to allow the Swedes to come with me in the hope it would lead to a gravy-train of TV funding. That bonanza never came, so the Swedes leeched off the banker and I leeched off them.

Drowning in tripods and cameras, film-stock and lights, the documentary team threatened to snuff out the frail flame it sought to preserve on celluloid. The vast quantity of their gear, strapped to the porters' backs, made for painfully slow progress. And now Pancho was pointing to the ridge.

I led him aside. Fine-boned, nervous of outsiders and unable ever to look me in the eye, he squatted on an uneven granite block and glanced away as I addressed him.

"Are you sure, Pancho?"

He did not answer. He never answered.

"Pancho, you know that climbing the ridge will kill the men?"

The fragile warrior of the Machiguenga tribe remained silent. He extended his index finger for a second time and poked it mutely at the solid canopy of trees.

"Is that the place . . . where you found the ruins as a young man?"

Pancho's cheeks lifted for an instant as he smiled, a faint glimmer of pleasure. "*Sí, arriba, arriba.*"

I instructed the men to untie their packs and gather round. They were suspicious of my charity. Never before had I granted permission to remove packs during a march. Ours was not a pleasure trip to the French Riviera or the Costa de Sol: we were on an expedition where the only certainty was pain. The porters might have hated me, but I do believe that they appreciated my consistency.

Very slowly, they rested their burdens on the pebbles, and clustered round.

"We have arrived at the crossroads," I said. "It is here that we leave the river and take a new road. Up there."

I motioned to the swirling fog seeping between the cordon of trees. It filtered down to the river like a phantom, rinsing our faces in moisture.

4

"There is no road there," said Julio, the tallest and most confident of the porters. Unlike the others, who had been broken long before, Julio remained resilient despite the appalling conditions. "There is no path, no way ahead," he declared. "*Entren en la selva Y morirán*, enter the forest and we are dead."

The other porters regarded him as their leader, and when he spoke, they listened. It would have been wiser never to have hired Julio, but I had done so in the hope that I could dominate him. Control their leader and I would control the porters. My plan had been flawed, for Julio was a radical. He had no fear, but used an abiding sense of terror to influence his peers.

"*Los hombres no entrarán en la selva*, the men will *not* enter the jungle," he said, with calm assurance. "There is danger in there . . . *El Tiger está esperando*. The Tiger is waiting."

That word was in the air again, that infuriating word. Our search for the last refuge of the Incas, known to the Machiguenga tribe as the House of the Tiger King, had been blighted by the fear of an imaginary cat. The entire team knew as well as I that tigers are not native to the Americas, but to them Tiger was not flesh and blood. They would have been able to deal with that. To them, the Tiger was a spectre, an apparition of an ancient empire, the ghost of the jungle. It was invisible, haunting, terrifying in the most elemental way. The porters would speak of it at night as they lazed beneath their flea-ridden blankets. Julio would tell them of the myth. He would whisper it as a slow incantation, syllable by syllable, word by word. My Spanish is unimpressive, but I would find myself drawn in, as terrified as the others.

The quest for a lost city erodes your body, damaging you beyond all reason. But it is your mind that bears the heaviest toll. Listen to the doubters, the worriers and the weak, and the vaguest hope of success evaporates. The men despised me because I pushed them as hard as I pushed myself. I was fortified by the prospect of triumph; I could already taste the glory. But the porters had nothing to keep them going.

The only tool I knew strong enough to mobilise them was to dent their sense of machismo. They might have been exhausted, covered in sores and riddled with worms, but calling them a soft-skinned bunch of sissies had a magical effect. Each one would grit his teeth, wearily pronounce his manliness, and carry on. But after weeks of overuse the efficiency of this mobilising device had weakened.

As we paused there on the riverbank, I launched into my usual harangue, lampooning the team's pathetic state as a sordid mishmash of femininity. None said a word, except Julio.

Raising himself to his full height, well over six feet, he lowered his eyelids, stretched his arms towards the trees, fingers splayed. Then, as we all watched, motionless, he began to whistle. Monotone, echoing, unforgettable, the sound swept round us. I wondered if it was a spell of some kind, but there was nothing protective about it.

The porters cowered together rigidly. Their leader was communicating directly with El Tigre, the phantom of the jungle. I shifted my gaze from Julio to the men. They looked on, like believers witnessing the miracle of a saint, the whites of their eyes swollen with conviction and with fear.

"*El Tigre me ha hablado*, the Tiger has spoken to me," Julio said, when he had finished. "Enter the forest and he will gorge on our blood tonight."

Forty minutes of silence passed. My mind was racing but I dared not speak. Utter the wrong words, and the expedition would end right there, on the rough pebble shore of the Palatoa river. I had come too far to give up the search for Paititi, especially now that Pancho was at last pointing to the trees. So we sat there, each waiting for the other to break.

All I could think of was Henry Stanley, the nineteenth-century explorer, celebrated for finding Livingstone in central Africa, and famed, too, for his barbarity. Stanley would think nothing of having dissenters thrown in irons, or lashed until the verge of death. He was heartless and cruel, but he had a knack of keeping his men going.

What would Stanley have done in my situation? I wondered. Perhaps he would have used force, threatening to shoot anyone who fell behind. But there comes a stage at which a man would rather die cleanly by a bullet than by the unknown terror of the phantom in the forest. I believe Stanley would have resorted to a more cunning tactic. He would have taken control of what the men held most dear.

I ordered the porters to unload their packs and display the contents on the lean stretch of beach. They complied willingly: they liked nothing more than to stare in wonderment at the tantalizing array of equipment and supplies. Even though we had stripped down again and again, there was still no shortage of gear: giant green tarpaulins for the evening camps, climbing tackle, machetes and sharpening stones, lanterns, shovels and saws, pots, pans, kerosene and gasoline, and even a metal-detector for finding gold. The food consisted of rice, beans, spices, dried jungle meat, and an assortment of dead birds trussed up in a sack. Beside the birds lay a rotting British army kit-bag. I spread its neck wide and observed the contents. As I did so, I realized I had found the men's one weakness. The bag contained Pot Noodles.

Ours was an expedition born of economy. There had been no funds for upmarket rations. I had spent my own meagre budget on the cheapest, lightest food I could find — six hundred Pot Noodles. I had never expected them to become an obsession, but however weary their state, the porters could always be coaxed to continue a little further through driving rain by the mere suggestion of a Pot Noodle at the end.

After months in the jungle we were down to the last dozen white plastic pots. The men regarded them as a symbol of extraordinary sophistication, fare fashioned from the most advanced additives and E-numbers.

I lashed up the neck of the Pot Noodle kit-bag and slung it on to my shoulder. The porters cringed anxiously, then gasped, as I tramped up the steep, root-encrusted bank into the jungle. Down on the shore I could make out Julio reminding the others of the terror of El Tigre: "Enter the forest and you will not come out alive!" he yelled.

But his companions did not listen: there was too much at stake for them not to follow. There were still Pot Noodles to be eaten. They scrabbled the equipment into the packs, fell into line and marched behind me into the twilight. Left with no choice, Julio joined the rear of the procession.

Entering the cloud-forest was like crawling beneath a great velvet curtain of secrecy to witness some clandestine ritual. What struck me first was the silence, and the lack of animal life. A million eyes might have been watching our wretched procession, and as many ears listening to the *Ting! Ting! Ting!* of machetes cleaving vines, but they were invisible. The only obvious form of life was that of the insects. The ground between the trees was crisscrossed with trails of soldier ants. The trees themselves were striped up and down with termite tracks, which ran to the nests, the great balls of clay, hanging like lanterns in the uppermost branches. Giant moths flapped across our faces, brushing the sweat from our cheeks, then flitted back to the instant camouflage of the jungle floor.

We pushed into the suffocation of trees, drowning in perspiration, impelled by a kind of madness. It must have been madness, for no sane man would ever have left the river and ventured into that green hell. The fact that the men were trudging forward gave me great satisfaction and renewed my energy. If I could keep them going a little further, the ruins of the lost city would be within reach. More comforting still was that Pancho had taken the initiative and, for the first time, he was leading the way. I had spent weeks courting him, coaxing him. Without Pancho there was no chance of success.

Like most Machiguenga, he went barefoot and, like all the others, he took delight in cackling at my clumsiness. Behind the pretended veil of political correctness, our society so often ridicules the primitiveness of tribal people. But spend a moment with them under the sprawling canopy, and you grasp at once the proficiency of their own society. The Machiguenga are masters of jungle movement, as serene in their world as ballerinas in ours.

The team chopped a route towards the ridge and, as they did so, my bitterness evaporated. Until then I had felt that Pancho was flirting with my greed, luring me on with a vision of unattainable victory. I would spend hours watching him, desperate to understand. I knew that if I could get inside his mind, and see what he was thinking, there was a real chance of success. Yet I realized now that Pancho wasn't going to do all the work for me. If I was lucky, he would point out the way, but if I wanted to find Paititi, then in many ways I was on my own. In Pancho's world you had to work out the answers for yourself.

Three hours after leaving the river, we found the first block of stone. Straight-edged and uniform, measuring four feet by two, it was obviously the work of Inca stone-masons. You could make out the subtle chisel marks on the sides. I wondered if it was a marking post of some kind, a pointer to the ruins. We excavated the surrounding area, hacking wildly with machetes. Three more of the stones were unearthed, and what looked like a lintel for a door.

I applauded Pancho and the others, and roared the order to continue at full speed to the crest of the ridge. Six of the men were armed with machetes; they sliced a narrow corridor through the oppressive foliage. The ascent was brutal beyond description. The porters heaved themselves up a step at a time, the agony framed in their faces.

Half-way up the ridge we made a camp. The men were reluctant to stay in the jungle, but the prospect of a piping hot Pot Noodle was too much for all except Julio. He stormed back down to the river with Alfonso's ancient shotgun, ranting that El Tigre would feast on our blood.

The ground was so uneven that we cut staves of cedarwood and created a crude platform across which we lay. We were used to a good deal of space at the camps pitched near the river's edge. The situation was different in the jungle. Every inch of ground had to be earned, and was done so through much exertion with the blade.

I was pleased that Julio had chosen to leave us: it quashed the talk of malevolent spirits. Giovanni, who usually prepared the food, heated a little water gathered from sections of giant bamboo and dished up the Pot Noodles. The porters fatigue was eased by the sudden injection of monosodium glutamate: the chemical had

11

an impressive ability to restore one's strength; I had noticed that it helped to protect us from mosquito bites as well.

The Pot Noodle appetizer was followed by the usual main course of jungle birds stewed with an assortment of extra-bony fish. Copious hot food is the only thing that can keep tired men from mutiny. My great fear was for the next day: after breakfast the treasured Pot Noodles would all be gone.

It poured with torrential rain all night. The water cascaded downhill and drenched us as we fought to sleep. I drifted in and out of consciousness, hounded by a recurring nightmare . . . a phantom with foot-long fangs, coarse whiskers and wicked soot-black eyes.

Before the first shafts of pale grey light had cut through the trees, we were woken to the report of Julio's gun. The sound was close by. A second later, a large, bulky creature was falling downwards, crashing through the lattice of branches. It smashed on to the bottle-green tarpaulin under which we lay huddled in a sodden line. From the weight I could tell immediately it was no bird. Julio leapt through the trees to claim his prize — a full-grown howler monkey, the size of a toddler.

As the hunter knew well, the one vice that appalled me was the killing of monkeys. The animal was skinned, dismembered, and sliced up for breakfast without delay. Pancho built a small fire, fuelled it with a fresh termite nest, and soon had the primate roasting. I had eaten monkey before, while a guest of the Shuar, a tribe in the Upper Amazon formerly celebrated for making *tsantsas*, shrunken heads. I cannot say that I shared the other men's enthusiasm for the meat, largely on account of the worms.

We set off once the last strands of flesh had been consumed, and the bones shattered for their marrow. Despite the protein, the porters were weak and getting weaker. They craved carbohydrate, but lack of it was not life-threatening. More worrying was that one might slip and we would have another casualty. As any platoon commander knows, an injured man is a terrible liability, requiring one or two others to attend him. A few days before one of the porters, Francisco, had vomited blood one morning. By lunchtime he had lost his sight. Going blind in deep jungle has to be the most fearful prospect imaginable. Fortunately Francisco's vision had returned. Suspecting he had had a mild stroke, I had been forced to leave him in a cave with a trusted companion.

The main thing on my mind now was to push on to the top of the ridge. From my research I knew the Incas built simple stone roads along ridges, and on high land, linking up distant points within their empire. Others who have searched for Paititi have talked of a secret stone road running north-west through the Cordillera. I was certain that if I could discover it, I would find the city. Every night for months I had studied the contours on the maps, and had replayed Pancho's story through my mind.

As a young man searching for new hunting grounds, he had ventured far up the Rio Palatoa, before hacking into the jungle. There, beside a deep expanse of crystal

13

water, he said he had found a series of large ruins. Digging at the foot of a towering stone wall, he had discovered a metal hatchet, its blade highlighted in gold. Pancho took the hatchet back to his father, who was the tribal chief. Rather than praising his son, the old warrior exhorted him to return the weapon at once, and to forget about it for fear of activating a curse. El Tigre was waiting to punish not only him but the entire tribe, he said. Pancho did as his father bade him. Three decades passed, but he could not forget about the ruins or the golden hatchet.

It had taken me months to get Pancho involved in the expedition, partly because the tribe had forbidden him to co-operate, and partly because he saw it as an empty cause. As far as Pancho was concerned, there was no reason to search for the ruins. Why look for a ruined city, overgrown and deserted, when there are plenty of *live* cities, bustling with people and traffic? Pancho had heard the tales of civilization from the missionaries. They had spoken of the wickedness of development, a wickedness that the warrior had found appealing. They had told him of Lima's dens of vice, the "high-class" brothels where girls line up in tall shoes, their mouths circled in paint, the colour of scarlet macaws. They had told him, too, of meeting-places where immoral men served up sinful, intoxicating drinks, places at which there was always plenty of liquor to go round. But, best of all, he liked the sound of the third fantasy: a house with drinks and coloured lights that flash on and off as music plays, even though no one's playing it.

14

Pancho's dream was the mirror image of my own. He longed to go to the place of which the missionaries had spoken, to carouse, to drink till he dropped, dance, and to have a look at how the other world lived. We had made a pact: if Pancho took me to the deserted ruins of Paititi, I would take him to the city of Cusco.

In the early afternoon we came upon more hand-cut blocks of stone. This time they were standing upright, like sentries. We scraped away the moss and lichen to find them gargoyle-grey beneath. My investigation of them was brief: I feared that a prolonged stop would cause the men to desert. Julio had been speaking of the spectre again, and someone had reminded him of the curse. Such talk had the immediate effect of obliterating what little optimism we had earned through the climb.

A few feet on we reached a sheering granite rockface. It towered upward like the supporting wall of a medieval cathedral, indomitable and encrusted in lichens and silky olive-green moss. The men slumped at its base. With Pancho's help I managed eventually to get a rope to the top. It was threaded through the mass of roots and the medley of branches. One look at the porters and I knew full well that they would not be going on. They were not tribesmen, but members of a chainsaw gang whose ancestors had emigrated from the mountains to the forest. For them, the jungle was an awe-inspiring backdrop, a twilight zone of life to be felled as swiftly as possible. None of them understood the attraction of seeing a tree in the perpendicular position.

The granite rockface was a natural parting point, a crossroads, a place of decision and indecision. I didn't ask for volunteers to accompany Pancho and me because the men had proved their honour. Perhaps it was at that moment I should have pressed them harder than before, but I had lost my nerve. The last push was my own challenge, a contest for myself against myself.

The film crew were tough beyond words, but their batteries were exhausted, and the Peruvian cameraman suffered from vertigo. We whispered goodbye, and made a plan to keep in touch by radio.

I slipped on the climbing harness, attached an ascender and began the excruciating climb in search of the stone road. Pancho had shunned the rope and scaled the rockface barefoot, with great ease. A glance up and I could make out his spindly frame waiting for me between the trees far above. A glance down and the cluster of men was smaller than before. A moment later I looked down for the last time, but they were gone.

CHAPTER
TWO

Qualifications of a Traveller
If you have health, a great craving for adventure, at least a moderate fortune, and can set your heart on a definite object, which old travellers do not think impracticable, then — travel by all means.

The Art of Travel

My search for the last refuge of the Incas had begun in the snug surroundings of our illusionary world. Only a man who has his health, a full stomach and wears clean clothes would ever entertain the notion of tracking down the greatest lost city on Earth, or venturing from such comfort into the bitter reality of the jungle.

My obsession with the ruins had begun a decade before, when my eyes had been drawn to the cursed name "Paititi" in the foot-note of an obscure historical text. From the first moment I read the word, I sensed it beckoning, daring me to try my luck. It would have been so easy to turn the page and move on. But, instead, I gazed coldly at the type, took a deep breath and shut the book.

Once inside me, the corrosive allure of Paititi ran wild. For months, then years, I tried to suppress all thoughts of the Incas and their lost treasure. I undertook other projects, other journeys, but Paititi was never far from my mind. Like so many before me, my motivation was founded on greed, an overwhelming greed. Not for gold, but for glory.

Locate a lost city and your name is etched in the history books. Find Paititi, and I would be transformed overnight from a humble traveller into the world's most famous explorer.

To have a hope of discovering the lost city, I knew the key lay in the archives of the Spanish *conquistadores*. They had documented their invasion of the Americas in fine detail, but they were too busy suppressing native people to piece together the clues. For months I studied the history, reading and rereading the chronicles of Francisco de Xeres, Garcilaso de la Vega, Christobal de Molina, and of Felipe Guaman de Poma. The clues would be hidden, for they had eluded explorers, adventurers, archaeologists and warrior-priests for almost five hundred years. Yes, they would be concealed well, waiting to be teased out — that is, if there were any clues at all.

In the West, we are brought up to solve a puzzle with fragments of collected information, rather than by placing ourselves in the mind of the person who devised the riddle. By steeping myself in the Spanish chronicles, detailing the Incas' daily lives, folklore and beliefs, I hoped to understand how they thought. Understand that and, I hoped, I would be closer to rooting out the trail to Paititi.

When the Spanish first arrived at the coastline of Peru, in the first half of the sixteenth century, they were searching for El Dorado, a land of unimaginable

18

wealth. An Indian chief in Panama had spoken of a kingdom to the south where the only known metal was gold: where it was used for pots and pans, plates and jewellery, for hunting bows, ritualistic daggers and flutes. The *conquistadores* made a beeline southwards.

They found a vast empire that had been established only a century before, known to its people as Tahuantinsuya, the Land of Four Quarters. Centred at the capital of Cusco, the realm stretched from Chinchaysuyu in the north to Lake Titicaca in the south, and from the Pacific Ocean in the west to the endless cloud-forest of Madre de Dios in the east. It was a land of contrasts: stark *altiplano*, seething jungle and snow-capped mountains, populated by a people whose barbaric rituals shocked even the cruel sensibilities of the *conquistadores*. The religious figurehead of the society was the scion of the sun itself, the Inca Atahualpa.

Had it not been cut short by such an unlikely foreign invasion, the Inca empire would surely have endured for centuries, amassing even more treasure than it did. And what of the treasure? The Spanish imprisoned Atahualpa, who feared imminent execution. He had noticed the invaders' obsession with gold and silver and, although surprised by it, he proposed what must surely be the most famous ransom in history. He scratched a line high on one wall of his cell, and pledged to fill the chamber once with gold and twice with silver in exchange for his freedom. Amazed and delighted, the Spanish readily agreed. One can only imagine their astonishment: the room measured more

19

than twenty feet by seventeen, and the line on the wall was higher than a man: a volume of more than two thousand cubic feet.

Gold and silver were ushered forth from across the Inca empire, a quantity that exceeded the Spaniards' wildest dreams. As one would expect, the pledge to Atahualpa was broken; the conquerors executed him, then set out to plunder his capital. But in Cusco they found relatively little gold. A rumour circulated that the bulk of the golden treasure had been hurried from the city by the Incas' supporters. It was said that they had retreated deep into the jungle, east of Cusco, where they established a magnificent city in the most inaccessible corner of the cloud-forest. They called it Paititi.

I tried to put myself in the mind of the Incas, asking myself how they might have secretly passed to one another the whereabouts of their El Dorado. With the *conquistadores* all around them, they would no doubt have resorted to ciphers, unlikely to arouse the suspicions of the invading Spanish. But they had no tradition of writing, no paper or ink.

We know that they placed relatively little importance on gold. A civilization without iron, they favoured the soft yellow metal for its easy malleability, and regarded it as utilitarian rather than as a valuable commodity. The Incas placed utmost value on their fine textiles, woven in alpaca and vicuña wool. Early *conquistador* reports tell of the first meetings with the Incas, who came alongside the Spanish ships in flimsy craft. They presented the European visitors with exquisite woven garments, their highest honour. Horrified at what they assumed to be an open insult, the Spanish set fire to the textiles and chased the Incas away.

The fabulous arts of weaving and embroidery had been developed by the ancient communities at Paracas and Nazca on the Peruvian coast, which flourished almost two thousand years ago. It was from them that the Incas acquired their knowledge and further developed the craft, using it to record information and ideas. These embroidered patterns, known as *quellca*, a word that is sometimes used to mean "writing", might well have been employed to conceal the location of Paititi.

I studied hundreds of Inca textiles, hoping to decipher the meanings of the geometric patterns; and I spent a great deal of time attempting to trace the finest Inca textile ever made. It was sent to King Philip II of Spain in 1570 for the monastic walls at El Escorial, but it has disappeared without trace. One of the greatest historical treasures ever to come from the Americas, it was probably thrown away.

My studies of the *quellca* embroideries led me to consider what treasure the Incas would have taken to Paititi for safe keeping. If they did not consider gold the ultimate possession, then perhaps they would have taken their textiles instead. I knew from previous experience that the humidity of the rainforest is ruinous for cloth. If Paititi had lain in the jungle, there was little hope of any woven riches remaining intact. None the less, the draw for me was the ruins themselves, the vast stone walls like those at Machu Picchu, which would surely form the foundation of the lost city.

My obsession with Paititi, and the glory that finding it could bring, gnawed away at me. I travelled to Peru in search of the Birdmen of the Upper Amazon, a project that culminated in a book on the subject. It gave me the opportunity to do much more research, and to quiz hundreds of Peruvians on what they knew of the Incas and their last place of refuge.

I spent months combing library stacks, trawling through miles of manuscripts, many written more than four centuries ago. There were so many books, but so few clues. The only one was the recurring name Madre de Dios, the vast impenetrable jungle, east of the Andes, on the southern cusp of the Amazon.

The lure of the last great lost city of the Americas had not attracted me alone: at least a dozen of the world's most seasoned explorers had just returned or were about to leave for the cloud-forest. Teams from the United States and the UK, Poland, Australia and Peru itself had isolated a relatively small "hot zone", which lay between the Piñi-Piñi and Palatoa rivers. Somewhere in there, they all claimed, lay the ruins of a tremendous civilization. Although, geographically speaking, the area is small, it's regarded as the densest stretch of jungle in the world. One adventurer told me: "You could hide New York City in there and walk right by without knowing it." He added that the race was reaching fever pitch. "If Paititi exists at all," he said firmly, "it will be found in the next six months."

That prediction got my blood racing. It might be the last chance I would ever get at easy fame. I had been fixated by the lure of the Inca stronghold for too long for the prize to be snatched by some other less deserving adventurer. I bought the cheapest flight to Lima I could find. It was scheduled to leave in a week's time, on Christmas Day.

Unlike most of the competition, I didn't have corporate sponsorship or a fat expense account. Nor could I boast a support team of scientists, or high-level contacts in the Peruvian government. I didn't have a headquarters either, or much in the way of specialist equipment. I owned a second-hand GPS, but hadn't a clue how it worked. It was just for show, proof of my serious intentions, as was my Gold Bug metal-detector, which I had bought on my Ethiopian search for King Solomon's mines. Like a rebel fighter in a guerrilla war, I viewed my weaknesses as strengths. I was lean and mean, free from excess people and a glut of equipment. I had no one to report to, and no one except myself to please.

My wife rolled her eyes when I explained that I had to leave our poky flat in London's East End almost at once. The jungle was calling me, I said theatrically. She was very understanding, considering our little daughter's first birthday was a few days away.

I bought a copy of *Loot*, a newspaper with classified ads, and withdrew two hundred pounds from my bank account. I spread the sheets of advertisements on the sitting-room floor, and searched for equipment worthy of a budget lost-city expedition. In less than an hour, I had found an old Zodiac rubber dinghy, a pair of used jungle boots, two shovels, six canvas kit-bags, three tarpaulins and a pair of cheap lanterns. With the money that was left, I went to a local hardware store and bought some plastic rubble sacks, the kind used by builders to carry gravel. I splashed out on some extra batteries and a roll of bin-liners too. Lastly, I went down to Safeway with my credit card and snapped up some packet soup and their entire stock of Pot Noodles. Previous experience had taught me that any expedition marches on its stomach.

It always amazes me how much money people spend on nonessential knick-knacks and mountaineering food at camping shops. A whole industry has developed touting nicely packaged rubbish to ingenuous adventurers. You're far better off buying everything second-hand, from a hardware store, supermarket or, better still, on a market stall in the country you're visiting.

These days, explorers tend to take with them from the start everything they expect to need. It's an inefficient way of operating; you get lumbered down and can hardly move. It's wiser to take only a basic core of equipment and to compensate by making anything you find you need. On rough journeys, ingenuity is the mother of success. The Victorians were masters of exploration and of solving problems, and they turned problem-solving into an art form. They could knock up just about anything from a few feet of waxed canvas, some stout cord and a cleft stick or two. For those who wanted handy tips on how to bivouac, build a camp, or cross quicksand in heavy rain, there was an invaluable guide entitled *The Art of Travel*. The book's editor was Francis Galton, a cousin of Charles Darwin and a renowned scholar and adventurer in his own right. Galton's book, which was first published by John Murray in 1855, ran to four editions, the final and most comprehensive one appearing in 1872. It was carried by explorers and soldiers, missionaries and government officials, and is an encyclopaedia of ingenuity. Much of it is regarded now as horrendously politically incorrect — especially the section on "the management of savages" — but it contains many titbits of invaluable information. Fortunately, *The Art of Travel* had recently been reprinted. It was the last purchase I made and, without doubt, the best value.

The day after buying the equipment, I was talking to a television-producer friend, blustering on about my grand plans to find the lost city of Paititi. Like my wife, he rolled his eyes for, again like her, he had heard of my grand quests before. Just before we parted, he said that a friend of his, a Swedish film-maker, might be interested in coming along. I barked at the thought of European company; my friend pointed out the benefit. Find Paititi, and the film-maker could record my discovery: surely it would only add to my glory. After all, who would have cared about the lunar landings if we had not received the grainy footage of Armstrong climbing down from the NASA module on to the dusty lunar surface?

I took the Swede's number and gave him a call. We arranged to meet next day in an East End coffee-house where the grease on the walls reflected the mud on the floor. I lurked at the back, away from the usual assortment of weirdos, a soft-covered book of Inca textiles on the table before me. As I sat there, staring at the geometric designs, two men approached. One was a good twenty years older than the other. They were both dressed in leather, the first in black suede, the younger in tan-coloured buckskin. The older was short, five foot three at the most, with dark, receding hair, swarthy complexion, pursed lips, and shoulders that were noticeably relaxed, so much so that his hands hung down at his sides like cured hams in a butcher's window. The younger had long, russet-brown hair, which covered his ears and curled down over the collar of a torn denim shirt. His face was tight and energetic, partially concealed by a straggly beard and moustaches. He looked as if he had stepped from a seventies pop-idol poster.

The pair introduced themselves as Leon and David Flamholc. They worked as a team, the father producing, the son directing. They made art-house feature films in Sweden, but they had come to London to break into the English language. Sweden was too small, too conventional, they confided darkly, and its people were too easily shocked.

I told them about my plan to venture deep into the densest jungle in the world on the trail of the fleeing Incas. "I could do with someone to document the ruins," I said.

I expected a barrage of questions, beginning with "Do you really think you'll find the lost city?" But the Swedes didn't ask any questions at all. They cackled enthusiastically in their mother tongue, and noted down a few details. As they did so, I noticed a man with a large video camera standing outside the café. He was pointing the device in our direction, filming through the filthy window. "Do you know him?" I asked.

"He follows us everywhere," said Leon, distantly.

That afternoon I visited the hallowed halls of the Royal Geographical Society in London's South Kensington. I was in search of a map. The RGS takes the subject of exploration very seriously indeed, and tends to frown on low-budget expeditions. As far as they are concerned, the business of exploration is best left to professionals.

The secretary wrote my name in a ledger and ushered me past long, dark oils of the great explorers, Stanley, Livingstone, Burton, and some others of equal fame. Then he marched me down a corridor, striding solemnly as if we were pall-bearers in a funeral cortège. A central carpet, laid over the parquet, cushioned the sound of our steps. Along the corridor ran a finely tooled display case. It housed the holy of holies, Livingstone's peaked cap and Stanley's jungle kepi, Amundsen's cooking stove and Sven Hedin's sextant. Each item bore the scars of ordeal: the ordeal of exploration.

The Map Room was lightless and cold, its walls lined with cabinets, each filled with charts and plans and miniature globes. Every inch of available space was stacked with clusters of maps, a million, billion maps. There were maps of hamlets in obscure corners of the southern African veld, city maps of Shanghai, Manila,

Santiago and Trieste; maps of rivers and mountain ranges, of endless deserts and deltas, Arctic tundra and trenches on the ocean floor.

A clerk asked me to write my destination on a scrap of paper. I did so, inscribing "MADRE DE DIOS" in small, neat capitals at the centre of the page. I slid it back across the counter. The clerk licked his thumb, scooped it up and strained through bifocals at the words. Then he scratched a rounded fingernail on his cheek.

"No, sir," he said, in a shrill tone. "No, sir, there is no map of Madre de Dios. There is no map at all."

Before I knew it, I had been ushered back to the street. I felt like an outcast, as if I had sought to embarrass the Map Room by seeking out its Achilles' heel.

Much time has passed since brave Englishmen dressed in tweeds were dispatched by the RGS to fill in the blank outlines of the continents. The business of exploration has changed. There is still danger, but these days when you embark on an expedition you expect to return alive. Adventure is no longer about providing a service to humanity, but about bettering yourself, testing yourself and striving for glory.

Two days later, I had a second rendezvous with the Swedes. We met in the immense tropical greenhouse at Kew Gardens. On a hard jungle journey nothing is so important as having a team you can trust. The Swedes symbolized a lucrative source of TV funding, but there was no point in having them along if they would crack up in the climate.

As before, they arrived trussed from head to toe in leather. And, again, they were being stalked by the broad-shouldered blond man, armed with a video camera and an oversized microphone. He tracked them through the undergrowth, moving between the shrubs and fronds with impressive nimbleness.

"Who *is* that man?" I asked.

"It's Boris."

"*Boris?*"

"He's a Bulgarian film student," David replied.

"Oh."

"We have a cult following in Bulgaria," he added, by way of explanation.

Miniature beads of condensation had formed on David's costume. They grew larger and larger and ran together, then dripped silently to earth. This time his outfit was complemented by a golden medallion, hanging at the centre of his bald chest. As he moved through the festering humidity of the hothouse, it caught the light, which broke occasionally through the layers of rubbery leaves.

I warned him and his father of the certain hardship that lay ahead. The Swedes seemed unfazed by the prospect of adversity. They had been preparing, they said, grinning.

"What do you mean, *preparing?*"

"We sealed up the windows in our flat," said Leon, "and installed a heater from a sauna. It's a hundred per cent humidity at home, and as hot as Hell."

I was struck by their dedication, and comforted myself that Swedes knew about saunas, and could probably endure the heat better than I. The conversation moved on quickly to money. I asked what their budget was for equipment and supplies. Their confidence plunged.

"There's no money yet," said Leon.

"But we're leaving in five days!"

"Don't worry, we have a patron."

"Who?"

"A banker, a very rich Russian banker."

"Excellent."

"There's a small catch," said David, wiping his medallion with his thumb. "We can sting him for lots of cash, but he wants to come along."

At first I disapproved of my expedition to find the lost city becoming an upmarket package tour for middle-aged bankers, arty Swedish film-makers and their Bulgarian groupies. But the more I thought of it, the more I came to understand that there might be strength in such an odd line-up. Ours was not going to be a clone of the usual expeditions, oozing with sleekness. It was clear from the start that oddity was our advantage.

There are two ways to find a lost city. The first is to rely on luck alone, the second is to control all the information. My historical research had filled in some of the gaps, but it was important to hear first-hand from other Paititi-hunters. I wanted to know where they had been and what they had found. To this end, I interviewed as many as I could find, pretending that I was preparing an article about the search for Paititi. The cover story seemed to put the explorers at ease. They spoke freely about locations and methods, without fearing that I was about to steal their information. It might have been underhand, but successful explorers have always resorted to scheming, even depraved methods to ensure success.

Exploration is a dirty game. I sometimes wonder with what red herrings the great adventurers like Captain Cook and Columbus, Walter Raleigh and Drake had thrown their competition off the scent. Perhaps they were more gentlemanly then as there were more unexplored chunks of the world to go round. But now, with so few jewels in the crown of exploration still remaining, the competition is cut-throat.

I would frequently root through library stacks only to find that the relevant page of a key text had been torn out. And seasoned trailblazers would often "shuffle" co-ordinates while recounting tales of their journeys. I didn't blame them. As I progressed in my search, I became as conniving as everyone else. Obsession and greed can compel a reasonable man to behave in the most appalling way.

Through a strange kind of geographic arrogance, Europeans like to think that the world was a silent, dark, unknown place until they trooped out and discovered it. They forget that when Columbus arrived in the Caribbean he came upon an orderly indigenous society, just as Pizarro did in Peru, and Captain Cook did in the Antipodes. Of course, these native peoples were regarded at the time as wild and untamed, to be taught discipline and the wisdom of the Bible.

In the same way that newly discovered landmasses had always been known about by the people who lived on them, a lost city can never really be lost at all. Tribal people know their territory inside and out. They always know where the ruins lie although, unlike us, they may have little or no interest in them. When tribal warriors stumble upon ruins overgrown in their ancestral lands, they don't waste time inspecting them. Their attention is focused on acquiring food, not antique possessions with which to spruce up their homes. Indigenous people are not gripped as we are with notions of ownership, urbanism or cultural history. Just as the British developed a mania for climbing the Alps in the Victorian era, searching for a lost city is a particularly European obsession.

For this reason, I became aware early on that the best way to find Paititi was to go directly to the people who surely knew where it lay. Most expeditions don't integrate with the societies through whose lands they travel. They remain apart, superior, judgemental. As a result they are mistrusted and disliked by the locals. I had heard of the Machiguenga, a tribe whose hunting grounds stretch across much of the Madre de Dios cloud-forest. They have been portrayed as a ruthless, warlike people, more eager to slay invaders than to welcome them. Thirty years ago they wiped out a French-led Paititi expedition, near the jungle village of Mantacolla.

My approach was to venture to that same village and gain the trust of the Machiguenga, the very warriors who supposedly killed the French group. We would come as equals, as friends, rather than adversaries. Gradually, with time, I hoped to broach the subject of the lost city itself.

CHAPTER
THREE

Size of the Party
In travel through a disorganized country, where there are small chiefs and bands of marauders, a large party is necessary.

The Art of Travel

Lima is a frenetic mass of people, all residing beneath an impermeable blanket of man-made smog. There are those who have and those who have not. You get the feeling that the haves are clinging on by their fingernails, and the have-nots could do wonders given half a chance. From time to time the people at the top are forced into exile, chased away with their bulging sacks of swag. They're simply replaced by the next tier of would-be swindlers, who start lining their pockets from the first moment of their first day in power. The clock is always ticking for such people, a fact of which they are very well aware.

Somewhere down at the very bottom, way below the *desamparados*, the Helpless Ones, who make up Peru's silent majority, are the tribal people. Their voice is less than mute. To most Peruvians they're at best a curiosity and at worst a faceless symbol of how far the urban society has come. The same people regard the asphyxiating clouds of pollution as an emblem of national prosperity.

The tribes have little contact with their national politicians. They hear from them only at election time, when the men in hand-cut suits send gifts in exchange for precious jungle votes. The lengths Peruvian politicians will go to in order to secure a few tribal votes suggest how desperate some of them have become.

Four years before I had ventured to Peru to make a long journey by boat through the Upper Amazon in search of the legendary Birdmen. These members of the Shuar tribe use a complex hallucinogenic preparation called *ayahuasca* to fly into what they say is the "real" world. The Shuar despised their political leaders, and boiled over whenever politics was mentioned. They shunned all politicians because they had placed their trust in another group of outsiders: evangelist missionaries from Alabama.

The missionaries had translated the Bible into the Shuar dialect, handed out little pink pills and condemned the tribe's ancient and perfected tradition of shrinking their enemies' heads to the size of grapefruits. I became outspoken on the curbing of the practice. Although it sounds barbaric, and it is, the custom held the society together and kept everyone on their toes.

My great fear was that the Machiguenga had, like the Shuar, succumbed to the beguiling charm of missionaries from the Bible Belt. As far as I was concerned, a little danger of head-shrinking is a small price to pay in return for a people who have remained true to an ancient code.

On my journey to the Shuar, I had been protected by a former American army ranger from 101st Airborne Division, named Richard Fowler. He was an expert on psychotropic plants, and had lived in the jungle since enlisting for two tours of Vietnam back in 1968. I would need a security man if, as I hoped, the missionaries had not got to the Machiguenga. Richard Fowler's name was the last on my list. He was an impossible character and I had vowed never to communicate with him again, let alone work with him. But time had tempered my resolve, and I had few options. The day after I arrived in Lima, I arranged to fly up to Iquitos, a small town in the Upper Amazon built a century ago by the rubber barons. It was there that Fowler could be found, when he wasn't living it up in the jungle.

The night before I went in search of Richard, the desk clerk at my hotel took me aside. "Señor, I hear you want to find Paititi," he said.

"Who told you that?"

"It is the word on the street," he said, with sinister intonation. "Listen, if you want to find Paititi, there is a man who can help you."

"Who?"

"*El Jefe de la Policía*, the Chief of Police, Señor Martín."

"Where can I find him?"

"At the cock-fight."

The clerk scrawled an unintelligible note and handed it to the security man at the front door. He flagged a cab and, in turn, passed the note to the driver. The

Swedes, the Bulgarian, the Russian banker and I squeezed into the car, which sped away.

The taxi ride was my first experience of "full on" documentary-making. The Bulgarian was filming the Swedes, as usual, and they were filming me. The banker was recording the sound and giving direction, too. As with most millionaire bankers, he wasn't used to doing as he was told.

Outside the taxi, downtown Lima was closing up for the night. I have never come across a city that's shut down as firmly as Lima. It was as if the shopkeepers were expecting street warfare to ensue. They unclipped the neon bulbs and wrapped them in newspaper. They bolted inch-thick sheets of steel to their windows, and wove strands of razor wire across them. They battened down hatches, fixed sharp spikes to anything left unprotected, chained double-locked doors, and positioned armed guards in bulletproof vests.

Previous journeys in search of treasure have taught me that a zigzag strategy is the best way to get ahead. It may seem like madness to the uninitiated, but the worst method is to head straight for the target. Do that, and you miss out on nuggets of information that can be invaluable later on. More importantly, the zigzag method sometimes reveals the trail to the goal.

At first the Swedes didn't appreciate the detour into Lima's cock-fighting underworld. They couldn't grasp its connection with Paititi. I said that I had been passed a tip-off by one of my informants.

The Russian, Marco, tapped a thumb to his nose. "Just like in the KGB," he said shrewdly, in his thick Ukrainian voice. "There's nothing like a good informant."

The taxi pulled up at a large *pollería*, a roast-chicken restaurant. Hundreds of birds were sizzling on spits outside, reflecting the cherry-red neon lights. The air was warm, perfumed with the pungent smell of roasting meat. Peruvians adore grilled chicken. They can't get enough of it. No Sunday evening would be complete without a roasted bird or two, washed down with a few bottles of Pilsten. Dozens of families were milling about expectantly, many with three or more generations in tow. Everyone was scrubbed clean, like potatoes ready for the pot, and decked out in their best clothes.

Marco pushed his way through the lines of families who were waiting obediently to be served. He buttonholed the manager and stuffed a hundred-dollar bill into his shirt pocket. The man clicked his fingers, like a gypsy performing a flamenco dance, then yelled a volley of orders to his waiters. The throng of honest, chicken-loving families was roped back, a moth-eaten scarlet carpet was rolled out and we were ushered to the far end of the hall.

The only thing Peruvians like more than gorging themselves on grilled chicken on Sunday night, then massaging the grease into their squeaky clean cheeks, is cock-fighting. The sport is a national obsession.

At the rear of the dining hall lay the Palicio de Gallos, the cock-fighting arena. I was stirred by the size of the place. The ring must have been sixty foot across, encircled by more than five hundred red plastic seats, with a low domed ceiling hanging above it like a Chinese parasol. Offset to one side stood a digital scoreboard. The fuchsia numbers flashed importantly from time to time, but no one took any notice. Everyone was watching the warring birds.

The audience consisted of about two hundred overweight middle-aged men. Some were scowling, others were drunk. They all had money at stake, and were clapping, screeching, roaring orders at the birds.

A man with no legs and cropped, oyster-grey hair was taking the bets. He lurched around the ring on his hands, raising his stout body up on the knuckles, a wad of betting slips and a pencil gripped in his teeth.

In the middle of the arena, the fight was a whirlwind of wings, beaks and sharpened spurs. It was hard to see which bird was winning. Both were stripped of their plumage and dignity, both drenched in blood. All of a sudden one collapsed sideways. The victor continued to attack. A few of the gamblers erupted in cheers and accosted the legless man, demanding their winnings. The dead cockerel's owner made for the stage, moving with fast, sombre strides. He scooped up his lifeless bird and peered into its eye, flipped the head, and peered into the other. There was no question about it: his prized fighting cock was dead.

Not far from the scoreboard, an awkwardly tall man in a blood-stained medical coat was binding spurs to a bird's ankles. His small, devious eyes were magnified by thick lenses. I watched him for a moment or two, as he fixed the spikes in position and clipped them sharp. He filled a syringe from a vial of clear liquid, which I suspected was adrenaline, and jabbed the needle into the rooster's thigh. After that, he put the bird's head into his mouth, and sucked it.

When the creature had been taken off to fight, I approached the medical man. He was tidying his syringes, scalpels and other implements. "I am looking for Señor Martín," I said.

The vet didn't look round. He could tell I had no interest in cock-fighting, that I had come on less important business.

"Go to the weighing-pit," he replied. "He'll be over there." Straightening his arm and index finger in one slick motion, he pointed to the far end of the arena. I could make out a simple leather sling suspended from a set of scales. Birds were being weighed, like boxers before a title fight.

I went over. The man in charge of weighing had a dirty crêpe bandage wrapped round one hand, and a patch of dry blood on the back of his shirt. He took great care in weighing each bird, then growled a number to his assistant. I moved in close, so close I could smell him. He reeked of black tobacco, the kind you get in the jungle, which they call *mapacho*.

"I'm looking for Martín," I said.

"*Sí, yo soy Martín.*"

"Martín, the chief of police?"

"*Sí. ¿Qué quieres?* What do you want?"

I felt like a fool, not because the Swedes were filming me and the Bulgarian was filming them, but because it seemed daft to ask anyone about the lost city in the weighing-pit of a cock-fight. But since we were there, I dived in: "I'm looking for Paititi," I said, with implausible confidence, "and I have heard that you may have some advice."

Martín called out the weight of the bird, and looked at me. Then he looked at the Swedes, the Bulgarian and the banker. "Are all of you looking for Paititi?" he asked.

"It's me, mostly," I said. "I'm going into the jungle to search for it."

"¿Traes protección? Do you have protection?" snarled Martín.

"I'm planning on taking a former soldier. He served in Vietnam."

"No, not that kind of protection ... Protección contra las brujerías, protection against witchcraft."

Martín paused from weighing fighting cocks and looked at me. The scent of stale mapacho hung between us like a veil. We stared at each other: he observing my inexperience, and I peering into his lizard-green eyes. Those eyes. They can only be described in cliché. They were haunting, tempting, wicked, supreme. They hinted of terror on an unknown scale, the kind of terror created by fantasy.

"Las brujerías pueden matar al hombre, the witchcraft can kill a man," said Martín, after a long pause.

"Do you know where I should look for Paititi?" I asked. "I've heard that the Machiguenga know."

"Without protection you are not prepared," he said frostily. "And without preparation you are a fool."

I was keen to ask Martín about his own interest in Paititi, but he was unwilling to tell me anything else. In parting, he said: "Get protection and prepare your mind. Prepare it very carefully. If you fail to do so, the jungle will make a madman out of you, and it will take your soul."

Richard Fowler had swapped his soul for the jungle long ago, in the dark days when his home was a foxhole east of Saigon. He said he went to Vietnam because the rainforest called him, and because its foliage gave reason to the chaos of his life.

As our passenger plane descended closer and closer to the mantle of green, I reflected on Richard. I was already mad, I mused, for only a madman would employ Richard Fowler once and then again. The jungle was his only friend. It listened silently to his endless saga of war, death and high times in Indochina a generation ago. On our long voyage up the Rio Tigre in search of the Birdmen, Richard had talked non-stop about his search for reality. At regular intervals he would pause to swallow a tonic, brewed by his personal shaman, Rodrigo. The blend of flora-based hal-lucinogens and nerve agents kept him functional. They helped him control the pangs of enmity that welled up in the night, when the suffocating jungle air choked us as we struggled to sleep.

The Swedish director, David, was sitting beside me on the flight. As if he had read my thoughts, he asked me about Richard. Like the others, he had seen the glowing account of the Vietnam vet in my book *Trail of*

Feathers and, like them, he was taken by the description of a real-life Rambo. As the aircraft touched down at Iquitos airport, I felt a sharp jab of anxiety in the pit of my stomach. I considered staying on the plane and going straight back to Lima, but the fact remained: I needed a security man. However impossible he was, Richard was a known entity.

Very little had altered in Iquitos, last outpost of the Upper Amazon. Wizened *señoras* still sat beneath their porches, tilting back on hardwood chairs, fanning their faces and dreaming of the wealthy tourists who had never come. The main street was still potholed, the café clientele still slurping *aguaje* juice at shaded tables, plagued by a thousand schoolboy salesmen. Even their wares were unchanged: stuffed piranha paperweights with open mouths, jaguar-tooth pendants, and pink-toed tarantulas pinned out in frames.

In 1854, a European traveller had described Iquitos as a "sparse and miserable hamlet consisting of no more than thirty houses and a straw-thatched church". Fifty years later it was a city with twenty thousand Peruvians and four thousand Europeans, all of them involved in the rubber business. With Charles Goodyear's invention of vulcanization in 1839, rubber became an invaluable product and was used for everything from making pavements to a covering for raincoats.

Along with Manaus, downstream in the Brazilian Amazon, Iquitos became a pleasure dome of decadence. The wealthy spent money like water. They imported crystal chandeliers, silk furnishings and entire cellars of vintage Champagne; they ate off the finest porcelain, gambled a fortune on the toss of a coin, and lit their cigars with five-dollar bills. But in 1912 an Englishman named Henry Wickham smuggled seventy thousand rubber seeds to Malaya. With no indigenous diseases to attack them, and arranged in neat plantations, the rubber trees thrived. Overnight Iquitos went from boom to bust.

As in many Amazonian towns, Iquitos had a mysterious surplus of women — about eight to every man. In an effort to win the female vote, and to boost municipal funds, the town's authorities had worked ceaselessly to lure gringos there. They had promoted lavish hotels, discos with outrageous "jungle" shows, beauty pageants, gambling parlours and cut-price beer. But tour companies had struggled to sell an outpost in the middle of the Amazon as the next big nightlife destination.

I headed for the favourite haunt of the resident foreigners, the appropriately named Gringo Bar. We pushed through the bustle of seductively dressed young women, each of whom was hoping to gain the attention of a gringo man. As we entered the dim light of the bar, they swooned and pressed close to stroke the Swedes' slick leather outfits.

Inside, a short, balding American barman was serving drinks. He was dressed in the same lilac Hawaiian shirt he had been wearing four years earlier. Behind him a display of jungle liqueurs was reflected in a tinted mirror. A middle-aged Englishman was propped up at the bar. He was sipping a cocktail through a straw that poked out from a clutch of paper parasols. On either arm hung a fifteen-year-old girl. The barman introduced him as Mad Mike. It was only later that I remembered him as a timid insurance salesman from Wigan, who had sold up everything and moved to Iquitos to reinvent himself and search for loose, easy women. I asked if he had seen Richard Fowler.

He motioned to a corner table, set back from the others. At first I couldn't make out what Mad Mike was pointing to but, gradually, I noticed a man sitting there, his head on the dim vinyl surface. I approached cautiously, with the Swedes watching from the front of the room. The man was snoring loudly, comatose, drunk. He stank of vomit and cigarettes, and was dressed in familiar rip-stop camouflage fatigues, Altama jungle boots and a black, Ninja-style singlet.

I uttered Richard's name once, and then again. The snoring rose in volume, reached a crescendo and died away. I prodded one arm. No reaction. I prodded the other, and the shoulders moved back, raising the head. A pair of worn military dog-tags scraped over the surface of the table as the torso became vertical. My eyes tracked up from the tags to the face. The cheeks were puffed up, bloated by the heat and drink, and in need of a shave. The whites of the eyes were jaundiced, a pale beeswax yellow. Their enlarged pupils strained to focus on me.

"Go on, buy a drink for an old soldier," he said.

"Don't you recognize me, Richard?"

"A whiskey will help my memory."

In the four years I had been away, Richard Fowler had fallen on hard times. The little work he had once secured as a guide had all but dried up. An increased dependence on mind-altering substances, gleaned from jungle plants, had made him unreliable and prone to fits of ferocity. The Swedes asked if this was the same Richard Fowler who had protected me so valiantly on the voyage to the land of the head-shrinkers. I assured them it was, and promised that he'd be back to top form in no time. He just needed a little time to detox.

A petite teenaged woman sidled over and sank her teeth into the lobe of Richard's left ear. She was wearing a strapless pink dress, with matching pink pouting lips. A strand of brunette hair hung over one eye, as if it had been trained to do so. She slid her sharp tongue over the flamingo-coloured lips and glared at me, then at the film team, anxious to be introduced.

"Meet my girlfriend," said Richard hoarsely. "Her name is Delicious."

The first stage of Richard's detoxification took two days. I told him that if he could get the poisons out of his bloodstream, there might be work with a pay cheque at the end. Delicious took charge of the treatment, which involved Richard sitting in a tin bathtub on the fetid landing of Hotel Peru, drinking gallons of *aguaje* juice. As he sat there, with Delicious rubbing a poultice of red *achiote* seeds on his chest, I revealed details of the expedition.

Richard listened as best as he could, pausing from time to time to vomit over the side of the bath. I lectured him on the lost wealth of the Incas, highlighting difficulties faced by previous explorers. Then I described my plan. "We will search out the Machiguenga tribe, get to know them and gain their trust," I said. "They must know where Paititi lies, and they'll take us. We just have to talk them into it. You'll be there to give us protection, to cover our backs. Are you game to come along?"

Richard didn't reply at once. A quantity of moss-green bile spewed from his mouth and ran down his chest. It was an involuntary action, but alarming all the same. I stared down at him. He was naked except for his dog-tags, his upper body tinted red with *achiote* balm. I cursed myself for being so stupid as to give him another chance. I opened my mouth, inhaled enough air to declare my change of mind, but he cut me short.

"I'll join you on one condition," he said.

"Huh?"

"It's that Rodrigo can come along."

Richard and Rodrigo were the odd couple of the Upper Amazon: a washed-up Vietnam veteran and his mate, a shaman who specialized in suspect preparations with hallucinatory effects. They were both out of work, largely because they were a danger to honest society. Any other expedition would have shown them the door. Perhaps it was for that reason that I changed my mind once again. I told Richard to gather his things together and find Rodrigo. We would leave for Lima on the morning flight.

In the afternoon I strolled down to the floating market of Belen, at the edge of town. The citrus-yellow light bathed the workers' backs as they parcelled up a thousand jungle products. Spend a few minutes at an Amazonian market and you get an idea of the jungle's wealth. There's nothing like it anywhere on earth. You see rolls of black tobacco, live turtles with primeval shells, and triangular fruits encased in feathery barbs. There are blind blue fish with tiger stripes, slivers of medicinal tree bark oozing amber-like sap, and pens of agouti rodents, shaking with dread, waiting for the knife.

Iquitos is a captivating place, the kind you only discover on long, insuperable journeys when you least expect to find anything at all. It's a blend of people, some wicked, some good, living it up at the edge of a great dreaded expanse. Most never venture beyond the city's perimeter, as they are terrified of reptiles, spirits and untamed tribes. I wondered if Paititi had shared the happy-go-lucky atmosphere of Iquitos. After all, if the city had lain in the uncharted depths of the jungle, its Inca citizens would surely have been touched by the awful fear of what lay beyond.

Before dawn Rodrigo appeared as if by magic at the blistered front door of Hotel Peru. I went down to greet him. He was about five foot one, and skinnier than he had been. The gauntness emphasized his long, pale cheeks, the deep-set eyes, and the flat, misshapen nose that hung at the centre of his face, like the shaft of a modelling tool. He was wearing flip-flops, chequered trousers pulled tight at the waist, and a faded velvet T-shirt, whose American slogan read "Beware of the

48

Werewolf". On the ground beside him lay a five-gallon cauldron, blackened and wretched, and a small denim satchel from which poked a spray of roots.

The shaman had no trust for me, and I little for him. We were acquaintances, the kind who endure each other and struggle to make do with a bad situation. Previous experience had taught me that without Rodrigo Richard would be even more trouble than he was likely to be. My main concern stemmed from the fact that where you had Rodrigo you also had an incessant stream of mind-altering drugs.

Before Richard came down from his room, I cautioned Rodrigo, warning him to refrain from brewing up any Amazonian psychedelia. On his mother's grave, he promised to resist, kissing his knuckles as a pledge. A moment later the sound of jungle boots could be heard rapping across the warped floorboards above. Then Richard was standing in the doorframe. Over one shoulder was slung a compact camouflage backpack, and over the other a twelve-gauge Brazilian pump-action shotgun, designed to kill rioting slum dwellers. The American was a shadow of his former self, his muscles were wasted from inaction, but at least he wasn't drunk.

The film team had been on the town all night, taking advantage of Iquitos' unlikely ratio of women to men. No one spoke as we drove to the airport for the flight to Lima. The silence was appropriate: we were at last the nucleus of a team, ready to undertake a grave duty.

At the airport Richard kissed Delicious, a long, passionate kiss, as if to prove to everyone in the departure hall that she was his girl. As soon as they were parted, she howled like a lamb being led away to slaughter.

"Fucking whore!" Richard said, under his breath. "That dog's got no self-respect."

CHAPTER
FOUR

Conditions in Success and Failure in Travel
An exploring expedition is daily exposed to a succession of accidents, any one of which may be fatal to its further progress. Interest yourself chiefly in the progress of your journey, and do not look forward to its end with eagerness.

The Art of Travel

In the hope of bonding with Rodrigo, I sat beside him on the flight to Lima and spent the time asking for his advice on finding a lost city. I thought the chatter might put him at ease, as he had never flown before. But the shaman wasn't in the least perturbed by his first experience of jet travel. Leaning back in his seat, with his knees pressed against his chest, he looked like a cheerful Amazonian leprechaun.

When he had listened to my question, he plugged his thumbs deep into his nostrils, sniffed hard, and pondered for several minutes. I thought he hadn't heard me, or had not made sense of my enquiry. But at length, he withdrew his thumbs, licked them front and back, then ranted about the danger.

The thing about shamans is that they aren't preoccupied by the matters that concern the rest of us. They don't care about brushing their teeth, eating healthy food, or what others might think of their overall appearance. Their feet may walk the earth, but their minds are roaming in another dimension.

Rodrigo reported dreamily that he'd flown over the jungle a thousand times "in the secrecy of his mind". There was danger all around, he said, nowhere more so than in the cold, spectral landscape of the Madre de Dios cloud-forest. I asked him to clarify what he meant by danger.

"The curses," he said coldly. "They run up and down the rivers and through the trees, hovering like humming-birds before a passion flower. Look at one and it will turn you blind. Touch one and you will drop dead."

"Can't you protect yourself?" I asked.

"*Seguro que tu puedes,* certainly you can."

"How?"

"Take someone who has a connection to the place."

"We're going to make friends with the Machiguenga and go with them," I said importantly.

Rodrigo thought for a moment, scratched a long thumbnail down his flat nose. "That's not good enough. The invisible curses will still be there."

"Well, who else has a connection with that jungle?"

"The Incas," said the shaman.

"But the Incas who lived at Paititi are dead, long gone. It's a *lost* city."

"You can take a dead Inca with you," he said.

"A *corpse?* You think we should take a corpse?"

"Not a corpse, but *una momia*, a mummy," Rodrigo corrected me meekly. "*Nos guiará a Paititi*, it will lead us to Paititi."

The shaman stuffed his thumbs up his nose again, lowered his eyelids, and began to hum.

I am all for respecting the advice of a spiritualist, but grave-robbing seemed a little extreme. I would have dismissed the shaman's suggestion as lunacy, but experience has taught me the power of trophies. You may have every knick-knack and useless contraption ever devised, but while they weigh you down, a simple trophy can go a long, long way. Such artefacts can keep the porters calm, boost morale and pacify a native people.

Better still, I reflected, I happened to know a good source of mummies within stabbing distance of Lima. I had once befriended a family of sympathetic *huaqueros*, grave-robbers, living in the Nazca desert, while on the murky trail of the Birdmen. The ancient communities of the Peruvian coast had predated the Incas by more than a thousand years. Their societies had placed great value on mummification, and had developed elaborate embalming techniques. Unlike the ancient Egyptians, who tended to preserve only aristocrats and royalty, the ancient coastal culture of Peru mummified everyone. The desert is still littered with tens of thousands of mummy bundles, entombed in the desiccated fringes of the Atacama. You know they are there because of the unmistakable humps on the desert's stark surface.

I had been drawn to learn about the ancient culture because of its expertise in weaving. A great many funerary textiles were decorated with flying men, Birdmen, clutching human trophy heads and what appear to be hallucinogens. When the grave-robbers dig them up, after they have been buried in the sand for almost two millennia, the colours are blindingly bright. The ancient coastal societies' knowledge and repertoire of textiles was passed down to the Incas, along with their mummification skills.

From the start of the journey, I had made it clear to the film crew that they would be documenting, not deciding. I didn't want their opinions influencing my own decisions. But I wondered how they would react to the idea of taking along a mummified body. I intended to run the plan past them that evening, once we were secure in the fortress of our hotel downtown. Rarely do I have difficulty in broaching a subject, especially one in which I have a deep interest, but I hadn't spent long enough with the team to judge how they would react.

Marco, the banker, had ordered a bottle of vintage Veuve Clicquot to toast the expedition. I was surprised that such an atrocious hotel would keep such a fine Champagne. Marco's appetite for the drink was considerable. He ordered it whenever it was available, which halved in likelihood with every mile we covered. Although usually unruffled, he snapped at the waitress because the bottle was insufficiently chilled. Warm Champagne, he scowled, was a drink fit only for pigs. The remark filled me with a new concern: how would the big banker deal with the jungle if he was so disturbed by the temperature of a sparkling wine?

54

In the awkward silence, as the waitress fumbled to find ice, I raised the idea of bringing a mummy to the jungle. The banker grimaced, but the Swedes clapped in unexpected delight.

"A mummy will look fabulous on film!" shouted the young director, forming a rectangular frame with his hands.

I tapped the Bulgarian, Boris, on the knee. He slid his eye away from the viewfinder of his video camera and squinted at me in confusion.

"What do you think about taking a mummy?"

"Mummy, Daddy, baby . . . Sure, no problem," he said, in his heavy accent.

"If Rodrigo says we gotta take a fuckin' mummy," said Richard, wringing his hands together, "then we'll take one. He *knows* . . ." Richard paused for dramatic effect. "He can see the invisible beams, the rays, the Curse Lines." He shaded his eyes with his hands, and pretended to seek out the invisible rays.

The decision to take a mummy trophy touched a vein of lunacy, and set us a little further apart from our competition. I had heard from the Explorer's Club in Lima that a famous Polish adventurer had just departed for the high jungle east of Machu Picchu, in search of the lost city. On the phone, the club secretary's voice was trembling as he listed the inventory of the equipment and supplies, the team of learned men and women who made up the expedition.

I, on the other hand, had almost no equipment, limited food stores, consisting chiefly of Pot Noodles, and a team made up of a washed-up Vietnam vet, a shaman, a Russian banker with a penchant for chilled Champagne, a clueless Bulgarian and a pair of ever-optimistic Swedes.

My line-up might have been suspect, but I felt sure we could gain the upper hand by putting ourselves in the mindset of the Incas. Think like the Incas, act like them and, I felt, we could only be strengthened. We know that the Incas took their mummies along on journeys. It's conceivable that some were even taken to Paititi, to form a kind of spiritual nucleus of the society. So, in some warped way, having an embalmed body with us made perfect sense.

Before setting out to acquire a mummy, I broke away from the team and visited the library at the ancient monastery of San Francisco, a few blocks away from Lima's central square. The whitewashed walls of the central courtyard were hung with paintings, some dating back to the time of the *conquistadores*. The floors were laid with large, waxed terracotta tiles, the colour of blood oranges, and a cedar ceiling above the stairwell, clearly inspired by Islamic geometric design. I ascended the wide, low stairs, turned right and slipped into the magical library.

Sombre wooden shelves ran the length of the room and every inch was caked with dust, oily and aromatic like rappee snuff. The subjects were clearly labelled — *Liturgia, Ciencia, Historia, Topografía*; the fragile vellum texts were pressed tight together, a reminder of the days when the written word was sacred. A pair of symmetrical staircases, rising in spirals, connected the

56

upper gallery to the one below. I was on the trail of a book written four centuries before, the lost manuscript of Aguirre, self-styled Spanish king of the Amazon. A scholar in Seville had contacted me out of the blue and said that the text had been written in 1622 by Hector Gomez of Castile. I was surprised the man knew about my quest, and would bother to track me down to pass on such invaluable research for free. He swore that the manuscript gave the true location of Paititi. What he meant by "true", I wasn't sure. But an original clue is worth its weight in gold. My source told me that he thought there was a copy of the manuscript at Lima's San Francisco monastery.

The monk on duty had permitted me entrance to the library on condition I donate generously in advance. I counted a selection of damaged Peruvian bills into his hand, until his voracious eyes shimmered like fire opals.

Like all Paititi-hunters, I had read the existing account of Lope de Aguirre's expedition, which is presented in a text written by Friar Julio Simon, published in 1625. It is hard to overstate the author's contempt for Aguirre, a veritable bad boy of Spanish exploration. Of him, Simon wrote:

He was the *Demonio* himself, this Aguirre! About fifty years, short of stature, sparsely built, coarse-featured, of a villainous weasand, which any hangman would have slit with pleasure. His face was small and lean, his neck and cheeks pock-marked, his beard black as coal, and when he looked at you, out of dark eyes piercing as a falcon, his gaze was stern and threatening. But withal, he was a noisy talker and a boaster, if well backed by the *companeros*, and bold and determined; otherwise, he was an arrant coward. So hardy was his habit of body that he could endure endless fatigue, afoot or on horseback. Never was he seen without two coats of mail, or a steel breastplate, and he always carried a sword, dagger, arquebus or lance. He slept mostly by day, being careful of his throat, for he was afraid of resting at night, lest one steal on him in the dark. Never did he take off his armour altogether, nor hang up his weapons. Turbulent was this Señor Aguirre, lover of the broils and breeder of mutinies, enemy of all good men and deeds.

Lope de Aguirre, a Basque, had been sent to accompany a Spanish general, Julio de Ursua, on his journey in search of El Dorado. The year was 1560. They were hunting for the secret Inca city hidden deep in the jungle, said by contemporary accounts to be abundant with gems and gold. It is a dream that has driven honest men mad for centuries.

The expedition was colossal: hundreds of Europeans — warriors, religious men and common adventurers — and thousands of Indians from the Andes. They descended from the mountains, down, down, down, with their horses, weaponry and palanquins, into the grotesque vastness of the jungle. The general, Julio de Ursua, had brought along his lover, a young widow. Her name was Inez de Altienza; either she was out of her mind, or the bravest woman ever to live. Soon after the procession arrived in the jungle, Aguirre slit the frail widow's throat, then killed Ursua and declared himself King of the Amazon.

My informant in Seville had described the lost manuscript of Aguirre as "the last perfect chiselled piece to the Paititi riddle". Find it, he assured me, and I would possess the key to the lost ruins. I hadn't told the film crew of the lead, partly through paranoia and partly through a desire to control the information. After nine hours, checking ten thousand books, I came to a horrid conclusion. The book did not exist . . . not in the library, not anywhere. Months later, I realized that the Andalucian scholar was a fraud, his story a fabrication, dreamed up by the Paititi-hunting competition to draw me away from real research and waste my time.

Talk of Curse Lines, black magic and embalmed bodies dominated the fifteen-hour journey to Nazca. The driver became so fearful of the conversation that he made a detour to a chapel, and prayed there all afternoon. Most visitors to the small desert town of Nazca take the air-conditioned luxury bus: the service had the distinct advantages of speed, comfort and reliability. But we were on a budget and so we hitch-hiked instead.

Never before in the history of television could a film crew — or, for that matter, a lost-city expedition — have hitched with so much gear. We split up into two groups to increase our chances. I stood out in the road with Rodrigo and Richard, surrounded by a sea of kit-bags and boxes. It was a long time before anyone stopped. Eventually a 1957 Chevrolet Bel Air ground to a halt two hundred feet ahead. It was a sleek vehicle, plum-red, dented, and missing the chevron from the front. The driver was a burly, dark-skinned man called José, with a scarred neck and impressively muscular hands. He was eager to talk about the jungle and the danger. At the same time I realized that he harboured strong suicidal tendencies; he was the kind of person who becomes addicted to horror movies, not because he likes them but because he can't help himself.

Every so often he would swerve the steering-wheel to the left, throwing the old wreck of a car into the oncoming lane as a truck approached. As a veteran of India's highways I am not easily frightened, but José would wait until you were drowning in adrenaline before veering the crumbling roadster back to the right side of the road. His enthusiasm for dicing with death seemed at odds with the fear he derived from talk of bewitching.

"The legend of Paititi is as true and as sincere as a newborn baby," he said. "Nurture the legend, love it as a mother loves that child, and it will return the love."

"Do you think it will be a dangerous journey?" I asked.

José flared his lips wide so I could see the rotten teeth hanging from bloodied gums, like crumbling tombstones in a deserted burial ground.

"*El peligro es diabólico*, the danger is diabolical!" he yelled. "It could make an executioner of a priest."

★ ★ ★

60

We must have been the only visitors to Nazca in fifty years who had no interest in seeing the famous "Lines" etched into the basalt surface of the desert. People come from every country in the world to soar above them in small aeroplanes and marvel at the mystery. No one is certain how the strange symbols got there, or when, so they show their foolishness by dreaming up implausible hypotheses.

We had no time to solve the mysteries of Nazca: we were already engaged, committed to a far darker business. These days, the town is prosperous, enlivened by the wealth of tourist cash, every cent of it lured there by the Lines. We found a cheap, squalid boarding-house at the end of the main street. It perched there like a sparrow on a branch. You had the feeling that a sudden gust of wind might send it crashing to the ground.

As soon as we reached the hotel, Rodrigo stripped down to his underpants and prepared a ritual. He said it was for the carcass, the cadaver of a man whom we would meet next day. The ceremony involved the shaman drinking a murky tar-like fluid, more usually stored in a Fanta bottle at the bottom of his bag. When the cork was pulled out, a putrid smell issued forth. Rodrigo refused to tell me what the concoction contained, but said it was to wake the sleeping. He chanted for an hour or two, rattling the dried fronds of his *chacapa*, drifting on the sound. Richard was on the journey too, having sucked the dregs from the bottle while the shaman wasn't looking.

The film crew and I turned in early and were up at dawn in time to see the fresh glow of pink rise like a halo above the horizon. The odd couple were passed out cold. They had both thrown up in their sleep, no doubt a side-effect of the medicine. We roused them, feasted on an economic loaf of dry brown bread, and made our way to meet the grave-robbers at the burial ground of Barillo.

A *campesino* gave us a lift to the cemetery in his sleek new pickup truck. He didn't think it odd to be asked to drive off the main road and veer on to the *pampa* in search of mummies. In the hope that he wouldn't enquire about our motives, I praised his vehicle's immaculate condition.

"¡*Sí, sí*, Señor!" He cackled. "It's all thanks to our ancestors. They scratched those mysterious signs out there. Why did they do a thing like that? That's what everyone asks. The answer is simple, my friend, it was so that centuries later their descendants would get an easy living."

The old farmer reflected on this for a moment or two, changed from third to second gear and went on: "We should be like them," he said, "and do something that will help out our great-grandchildren a century from now." He turned up the air-conditioning a little higher, for the heat outside was already fierce. He accelerated, swerving down on to a dry riverbed, the same route I had taken four years before. The sand was fine, like sieved cake flour, and it exploded away from the wheels as we swept through.

We glided past a grove of *warango* trees, then caught sight of the farmhouse: a low adobe building with a rusted tin roof, circled by a slapdash fence of thorns. A pair of savage dogs rushed at the car, blurred in movement.

"Who's there?" shouted a man. We couldn't see him, but he was close. "Who's there?" he called again.

I shouted my name, exclaiming that I had visited four years previously. The voice whistled back the dogs. A minute of silence passed, and a man appeared. He stood before the vehicle, his back arched over, his grimy shirt ripped like a rag mop. I stepped over to him and put out my hand. The figure did not offer his.

"Juan! *¿No me recuerdas?* Don't you remember me?" I asked. "You showed me your mummified trophy head. You took me to the cemetery over there."

I pointed beyond the *warango* trees, but the farmer didn't see the sweep of my arm. He was sightless. Stooping a fraction, I observed his face. It was crafted from the same sheet of coarse leather as before, chapped and blistered like rawhide. His eyes were open but damaged in some way.

"The head's gone," said Juan sullenly. "It was taken by the thieves."

"*Thieves?*"

"*Sí, vienen por la noche,* they came in the night. They said we were taking too much loot from the cemetery. They wanted it all for themselves. So they killed my wife, took my sight and beat me with a cane. If I took anything else from the graveyard, they said that they'd return and cut off my hands."

"When did this happen?"

"*Dos años atrás,* two years ago."

"Did you tell the police?"

Juan spat at the dust. "*Police?* What good are they?"

He might have been blind, but Juan could still lead the way unaided up the steep embankment to the burial ground. He had walked it a thousand times for sure, so often laden with riches from newly opened graves. We ascended the natural bulwark of sand, and went over the top like soldiers at the Somme. The cratered panorama was like a repulsive no man's land. Bleached white bones were scattered all around, tattered clothing, scalps of brunette hair and fragments of human skin: a postcard of apocalypse.

The grave-robbers' front line had advanced considerably since my previous visit. The *huaqueros* were far more organized now, using bulldozers and chainsaws to open the graves.

The Swedes were shocked by what they saw. They shot a few feet of film uneasily, as Richard knocked the teeth from a broken lower jaw. "I'm gonna make a necklace for Delicious," he said.

We all looked at the Vietnam vet, appalled at his insensitivity. But I was as guilty as he. I had conspired with Rodrigo to pilfer a mummy for our protection.

I asked the slim shaman for an alternative defence against the invisible Curse Lines. "If we take a mummy," I explained, "Juan here will have his hands cut off, and we don't want that to happen."

The shaman tightened the strap of his wide-brimmed cloth hat to his chin, and nodded vigorously. "I will ask the spirits, the dead, to leave their graves," he replied, "and to join us on our journey to find Paititi."

Crouching low on his haunches, Rodrigo opened his denim bag, and pulled out a homemade cigar. It was stuffed with *mapacho*, black jungle tobacco, and was as thick as my wrist. He lit it, sucked at it, kissing with his cheeks until the tip was burning evenly. Then he took a long, measured drag, his chest swelling with smoke, as he traversed into another cerebral plane.

While the shaman called the spirits from their sleep, I escorted Juan back to the farmhouse. We sat there on rough-cut logs fanning our faces with our hands. On the far cracked mud wall the poster of Diana, Princess of Wales, was still hanging, a little dustier and more yellowed than before. Nothing had altered since my last visit, except three new pieces of furniture, positioned in the corners of the room. For some reason they were hidden under dirty sackcloth sheets.

"My wife is dead, *mi amada esposa*, my beloved wife," said Juan forlornly. "She was the light of my life. How I miss her!"

I tried to console the retired grave-robber as he squatted on the log, his blind eyes weeping. "She lives in your heart," I said. "She is with you. She is here. Fight the loneliness."

Juan stared blindly at the poster of the princess. "*¿Soledad?* Loneliness?" he whispered. "I am not alone."

I assumed that he was referring to his children, or to the image of the dead princess. But he was not. Leaning over to one of the sackcloth sheets, he fumbled for the corner and tugged hard. I am not easily surprised, but I was certainly taken aback by Juan's secret friend. For under the cloth was the embalmed cadaver of a man, crouched in the foetal position, all leathery and calm. His hands were grasped together, the fingers contorted like tubular roots; his spindly limbs were slender and crooked, and his face a crazed, glaring mask of disbelief.

Juan got up, and lifted the veils on his other two mummified companions. He did so with extraordinary composure, as if pulling the coverings away from disused chairs. The other two people were similar to the first, one male, the other female. They were perched awkwardly, wrapped in gloomy layers of cloth, their desiccated features leering like grotesque fiends from a child's imagination. Juan could not see his embalmed friends. But he stared at them all the same, caressing his rough palms over their faces, moving his fingers lovingly over the furrows and the grooves.

As I sat there, watching, part in horror and part in awe, I reflected that, in any other society, an old man who lived with mummies might have been dragged off to an institution. But Juan wasn't harming anyone. He was the one who had been duped by society.

A long while passed. There was still no sign of the film team or the odd couple. Juan and I sat in silence, reflecting, thinking, hoping. Then, spontaneously, he wept again.

"*Estamos maldecidos*, we are cursed people," he said, in a dry, raspy voice, when the tears had dried. "All of us, cursed, certain to face damnation. *No hay salida*, there is no escape."

CHAPTER
FIVE

Presents and Articles for Payment
It is of the utmost importance to a traveller to be
well and judiciously supplied with these: they are his
money, and without money a person can no more
travel in Savagedom than in Christendom.

The Art of Travel

A journey to Peru would be meaningless without at
least one fifty-hour bus ride over the Cordillera, the
mountains that run down the country like the spine on
a chameleon's back. The distance between Nazca and
Cusco is pitifully small, but the drive is an endurance
test of jolting, the kind used to see if a new model of
car is roadworthy or not.

The trip was made worse by Richard, who
entertained himself by boasting about every girl he had
savaged. The list was long, the details obscene,
especially the conquests of prepubescent girls in the
riotous days of Vietnam. "There's nothing like a French
whorehouse to service a man's needs," he said, rattling
the mummy's teeth in his hand like dice. "Those little
Asian *chicas* could bring tears to a grown man's eyes.
I'll tell ya, I've killed people, what the heck? I'm not
ashamed of it. War's just like that. Sure, I've killed
gooks, scalped 'em too, but I've never shed a tear over

it. They're dead and that's that. Then I hustle down to Saigon with a couple of chums, and I'm weeping like a kitten within the hour."

I asked about taking scalps.

Richard stared out at the coffee-brown panorama, lost in concentration. "You need a sharp knife," he said slowly. "It's got to be real, real sharp, so sharp you could do someone an injury. You lie 'em face down with your boot on the back of their neck. Then you slice from the temple, at the hairline, cutting down through the fat, real gentle, with an arc-like movement. You have to make sure to get enough of the flesh, otherwise it'll go wrong and you'll start losing the hair." Richard paused, his eyes wide as he peered into the past. "I did a lovely one once. It was a woman's scalp. Had it hanging from my belt."

It was too easy to judge Richard, to condemn him. His first experiences as a man had carved out his life, charging him with hatred, a terrible bitterness. He was traumatized beyond the point of redemption, broken, unwanted, loved by no one except Delicious. Richard had his sight, but was sightless; just as Juan was blind but could see.

The bus rolled on to the east, lurching over the mountains like a fairground ride. It stopped frequently and, when it did, an army of short round women with plaits and black sombreros scuttled up and touted purply-pink jelly. They completed the carnival atmosphere, howling with laughter for no reason at all.

I sat with my face pressed up against the window, pondering life and entertaining dark thoughts. I shared Juan's sadness, then found myself raging that Richard should have been wounded by the generation he had served. After that, my thoughts turned to Paititi.

Perhaps the lost city wasn't a haven for the Incas' mummies or their gold, I thought. Instead, it might have been a place of sacrifice. The carved sacrificial stones at Machu Picchu, with their cupped conduits for blood, have been well discussed. So, perhaps it's conceivable that Paititi was in fact a killing ground, a zone dedicated to ritual sacrifice. After all, the Spanish frowned on the slaughter of innocent child victims, a practice to which the Incas were rather partial. Without such executions they had no way of placating the wrath of the Sun. Down there in some corner of Madre de Dios, I reflected, perhaps there lay the remains of ten thousand dismembered children: their blood tapped by a deranged officer, veteran of a depraved campaign, an Inca Colonel Kurtz.

After six punctures and fifty-one hours we arrived at Cusco, broken and dishevelled. I suggested to Leon, the producer, that he suck some funds from the Russian banker. But he said Marco was enjoying the hardship: it was new to him, a feature of life he had not tasted before.

As soon as we had settled into a fleapit off Avenida del Sol, I set about tracking down a man called Sanchez Esmeralda. A friend of a friend had slipped me the name in London, exclaiming he'd found more lost cities "than Indiana Jones".

Finding Sanchez took about twelve minutes. This was partly because Cusco is quite a small town, the kind where everyone knows everyone else; and partly because he happened to sell ice-cream from a booth a hundred yards from where we were staying.

He was an earnest-looking man, bespectacled and bald, with bushy eyebrows that hung above his face like thunderclouds. He smiled between sentences, and talked very fast, about ice-cream, mostly. He gave me an ice lolly for free. It was shocking pink and tasted of walnuts.

"It's a new one," he said smugly, "getting quite popular . . . It's called la Sangre de los Incas, Blood of the Incas."

I asked him about lost cities.

"There's no such thing," he said quickly.

"But I thought you'd found lots of them."

Sanchez ripped the wrapper from a second ice lolly and sucked on it hard. "Cusco's full of people searching for El Dorado," he said, "*pero son idiotas*, but they're idiots. They have no brains. Sure, I did have a quick look in the jungle, dipped my toes into it. But I've got brains, so I came back and settled down to an honourable life. Search for a lost city and you understand there's no honour in it . . . that it's a worthless way to spend your time."

I swept my tongue over the Blood of the Incas, and grimaced at the taste. "What about Paititi, then?"

70

Sanchez giggled and slid the bridge of his glasses to the top of his nose. "Paititi is a myth created by *los que están en la sombra*, the men in the shadows."

"Who are they?"

"The men in grey suits who run the country."

"You mean the President?"

"No, no," Sanchez corrected me. "Presidents come and go, but the men in the shadows are always with us."

"But why spread a rumour, a myth, *the* myth of Paititi?"

"*Por el petróleo, por supuesto*, because of the oil, of course."

Sanchez stopped talking, and paused to serve fluorescent yellow ice-creams to a group of schoolgirls.

"*Oil?* What's oil got to do with Paititi?"

"Have you seen the oil charts for Madre de Dios?"

"No."

"Well, go to INRENA and take a look," said Sanchez, smiling. "There's ten million barrels of oil under the trees. If the government started drilling, there'd be an international outcry. It's virgin jungle after all. So they've closed the area off, saying it's to protect the nature and the ruins ... the ruins of Paititi."

Sanchez's conspiracy theory and the Blood of the Incas gave me a terrible stomach-ache. I did not agree with his theory that Paititi simply didn't exist. But I was alarmed by the government's eagerness for oil. I have come across suspect oil projects before, and where you find them, you find problems. Next morning, with the film crew trailing me, and the odd couple still asleep, I went to ask hard questions at the National Institute of Natural Resources, otherwise known as INRENA.

The department had that odious air of officialdom, the kind that drains the life out of visitors and employees alike. Everyone who worked there staggered around with furtive movements, clutching dusty files to their chests. They spoke in whispers — if they ever spoke at all. It was as if an invisible sign ordered silence on pain of execution. The only sound was the clunk-click of manual typewriters spewing out official reports on reports.

Not daring to speak, I waved at the clerk to attract his attention. His index fingers were pecking at the keys of an antique Remington typewriter, like a pair of peahens feasting on grain. Eventually he looked at me and came over. There was a patch of grime in the middle of his shirtfront, where dusty files had pressed while being transported surreptitiously from one desk to the next. "¿Sí, Señor?"

"I am interested in going into Madre de Dios," I said.

The clerk didn't reply at once. He stooped low, pulled back a deep wooden drawer, and snatched an inch of papers. "Fill them in triplicate, all triplicate," he hissed.

It was then that on the far wall, beyond a sea of grey-skinned clerks with grime patches on their chests, I saw a map. The reason it caught my eye was that at the top, printed prominently in brash type, was the name of an oil company, a household name all over the world. The map was green. It was a map of the jungle, the Madre de Dios jungle.

I motioned for Marco to engage the clerk in grave conversation. As a banker, he was good at such things, while remaining charming. Then I hurried between the maze of desks, bobbing and weaving like a frail sailing-boat balanced upon a curl of ocean wave. I was soon standing at the great lime-green jungle chart, struggling to make sense of the contours and waterways.

I found the Madre de Dios river. Some distance north-west a clutch of pins, with miniature flags attached, poked triumphantly through the sheet, like markers of an immense treasure. All around, a zone had been drawn with a red Chinagraph marker, warning ordinary folk to stay away.

Until that moment, as the clerk chased me back through the labyrinth of desks, I had considered ice-cream-selling Sanchez to be a bit of a crackpot, the sort of man who kills someone famous for no reason at all. But the map pins had suggested there was oil, and if there was oil there was money at stake. I rushed back to have a chat with Sanchez. But, mysteriously, his booth was boarded up.

"*Él se ha ido*, he's gone away," said a shoeshine boy. "Two men came this morning and took him away."

"Where? Where did they go?"

The boy shook his head. "*Al infierno*, to Hell," he said.

I'm not good with forms or official documents, so we got Marco to complete the application. He pored over it for hours, while the Swedes and I went to the market to buy supplies with his money.

Cusco is the Kathmandu of South America. The main square, Plaza de Armas, was flooded with sickly yellow light, backpackers and prim little boutiques selling junk: llama-shaped toothpick holders, condor-feather fans and paperweights crafted from rusty tin cans. On the other side of town there lay a fabulous covered market, where stout Andean women scurried past, heaving bundles on their backs. We bought a pair of blue plastic barrels with tight-fitting lids and filled them with basics: rice, raisins, coca leaves and nuts, flour and cooking oil, garlic and spices, spaghetti, canned fish and plenty of sugar. Elsewhere, we stocked up on size-nine rubber boots for the porters, fishhooks and plastic sheeting, pots, pans, cutlery and plates. We bought some cheap Chinese flashlights, too, and batteries and candles, and a Manchester United football. My journey to the land of the Shuar tribe had taught me the importance of practical gifts. Last time I had made the mistake of buying beads and trinkets, and learned quickly that tribal people all want the same thing: twelve-gauge shotgun cartridges. So we bought six boxes of them. The only thing they valued higher than ammunition were Man United footballs.

Back at the hotel, Richard and Rodrigo had been experimenting with a shrub called *sinicuichi*. More commonly found in Mexico than Peru it was used by the Aztecs. Ingestion of the plant leads to strong auditory hallucinations, radically distorting any sound.

Richard's condition made it quite impossible to have a sensible conversation, so I went downstairs.

In the foyer, the manager had heard about Sanchez. "They've taken him away," he explained glumly.

"Because of his outspoken views on the government?"

"No, no, on account of his ice-creams. He makes them himself, and they keep poisoning people."

We got talking about Paititi. The manager dabbed a handkerchief to his temples, as if trying to soak up a stain. "Have you spoken to Navarre?" he asked.

It took another twelve minutes to track down Señor Navarre. He was a professor of tourism at the university, and had written a treatise entitled *Paititi: The Truth of the El Dorado Legend*. I flicked through it and realized the book was designed to throw other Paititi-hunters off the trail. Its author was about forty-five, had sleek Mongolian eyes, a thick beard and a slippery disposition.

"Why are you interested in Paititi?" he asked at once.

"We're making a film about great explorers who have searched for the ruins."

"You'll never find them," he said. "You have no hope at all."

"You mean we'll not find *explorers*?"

"No, the ruins. I know you are hunting for them. I can see it in your eyes."

I lowered my head and stared wide-eyed at the floor. Gosh, I thought to myself, this man's really good.

"I suppose you want me to tell you where to find Paititi," Navarre went on. "Well, I won't. I won't help you at all. I'll just give you some advice: keep your team small, a handful of men at the most. Take the bare minimum of food, and plenty of coca leaves for stamina, and don't forget the *lifta* to activate it. But, most important of all, take your time. A man with no hope has even less hope if he has no time."

We waited and waited, and hoped, and waited some more, but our permission to enter the restricted area didn't come from INRENA. The morning before we were scheduled to leave Cusco for the jungle, I rose before dawn and walked out of town, up the hill to the ruined fortress Sachsayhuaman. It's said that the Incas built Cusco in the shape of a puma and that the stronghold of Sachsayhuaman formed its head and jaws. The puma, or *tigre*, as everyone in Peru calls it, was regarded as a sacred animal by the Incas. No one is quite sure how long it took to construct the unfinished fortress, or how the stone blocks were moved into place.

Sachsayhuaman is undoubtedly the most impressive feat of known engineering left by the Incas. The stones range in size from small rocks to colossal shaped granite boulders, which weigh more than three hundred tons each. They are fitted together without the slightest gap between them, a fact that has bewildered archaeologists for generations. As usual, the mystery has led to a great number of theories, some of them possible, others far-fetched. One of the least plausible suggestions was that a plant-based potion was poured on the stone. When left for an hour or two, it supposedly softened even the hardest granite to the consistency of clay.

As I climbed up to the fortress, a family brushed past me, all dressed up in tight Andean clothes, a pet llama led behind on a frayed string. They, and hundreds of other Cusqueñias, made the same trek each morning, posing for tourist pictures in the alleyways of the Plaza de Armas. For such people tourists are manna from heaven, ever-willing to sprinkle a few coins in return for a glimpse of how Peru might once have been.

The mighty fortress was still sleeping, enshrouded in darkness, cold and surly as if betrayed by the people who had built it. I walked down into its heart, and marvelled at the massiveness of the stones. They sit flush, cheek by jowl, taller than a man, daring you not to be impressed. You can set eyes on those blocks a thousand times, and each time you are forced to regard them with the same awe, the same fascination.

I was certain that somewhere, deep in the jungle, there were other immense walls like those at Sachsayhuaman. They would be overgrown with foliage and vines, but they would be there all the same. Of that I had no doubt.

Later that day Marco went to the INRENA office to see if the paperwork had been approved. He was armed with a roll of hundred-dollar bills and a box of Cohiba cigars. He returned an hour or so later with our application. It had been stamped all over: "REFUSED".

"What shall we do?" the Swedes asked nervously.

"We'll go without a permit, and get on with it," I said.

I suggested we prepare the equipment to take the film crew's minds off the paperwork. We took great care that all the bags were waterproof, their contents double-wrapped in polythene. For an expedition with a non-existent budget, we had accumulated a striking amount of gear. Most of it was the Swedes' camera equipment. They were shooting principally on film, digital video as backup. Film gives much grander results; the other advantage was that the 16mm Arriflex camera was virtually indestructible, a sharp contrast to the video, which was to seize up frequently in the humidity. They had eighty cans of film stock, each ten minutes in length. That alone weighed ninety pounds. Then there was the tripod, another fifty pounds; and a bag filled with tapes, chargers and batteries, a clapperboard, cables and lights, weighing another hundred and forty pounds. They had a seventy-pound Honda generator, too, for charging batteries and to run the hair-dryer, needed for drying out circuitry. There was sound equipment as well, and spare lenses for the Arriflex, the video system, and a mountain of other odds and ends. Another expanse of technical paraphernalia was positioned nearby in the shade. There were three steel boxes with padlocks, and a set of four black indestructible cases, more lights, another tripod and half a dozen tote bags, which felt as if they were filled with lead.

"That's not our stuff," said the Swedes, icily. "It's Boris's gear."

"But he's just a film student," I snarled. "Why does he need all this junk?"

Leon looked over the sea of technical apparatus. "Bulgarians are like that," he said.

I begged the film crew again to cut down their equipment, but they chased me back to my room. There, heaped against the far whitewashed wall, was the food and my own odds and ends. The pile rose up to the ceiling, like a bonfire waiting for the touch-paper. The Pot Noodles were still stowed in cardboard cartons, the size and shape of coffins. The food and supplies we had bought in Cusco had been stashed in the plastic barrels. Beside them was a set of tatty climbing gear and ropes, and the thirty-six-year-old Zodiac dinghy, deflated and packed, then a dozen machetes with various lengths of blade, the sharpening stones and shotgun cartridges, shovels, kerosene, lanterns and saws.

Previous journeys had taught me the danger of taking too much stuff. You end up spending all your time bogged down, feverishly protecting gear that's of little value anyway. The worst part is that you need an army of men to carry it, and an army of men needs food. It's a vicious circle: the more gear you have, the more men you need, and the more men you need, the more food you must have for them, and the more food you have, the more men you need.

On my expedition to the Shuar I had found that any item that couldn't be broken up, or cannibalized into something else if required, was worthless.

With gnashing teeth, I marched over to the Swedes' room and told them that if we hit hard times, nothing could be regarded as too precious. We had to be prepared to cannibalize everything.

"*Everything?*"

"Yes, *everything*, even the Arriflex!"

It might have been cruel to taunt them with such threats but, as I saw it, a little threatening was a good thing. It kept the men on their toes.

In the next room, the odd couple were waking up for the day. Their room stank of excrement, as the toilet had overflowed, sending a tidal wave of sewage as far as the beds. The film crew had come to my room in the night to tell me of their fear. Lined up, like cadet officers on parade, they reported the problem.

"It's Richard," said Leon, gravely. "He's very unstable."

"He's a Vietnam vet," I said. "He's been trained to kill a man with a single blow. A guy like that finds it hard to adapt to the city. He'll be fine once we're in the jungle."

Leon and the others didn't actually say it, but they were hinting Richard should be left behind. What passed for his usual conduct put the fear of God into ordinary men. I was no longer troubled when he pulled out a machete in a crowded bar, tried to pick up schoolgirls, or threatened to scalp us, then rip off our heads and scoop out our brains. To me it was quite normal, the kind of behaviour one would expect from a man who had walked the fine line between life and death.

A worn-out bus ran the route twice weekly from Cusco to the brink of the Madre de Dios jungle. We loaded up our gear and scoffed omelette sandwiches before the bald tyres grumbled away down the cobbles. There can be few drives on earth quite so spectacular as the one from the highlands to the cloud-forest east of the Andes. The landscape began as desolate, forsaken, abandoned, a thousand shades of grey. There was the odd thicket of eucalyptus trees, tall and huddled, like giants sheltering in the wind. The stark beauty was bisected from time to time by rivers, their high waters rolling down from the hills towards the secret heart of the jungle.

We passed infrequent hamlets, thatched houses crafted from honey-coloured blocks of mud. Outside each one an old man was chopping wood, and a pair of savage dogs basked in the late-morning sun. There were children, too, tossing marbles in the dust, and llamas striding about haughtily, as if they owned the world.

Drive down from the *altiplano* and you get a sense of how little the Peruvian countryside has changed in centuries. I wondered whether the Incas might have taken the very same route to Paititi with the Spanish at their heels. There would have been thousands of them on the move, some carrying the treasures perhaps, whatever they had been, as well as stone-masons and artisans, engineers, soldiers and priests. The Incas had scant understanding of the jungle. They traded with the tribes, but to live in the jungle themselves, they would have needed know-how. For me, that was the greatest mystery of Paititi. How did the Incas, a mountain people, learn to adapt to the ferocious jungle environment? How did they endure the mosquitoes and the damp, and stay safe from the predators and the tribes?

As the road spiralled downwards, the vegetation changed. Gone were the meticulous eucalyptus groves and the filigree of ferns, replaced by a riot of lichen-encrusted trees. From the moment I saw it, something clicked in my mind. This was an ancient, mesmerizing place, the kind the fleeing Incas would have found irresistible.

In a handful of miles, the meagreness of the highlands had been exchanged for a realm of prehistoric flowers with bronze-green fronds, of *cecropria*, bamboo and bromeliads, a place where every square inch of flora was a world of its own.

There were sheering rockfaces, too, shadow mountains, veiled by the variation in light, and sleek waterfalls, tumbling from one ledge to the next. Through it all, permeating like a dragon's breath, was the vapour. It was moist and haunting, cool, but above all it was cautionary, warning intruders to turn back while there was still time.

As we travelled into the jungle, I gave much thought to the ruins and what we would do when and if we found them. My concern from the start was that the

Peruvian authorities would muscle in and try to take the place over. We were on tourist visas, after all, and had nothing in the way of formal accreditation: a point that was sure to be held against us. One possibility was the idea of licensing Paititi, or buying it outright. It may sound far-fetched, but there was a precedent. In 1839, while travelling through the jungles of Honduras, the American traveller John Lloyd Stephens discovered and then bought the lost Mayan city of Copán. On buying a lost city, he wrote:

> The reader is perhaps curious to know how old cities sell in central America. Like other articles of trade, they are regulated by the quantity in the market and the demand; but, not being staple articles like cotton and indigo, they were held at fancy prices, and at that time were dull of sale. I paid fifty dollars for Copán. There was never any difficulty about the price. I offered that sum, for which Don José María thought me only a fool; if I had offered more, he would have probably considered me something worse.

The bus driver stayed alert with a quid of coca leaves stuffed up in his cheek. He was a timid man who took each bend with hesitation, as if it was his first day out. His face was long and anxious, with chicken-feet wrinkles to the sides of his eyes, and a field of deep furrows on his brow. His wife sat beside him, swivelled in her seat. She was a buxom woman, whose alluring eyes scanned the male passengers flirtatiously. The

Swedes, the banker, the Bulgarian and I managed to avoid her gaze out of respect for her husband.

The further the decrepit bus lurched down towards the jungle core, the more suggestively she teased the audience, until Richard could stand it no longer. He beckoned her over. In a heartbeat, she had flown from the front, and was perched like a bird on his knee. She clung there precariously, whispering into his ear, pouting with delight.

When eventually the bus slunk into the modest town of Pillcopata, Richard disappeared with the woman. He whooped loudly, declaring in his atrocious Spanish how he would give her a night to remember. As his employer I felt responsible in some way. I was unhappy that the bus driver's honour had been flayed so publicly. So, I went to apologize.

He was sitting alone, timidly, at the only bar in town, with a glass of warm beer and a damp cigarette. A rumba was playing in the back, the melody wafting through the evening air. I nodded in greeting and the bus driver pointed to a chair.

"I am burning inside," I said. "I feel terrible for the way my colleague has behaved. He has no manners. If you can forgive him . . ."

"*¿Porqué te preocupas?* Why do you worry?" asked the bus driver.

"Because I am embarrassed, and ashamed."

The man said nothing for a moment or two. He took a long, refreshing sip of his beer, stared out at the dismal mud street, and then he smiled very gently. "*Mi* esposa, my wife . . ." he said, under his breath. "She's got two gifts for your friend tonight."

"*Gifts?*"

"*Sí. El primero es gonorrea*, the first is gonorrhoea," he said, "and the second is syphilis."

CHAPTER
SIX

Reputed Dangers of Travel
Savages rarely murder newcomers; they fear their guns, and have a superstitious awe of the white man's power: they require time to discover that he is not very different to themselves, and easily to be made away with.

The Art of Travel

Pillcopata was hardly a town at all. There were no more than a few hundred residents, a blend of urbanized natives and adventurers, who whiled away their days in the broken shade. You wouldn't have realized it at first, but they were all waiting for the same thing: a tourist bonanza to roll into town. The men sat on the jerry-built verandas, smoking black tobacco, with their wives flustering in the gloomy wooden houses behind. Sometimes the sweltering silence of midday was pierced by the shriek of a small child being mauled by a savage dog. The dogs of Pillcopata had a vigour that I have encountered nowhere else. They could withstand the blazing temperature, but were exceedingly ferocious as a result.

Next morning the manager of the only hotel sat down beside me on the verandah. He was meek, yet severe, had a swarthy complexion, short greying hair and small hands that never stopped moving. He told me, almost as an apology, that his name was Walter.

He asked me to describe in detail the desert town of Nazca. I began to explain about the famous Nazca Lines.

"No, no, Señor," he said, with a smile. "I know about the Lines. But tell me of the tourists. What are they like?"

"Well, there are all kinds . . . from all over the world. Some are rich, others less so, but they all want the same thing — to fly over the symbols on the desert."

"¿De todas partes del mundo? From all over the world?" said Walter dreamily.

"Yes, they come from everywhere."

"And they bring money?"

"Oh, yes," I said authoritatively, "they have made Nazca very rich."

Walter puffed on a hand-rolled cigarette, and flicked the ash on the floor. "One day Pillcopata will be like that," he said, with certainty.

"But you don't have the Nazca Lines."

"We have something better, far better."

"What's that?"

"The ruins of the Incas."

I slid my tongue over my parched lips. "You mean, Paititi?"

"That's it," said Walter. "It's there, out there. It's just a matter of days now, weeks at the most, and it'll be found."

"Do you really believe it's there?"

"*¡Claro!* Of course! Why do you think I have this hotel? I'm waiting out the bad times, ready . . . ready for the shout, '*¡Paititi!*' When it comes, I'll be a millionaire."

I took a sip of my coffee, leaned back on my chair, and scanned the main street. "If the lost city was discovered," I asked, "how would Pillcopata change?"

Walter jumped to his feet, the veneer of meekness gone. "We'd build a line of hotels with fifteen floors on each, and a dance hall, and a bus station, restaurants and shops. There'd be banks and beauty parlours, too, and an international airport, and Tarmac roads carving their way deep into the jungle . . . to Paititi."

"But what about the native tribes?"

Walter clicked his tongue. "They'll all have jobs," he quipped. "It would do them some good. They'll help with the tourists, carrying their bags, that sort of thing. Think, my friend, think!"

"Of what?"

"Think how quiet and terrible Machu Picchu must have been before the ruins were discovered! Now there are helicopters and hotels and shops selling nice little things, and tourists . . . so many lovely tourists!" We were on the verge of entering the jungle to make contact with the Machiguenga tribe, but my conversation with Walter somehow soured my eagerness for the search. I sat gloomily in the sunshine, away from everyone else, fending off the ferocious dogs. I am outspoken against missionaries, who force an alien framework on people who don't need it. But, as I see the world, there's one element that's even more corrosive than missionaries: tourists. It's not that I feel above them in any way, but that the very places they patronize are destroyed by their affection.

Suddenly I understood the great curse. It was the real curse of Paititi, which will be activated only when the lost city has been found. The virgin jungle will be opened up, vast towering trees hewn down to make room for hotels and themed restaurants. Highways will be laid, crammed with a snake of gridlock traffic, all the way to the mountains. As for the tribes, their culture will be erased within weeks. Within a year or two, they will all be studying tourism at a local university, just as they are in Cusco.

I left the dogs in the heat and rushed to the rank-smelling bathroom at Walter's hotel. Standing there, sweat running down the edges of my face, I stared into the mirror. How could I be so stupid? How could I yearn for glory if its price was so high? I ran out of the bathroom and down the corridor to the room where the film crew were huddled, wrapped in wet towels. "I know the future," I said bleakly. "I've seen it at Machu Picchu."

The crew must have thought the heat was getting to me. They didn't say anything.

"You must promise me something," I said. "If we find Paititi, when we find Paititi, we'll take a good hard look and then we'll walk away."

"No pictures?" asked David.

"None."

"What about GPS co-ordinates?"

"We'll erase them," I said. "It will be hard, but we'll go to great lengths to pretend we didn't find it at all."

The tin-roofed market at Pillcopata was the last chance to stock up on kit. Most of the items on sale had been shipped in from mainland China. The developing world is flooded with such gear: functional, durable and tantalizingly cheap. When it comes to affordable Chinese goods, I'm a shopaholic. I can't help myself. I cadged some pocket money off Marco, and snapped up two dozen enamel mess cups, adorned with views of the Great Wall. I bought cheap sewing kits, too, to hand out to the tribe, and a sack of salted pork bellies. They looked vile and smelt even worse, but I remembered how the Shuar had lusted after salted meat.

Then I went to the health post, where a doctor sold me a box of fifty morphine vials and a handful of syringes. I had a good medical kit from London's Hospital of Tropical Diseases, but it didn't contain anything strong enough to keep an injured man comatose. From reading accounts of other lost city expeditions, I had learned the high risk of snapping ankles while wading through rivers and traversing steep jungle.

Richard sloped into the hotel at noon. His neck had been badly bitten, but there was no sign of the bus driver's wife. He joined Rodrigo upstairs for a "smoke bath". The shaman had spent most of the night engaged in the mysterious smoke ritual. I'm all for shamans doing their ceremonies, but as a diehard anti-smoker, I found sleeping in the room next to the makeshift smoke tent too much to bear.

"Rodrigo is being taunted by the Curse Lines," Richard said later. "The invisible spirits are firing darts at him. The only way to keep them at peace is to smoke those bastards out. He says he's brought seven spirits from Nazca. They're looking after us, and if we're lucky they'll point the way to the ruins."

We spent most of the afternoon, and that of the next day, trying to find transport to the end of the road. It seemed to extend about another thirty miles, twisting close to the east bank of the Madre de Dios river, ending at a village called Shintuya. I had heard that the settlement was a point of contact for the Machiguenga tribe. The problem was that there were no vehicles at all.

Being becalmed in a small Peruvian town is possibly the worst feeling in the world. We were soon getting on each other's nerves. The Swedes felt it necessary to document my frustration, filming from every angle, as I sat in the shade, swishing away the packs of malicious dogs. The odd couple stayed in their room for more than twenty-four hours, smoked out to the very limits of life.

When explorers get home from a trip, they always bask in the wonder of it all. But they forget to mention hours, days, weeks of sitting around waiting for something to happen. In the West we expect time to be filled with events. Not so in the Peruvian outback.

Entire lifetimes begin, mature and end without a single major event happening.

Walter must have taken pity on us. He staggered out of his bedroom from a long siesta with a cardboard box weighing heavy in his hands. He placed it on the hotel's dining-table. "This stuff was left by another expedition," he said. "Help yourself."

I sifted through the contents, a variety of notebooks, printed booklets and maps. The notebooks were packed with tight black handwriting, interspersed with sketches of birds and details of flora. All the writing was in Czech, a language none of us understood. We studied the maps. They had been prepared by the Peruvian National Institute of Geography to a scale of 1:1,000,000. They showed the Pillcopata area, the Madre de Dios river and the jungle to the north-west, where the oil exploration was going on. They were extremely useful, the only drawback being that vast swathes of white cut across the green. These were marked with the words *datos insuficientes*, insufficient data.

I asked Walter who had left the notebooks and maps.

"*La expedición grande*, the great expedition," he said. "They came through about four months ago."

"How many people?"

He slapped a hand to his cheek. "*¿Fue magnífica!* It was tremendous!" he claimed. "I've never seen anything like it. They were like an army, their supplies glistening in the sun. They were like warriors heading to battle. There must have been fifty men: scientists, anthropologists, engineers and porters. They had computers and special tents that self-inflate, and food from New York City."

"Where were they from?"

Walter thought for a few moments. "From Czechoslovakia," he said. "They were led by a man who seemed to have a confidence like no other man alive. He was dark-skinned and handsome. The women in town went wild when they saw him. They begged him to sit in their homes and take a drink. But the man waved a finger in the air. 'No, no,' he said to them all. 'I am on a mission, a mission sponsored by my government, for the benefit of all free men!' And, with that, he waved his army forward, and it rolled on out of Pillcopata into the jungle."

The Czech explorer sounded like the kind of man who makes a mockery of ordinary adventurers. We hadn't been fêted or invited into anyone's homes. The only attention we had attracted was from a married monster of a woman with raging syphilis. The Czech expedition might have been overloaded with gear, but they hadn't found Paititi. The lost city was still out there, still hiding in the foliage.

Eventually we negotiated a ride to Shintuya on the back of a truck full of pigs. The vehicle was in truly terrible condition, destroyed by the weekly runs from Cusco. On Thursdays it drove with pigs to the end of the road, and returned with bananas each Monday. Richard and Rodrigo, the odd couple, were both gasping for breath after the marathon smoke session; they spread out across the floor planks and tried to sleep. They didn't seem to mind the pigs charging all over them.

In one corner of the truck, away from the pigs, there was a knot of people, a mother with her twin daughters, and an old man whose arm was paralysed. A young Chilean man called Jorge was squatting near them. He had a hooked beak of a nose, big teeth and hazelnut eyes, which made you feel warm inside when he looked at you. I trusted him at once. Like every other foreigner passing that way, he was searching for the last refuge of the Incas.

He explained that he had hunted for the ruins for a decade or more, mounting regular trips into Madre de Dios, from his adopted home of Cusco. "You don't need fancy equipment to find a lost city," he said, "you just need time. Don't expect to find anything if you don't put in the time."

I asked if he'd heard of the Czech team. "Yes, of course," he said quickly, "everyone knows about Count Josef Capek. He's an aristocrat who likes to put on a big show. It makes him feel important. He's nothing but a Boy Scout."

"The taste for glory can make ordinary men behave in extraordinary ways," I said.

Jorge held on tight as the truck speeded up to ford a stream. "There are easier ways to find glory," he replied. "If you want glory then stay out of the jungle."

"What about the Machiguenga?

"Be wary of them," said Jorge. "They are sick of people searching for ruins in their lands. Haven't you heard of the French expedition?"

"The one that was wiped out?"

"Yes, the French-American group, headed by Nichols. They ran out of food, entered a Machiguenga village and found it deserted. So they helped themselves to some of the tribe's food. While they were eating, the villagers came back from their hunting trip, and shot them all with their three-foot-long arrows."

On either side of the track, the undergrowth was seething, insect wings echoing like the whine of a radio searching for a station. From time to time we glimpsed the mighty Madre de Dios, its furious current boiling with life. The pigs rattled around us like white mice in a box, as I took stock of our situation. Things were falling into shape, I thought. We must be in the right area, because everyone we met seemed to be looking for Paititi, or had something to say about it. The jungle was dense and, with each hundred yards, it grew denser. Like a giant web of concentric silk spirals, it became more perfidious the closer one got to the centre. At the outset of the journey I had worried about the film crew: their mountain of luggage was a great concern. But as we moved closer to the tribal lands of the Machiguenga, my anxiety shifted from them to the shaman and the Vietnam vet.

Rodrigo had started moaning about missing his family, even though he had little to return to. His children were grown up, and his wife had recently taken a lover, who had moved into their shack upstream from Iquitos. She had kicked Rodrigo out, along with his cauldron, and the ever-present bag of psychotropic vines. As I understood it, Rodrigo had become the laughing-stock of the Upper Amazon after a love-spell he had cast had gone horribly wrong. His patient had been treated with a potion to increase his sexual desire. The potion worked, but instead of lusting after women, the man found a new and insatiable urge for men. Our expedition provided the shaman with a chance to lie low for a while, to earn some money and have his shamanic skill taken more seriously again.

As we descended, closer to the river, Richard became increasingly unstable. We had hardly arrived in the jungle and he was picking fights with us all. His brief flirtation with detoxification was over. He now chewed coca leaves incessantly, took hallucinogenic snuff each morning, and spent the afternoons passed out after guzzling a bottle of "jungle juice". The preparation, brewed up fresh by Rodrigo each night, contained a variety of hallucinogens. In his waking hours, Richard behaved like a petulant teenager. But the danger was that he was armed with a Brazilian riot shotgun, its magazine packed with enough ammunition to dispatch us all.

At Shintuya, six or seven houses clung to a ridge above the riverbank like molluscs on a sea wall. They were built of upright planks, gaps between them, with ragged tin roofs, amber brown with rust. We unloaded our immense assortment of equipment and food, and erected a tarpaulin over a makeshift wooden frame, following the diagram in Galton's book, *The Art of Travel*. As we prepared the camp, the pigs were hounded out of the truck by its driver, and corralled in a crude pen at the water's edge. They knew instinctively that something of importance was about to take place. I think they could smell it; either that, or they had caught a glimpse of the crazed eyes of their assassin. Without wasting a second, the truck driver stormed into the pen, wielding a sharp-pointed knife. The pigs screamed loudly, as you would have expected them to do, their final, frantic cries dissipating into the descending darkness like the exclamation of condemned men. By the end of it, the truck driver was drenched. His face, bare arms, hands and clothes glistened with scarlet blood. It was a horrible, yet beautiful sight.

The only place to buy anything in Shintuya was a shop owned by a large, boisterous woman with warts, called Gloria. She was covered with them. They ran up and down her arms, and across her face, like the miniature bumps on Lego. I entered her shop to relieve the instant boredom conjured up by the community. She greeted me loudly, smiling, eyes creased.

"*¿Has venido por* Paititi? Have you come for Paititi?" she asked, as if it was a funfair ride at the water's edge.

"We've come to meet the Machiguenga," I said.

Gloria scoffed. "*Son piratas*, they're pirates," she said knowingly. "They will kill you and steal your stuff. Watch out!"

I thanked her for the advice and bought a can of tuna, not that we needed it but it seemed like a way of showing that we had come in peace.

As I left the shop, I spotted a group of short, lean men getting out of a hollowed-out canoe. There were four of them. They walked without shoes, and were dressed in tattered Peruvian football strip, green and blue. Two were carrying sturdy bows fashioned from black wood; the other two were holding arrows, each well over three feet in length. The arrows ended in serrated wooden barbs.

"There are your Machiguenga," said Gloria, who had moved into the veranda's shade. "They have come here to buy salt."

"Where do they live?"

"Not far," she said, "a few miles upriver, at Mantacolla."

I felt like rushing over and shaking them by the hand. But experience has taught me to go slow.

At the camp, Richard was out cold. Rodrigo was staring down at him in disappointment. "He didn't take much of the drink," he said, "but it is very, very strong."

"What was it? What did you give him?"

"It's *datura*," he said. "I found it growing over there."

The shaman pointed to a low tree, with thin foliage and a multitude of giant lemon-coloured flowers: *la trompeta del diablo*, the so-called Trumpet of the Devil. I had taken that wicked plant myself as an admixture in *ayahuasca* with the Shuar. They use it as an agent, a way to fly into the next world — a world they claim is reality. The alkaloids in *datura* give a sensation of flight, of soaring above the jungle canopy like a bird. So potent is its effect that the Shuar rarely take it these days. Instead, they reserve it for their hunting dogs and their guests.

Datura was known to the Incas, and its alluring flowers were soon noticed by the Spanish invaders, who brought the plant back to Europe in the sixteenth century. Medieval witches got hold of it and used it in their flying potions. They prepared a paste with the flowers, and applied it to their inner thighs. They would stand astride a besom, easing the ointment into the skin with the shaft, hence the idea of a witch riding on a broomstick. Within a few minutes they would pass out, and when they woke many hours later, they assumed they had been flying.

That evening we discovered that three sacks of food had been stolen since we had got down from the truck. I cursed Richard for having become so ineffectual, and yelled at Rodrigo for feeding him so many drugs. From that moment on I outlawed the serving up of any more hallucinogens. Rodrigo was forbidden to prepare potions; he could cook potatoes instead.

We sat under the stars on a sheet of blue plastic, brooding on Richard's shortcomings, while the film crew rubbed sun cream into their charred skin. The veteran was supposed to be protecting us, but was instead plunging the expedition into danger. I could not trust him with the Machiguenga. He would have to be left at the camp.

Sitting there, bristling with anger, I counselled myself to be harder on my employees. As the head of an expedition, you can't pussyfoot around being polite to everyone. You have to show your teeth once in a while; a little growling goes a long way.

The next morning Richard was still unconscious. He had soiled himself in the night, and was covered with ants, rather like a corpse abandoned in the woods. It was a deplorable sight, a grown man capable of so much and reduced to so little. We stood around him in a huddle, the film crew shocked that I had ever placed my trust in the former soldier.

As the sun's early rays touched the river like a wand, I questioned aloud how we would get to the Machiguenga village.

A local man meandered over. He had long arms, a vice-like handshake and a slow manner. After introducing himself as Jesús, he looked down at Richard despondently. "I bet he's not a Christian," he said coolly.

"He was in Vietnam," I replied. "It messed him up inside."

I asked Jesús about the tribe.

"I've got a *peki-peki*," he said. "*Te llevaré*, I'll take you."

We negotiated a price, and the film crew and I clambered into the canoe. Squatting at the stern, the boatman whipped the starting cord and the engine came alive. Roaring like a steam train into the wind, the narrow canoe pushed out into the river's current. The camp grew smaller and smaller as we gained our distance. My anger with Richard gave me strength, strength from fear of the tribesmen. We didn't have a weapon between us. I felt strong, resilient, like a condemned man before a firing squad.

The hum of the *peki-peki*'s engine resounded off the steep mud banks as we inched our way up towards Mantacolla. The river quickly narrowed, and was suddenly no more than fifty feet wide, but the current was fast. A *peki-peki* engine, which cannot provide more than five horsepower at best, feeds a cheap aluminium propeller at the end of a long shaft. The system's advantage is that the propeller can be swung out of the water in a split second at any sign of shallows.

It took about an hour to travel the short distance to Mantacolla. I was half expecting a village set on the riverbank, with people and commotion. Jesús stopped the engine and jumped into the water, guiding his craft up on to the shale beach. There was no sign of anyone.

"Wait here, and the tribe will come," he said. "I'll be back for you this evening."

"Are you sure we're in the right place?" I asked.

But Jesús didn't reply. He slid the canoe out into the water and hopped in, allowing the current to ease him back to Shintuya.

We sat there for an hour, blinded and burnt by the sun. Then a boy appeared from nowhere. He was naked, about seven years old, and had a fish skewered on a stick. He watched us from a distance, taking occasional nibbles at the meat. We waved, then gesticulated wildly. The child ran off into the undergrowth. A few minutes later a line of figures stepped out on to the beach. Like the men we had seen at Shintuya, they carried long arrows and black *chonta* palm bows. But these men had saffron-yellow faces. They didn't look up, but gazed at the ground before them as they approached, as if lost in thought. The man at the front walked with a limp.

When they were close we smiled falsely, baring our teeth in friendship. Now I think back to it, it seems mad to greet strangers with a display of teeth, as we do in the West. But I don't suppose the warriors saw us smiling. They never lifted their heads, as if eyecontact would afflict them with a disease of some kind.

Leon, who spoke the best Spanish, began the conversation. "*Hace calor*, it is hot," he said.

"*Sí, mucho calor*," said the man with the limp.

"The sun is bright, too."

"Yes, yes, the sun is bright," said the tribesman.

"We have come here as your friends," Leon went on, "and we have gifts."

The men looked nervously at each other. I sensed a silent wave of expectation pass between them.

I dished out some shotgun cartridges from a tattered plastic bag, as if they were boiled sweets. The men smiled and took a handful each.

"We have food as well," said Leon.

"Food," said one of the other men. "*Comida es bueno*, food is good."

We all agreed, nodding animatedly, that food was a good thing.

"There were some foreigners here once," said the third man. "They didn't have any food. They came into our village and stole food. *Fueron malos*, they were bad men."

"The French," I said softly. "It must have been the French."

But to the warriors, all white men looked the same.

"It is bad to steal food," I said.

"Yes," intoned the first man, "it made us sad. We were very sad. *Toda la villa estaba triste*, the whole village was sad."

The tribesmen looked at each other and chattered in a high-pitched language for a minute or two.

"If you want to go through our territory," the first man continued, "you will have to pay us money." There was a pause. "If you do not pay us money we will be sad."

The film crew and I exchanged worried glances. The last thing we wanted was for the Machiguenga to be sad again. Sadness appeared to bring out their violence.

Again, there was a long pause. After which the man with the limp said we could come to the village and talk about money. I was reluctant to discuss matters of business so early in the palaver, but there was little choice. The tribesmen stood up and led the way from the pebbles into the undergrowth. We walked after them down a track no wider than a doorway, the jungle rearing up on either side. Despite their reputation, the warriors seemed quite a straightforward group of men. As long as we kept handing out shotgun shells, I thought, we would stay on their good side.

Eventually we came to a clearing. A large number of trees had been felled, creating an open grassland, with a smattering of *malocas*, frail wooden houses, at the far end. They were made from narrow strips of hard wood and thatched with hay. Each one had a low door, necessitating extraordinary limberness to enter or exit. Between the huts there stood a hearth, protected by a shelter of woven banana leaves; in the hearth a fire was smouldering, and on the fire there was a pot. A woman, whose face was caked with yellow paint like the others, was stirring the pot. It was blackened, and filled with a mushy white porridge. I recognized it from my time in the Upper Amazon.

"*Masato*," I said coldly.

"*¡Si! ¡Si!*" said the Machiguengas, grinning. "*Masato.*"

A bowl of dirty river water was mixed into the brew, and stirred by a clumsy hand. The bowl was dipped into the liquid, which now resembled pancake batter. It was passed to me. I closed my eyes tight and gulped down about two pints. The Swedes went next, then Boris and Marco. Unlike me, they had the benefit of ignorance — they had no idea how the beverage was prepared. *Masato* is drunk across the western Amazon and the surrounding jungle region. It is made from *yuka*, the tubular cassava root, which is boiled in water and mashed. Then the women making it, invariably the oldest, ugliest crones in the community, stuff handfuls of the mashed *yuka* into their mouths, chew for a minute or so, then toss it back into the pot. Within hours, the cassava has fermented in the saliva and is mildly alcoholic.

Masato featured prominently in Machiguenga hospitality, as did roasted armadillo meat. I picked restlessly at the jumble of armadillo bones on my lap, the leftovers of an animal that had been killed a few days before. It had been cooked over a termite nest in the usual way.

When the man with the limp had downed almost a gallon of *masato*, he addressed us again. "Some white men came here recently," he said slowly. "They told us they were looking for the walls of Paititi. Then they said they would give us money and gifts if we showed them where to find the walls."

"Paititi?" I said keenly. "Isn't that just a myth?"

"Yes, it's a myth," said the headman, gnawing at the armadillo's jawbone. "It's very nice, though. People come here looking for it. They give us lots of money for passing through our lands. If they don't give money we get sad."

The film crew and I exchanged a firm look. We understood what he was saying. In the world of the Machiguenga, sadness could be equated with anger, and was a perilous emotion, by which a foreigner could lose his life.

I asked how much people paid to travel through their stretch of the river.

"We charge twenty thousand *soles*," he said.

"That's more than *five thousand dollars*," I said.

The headman did not reply. But he seemed pleased that the figure was regarded as large.

Late that afternoon, we heard the rumble of Jesús's *peki-peki* pushing upstream. I didn't feel we had yet made the breakthrough we needed with the tribe, but it seemed that we had covered as much ground as possible in the initial meeting. We thanked the tribal leaders and walked back to the beach, each of us wondering how we could evade paying the fee, while at the same time keeping the Machiguenga happy.

CHAPTER
SEVEN

Engaging Natives
On engaging natives, the people with whom they
have lived, and to whom they have become attached
and learnt to fear, should impress on them that,
unless they bring you back in safety, they must
never show their faces again, nor expect the balance
of their pay, which will only be delivered to them on
your return.

The Art of Travel

Back at the camp, Richard had wakened from his
hallucinogenic sleep. He was sitting in the twilight with
his trousers down. Rodrigo was shining the beam of a
flashlight carefully at the veteran's genitals. It made for
a curious scene. As soon as he saw us approaching,
Richard struggled to pull on his camouflage fatigues.

"Itching?" I said.

"That's my business."

Our conversation was cut short by the sound of
English being spoken on the road. A few minutes later a
hippie was standing before us. He was five foot tall,
with a gangling frame as if he had suffered from
recurring malaria; a long carpet of beard ran down
from his face. His legs were hidden by what appeared
to be homemade tie-dye trousers, and he wore

bedroom slippers on his feet. He was an Australian from Darwin, who, coincidentally, was called Darwin as well.

"Let me guess," I said, "you're looking for Paititi."

But Darwin didn't know what I meant. He had never heard the name before. "I've come to stay with the monks," he said.

"*Monks?*"

He pointed downriver.

"It may sound weird, man," he said, "but someone in Cusco told me that ten miles south of here there's a community of monks. When the leader of their fraternity dies, they cook him and eat him."

"Cannibals?" I asked.

"In exceptional circumstances," said Darwin.

Normally, I would have been the first to go in search of cannibal monks, particularly as I had heard of a similar tradition at a nunnery in the Philippines. It's the sort of quest I can't resist. But Paititi was still beckoning, and I felt as if we were making real progress. I left Darwin to listen to Richard's tiresome repertoire of Vietnam tales, and walked up to the shop to extract more information from Gloria.

She was sitting in the dimness on a bench, caressing a kitten's back with the tips of her fingers. As soon as I stepped up on to the floor-boards, she let the cat slide from her lap and turned up the flame of her paraffin lamp. "Did you meet the Machiguenga?" she asked.

"They gave us *masato* and armadillo meat," I said.

"Don't be misled by their hospitality. They'll rob you blind."

"If someone wanted to find Paititi," I said cautiously, "who would he talk to?"

"Not the tribesmen, for sure," said Gloria.

"Then who? Who *knows*?"

The shopkeeper rubbed a palm across the warts on her cheek. "*Hay solo un hombre*, there is a man," she said.

"Does he know about Paititi?"

"*Sí. Él conoce*, he knows."

"What's his name?"

"He's called Hector. He lives across the river."

"Is he a tribesman?"

"No," she said, "they're not from the tribe over there. They follow the way of Jesus."

We hadn't been down at the edge of the jungle for long, but our presence there was already paying dividends. Perhaps, I pondered, as I wandered back down to the camp, we would have beginner's luck and we would find the ruins with no trouble at all.

At the camp the Australian had succumbed to the noxious effects of *datura*.

"It seemed a shame to waste it," said Rodrigo.

Next morning, Leon and I left the others on the riverbank, and took a ride across the mighty Madre de Dios in a hollowed-out canoe. The water was much faster than it had been the day before, and the young boatman fought with the flat paddle as if our lives depended on it. He shouted that it had been raining heavily upstream, that the water would rise much higher in the coming days.

I asked if he knew Hector.

"*Sí, el hombre es el Mesías*, that man is a Messiah," he said.

"What do you mean?"

"*Él tiene un aura, carisma*, he has an aura, a presence. He has been touched by God."

On the far side of the river, we jumped into the water and marched up to the wall of jungle. With time we eventually found a path, and took to it, slipping on the mud like half-wits tramping across ice. On either side of the track there were banana plants and breadfruit trees, suggesting a village nearby.

We walked for about forty minutes, the morning sun scorching our necks, the flies bathing in our sweat. Then, quite suddenly, as we came to the village, the skies opened and it poured with torrential rain. Within five seconds we were drenched. A man waved to us from his porch. We ran over and took refuge in his house.

He had a big square head, broad shoulders and short-sighted vision, which caused him to scrunch up his eyes when he was talking to you. He announced modestly that he was the headman.

"We are looking for Hector," I said.

"You mean El Maestro, the master?"

"We were told he knows about Paititi."

"Ah, yes," said the chief, "*él conoce, sí, él conoce*, he knows, yes, he knows."

"Where does he live?"

"Usually he's here in the village, but now he's out at his *chacra*, his farmstead, planting a crop of *yuka*. He'll get back in a week."

"We have to go there now," I said.

The rain was growing heavier, and in the jungle heavy rain can fall for many hours without letting up. The headman peered out at the mud. "You could wait until tomorrow," he said.

"I cannot wait a moment longer," I replied.

The inertia of a jungle village is a dangerous thing. Before you know it your whole life has slipped by and you are still sitting there. I tapped my watch. "*Debemos irnos ya*, we must leave at once."

"Then my boy will take you."

He called to his oldest son, Sergio, and instructed him to take us to meet El Maestro.

We set off at once, sliding up and down the narrow path as it wound through the undergrowth like the body of a snake. Sometimes we scrambled to grasp at roots; at others, we forded streams up to our waists. All the while it poured and poured with rain, freezing us to the bone. Then, after four hours of misery, we spotted banana trees again. Our pace increased. A cluster of simple shacks came into view. There was no one about, just a few chickens looking wretched in the wet. We called, but no one came. We took off our shirts and wrung them out.

Our guide, the headman's son, said that Paititi was thirty days' walk through the jungle. Even then, I knew better than anyone the local inaccuracy of distance. In the Upper Amazon, I had found that the Shuar hardly

110

ever ventured more than a few miles in any direction. They had a reasonable knowledge of the surrounding area, but their language did not contain the words to express distance, weight or any other measurement.

"The government air force fly over our village very often," said the teenager. "My father believes that they may have already found Paititi, and that they're clearing out the gold bit by bit."

"How much gold does he think there is?"

The boy stretched his arms above his head and swung them down to his waist. "That much, or more," he said.

A few minutes passed, and then a young, athletic-looking woman appeared. She was no more than about twenty. Unlike everyone else in the region, her teeth were not rotten. It was as if she was from a different genetic stock. Her name was Mariella; she was Hector's daughter.

"Where is your father?"

"He will be here soon."

Five minutes more, and I glimpsed a grey-white beard moving through the trees. It was wrapped round the cheeks of a muscular man. His shirt was unbuttoned, its tails tied in a knot about his waist. Over one shoulder hung an axe, the blade ground down by years of sharpening. His expression was focused and the glint of a secret obsession shone in his eyes. From the first moment I saw him, I knew he was a key that could help unlock the puzzle of Paititi.

Hector did not seem surprised to find a pair of drenched strangers, shaking with cold, taking shelter at his shack. He strode over and introduced himself. A silence followed, a silence that called for explanation.

"We are here because we share the same interest as you," I said.

"You like growing *yuka*," he replied, regarding our soft hands. "No, I don't think so."

"We are on a quest," I said solemnly, "searching for the lost city of Paititi."

"*Aaaaah*," said Hector. "You are the fresh moth attracted by an old flame."

"We were told that you have experience."

Hector took off his shirt and wiped it across his face. He seemed very serious. "People have died searching for Paititi," he said. "Others have returned *different* from when they set out. They all made sacrifices."

"You mean they went mad?"

"*Locura*, madness." Hector uttered the word slowly, studiously. "Why do you want to find Paititi?" he asked. "*Por el oro*, for the gold?"

"At first it was for the glory," I said, "but now I'm not so sure."

"Paititi is up there," said the old man obliquely. "There is no doubt. If you have doubt, then turn and walk back on that path."

Hector was quite different from most other Peruvians. He had the charisma of a politician, and a form of compacted energy I have only ever encountered in men with resolute belief. It came as little surprise that he was a Seventh Day Adventist.

I asked if he was a missionary. He said he was not. He had never converted anyone, he explained, for he saw it as each man's right to seek out his own faith.

"I came here from Arequipa with my young family eighteen years ago," he said. "I was searching for something. If you are searching, the jungle is a good place to find an answer."

"Was it Paititi?"

"No, no, that was long before I'd heard about Paititi," he said. "I was searching for a cure for deafness. I'd been working in the mineral mines in the north of Peru, drilling in tunnels. I lost my hearing as a result, so I threw in my hard hat and came here, dragging my wife and children along."

"You obviously got healed," I said.

"Oh, yes, by a shaman. He's dead now, but he was a remarkable man. He forbade me to speak for an entire year. Utter a single word, even to myself, and, he said, I would never hear again."

Hector brushed his sinewy hands over his face. "¡Que difícil fue! Oh, how hard that was!" he said, laughing. "I thought I'd go mad. But then one morning I woke up and heard a cockerel crowing. It was the most wonderful sound I have ever heard. There were so many delicious sounds!"

"What of Paititi?"

"Ah," said the old man, "the shaman used to tell me about it. He said it was upriver, that his father had been there. Naturally, I was interested."

"Have you mounted expeditions for Paititi?"

"You need money, lots of it," he replied, "and time to prepare. Without preparation you could lose your life."

"You mean to prepare your body and build up your muscles, that sort of thing?"

"*No, no tus músculos*, not your muscles," said the old man, "but your mind."

Hector stopped talking and stared down at the swirl of smoke spiralling up from the fire. He sat down on a homemade chair and looked at me, studying my face. "To find Paititi," he said, "you must not look for it. But even then you have to purify your spirit, cleanse your soul."

"How long will that take?"

"*Nos llevará seis meses*, it will take six months," he replied.

Leon and I glared at each other.

"I feel quite pure inside," I said. "I think I could get away with a quick bout of purifying, a few days at the most."

"Me too," said Leon earnestly.

El Maestro gazed at me, not to examine my face or clothes, but my soul. I struggled to think pure thoughts, as Hector sucked out my psyche with his eyes. When he had finished, he glanced down at the fire again. Like the Indians, his vision seemed unclouded by trifling insignificances: his mind had been washed clean by the jungle.

"What of the Machiguenga?" I asked, hoping to draw him from his inquisition. "Do they believe in Paititi?"

114

"Of course they believe," he said, without hesitation, "but don't mention the word to them. It will turn them wild."

"With envy?"

"*No, con temor,* with fear."

Hector suddenly seemed overcome with tiredness.

"*Hay peligro,* there is much danger," he said sternly.

It sounded like a line from a B-grade horror movie, but he really meant it.

"I will be back at the village in a week," he said. "Come and see me. We can talk further then."

Two days after drinking the preparation of *datura*, Darwin, the Australian hippie, came to. He couldn't stand at first, and complained of severe soreness in his arms and back. "I flew, man," he said gently, as if he believed it.

"Where did you fly?"

"Up the river, and over the jungle, low above the water, over the tops of the trees. It was magical. I smelt the wind."

The film crew and I didn't pay much attention. We discussed what the next course of action was to be, and agreed unanimously that Hector, El Maestro, was our best bet so far. Although sitting there for a week was an unwelcome prospect, we had little choice. Meanwhile, Richard listened intently to the hippie's story. His eyes were encircled with shadowy rings. He looked worse than I had ever seen him, like a man woken from death. "Did you speak with the spirits?" he asked.

Darwin appeared confused by the question. "Yes, spirits, there were spirits," he replied at length. "They washed me, they touched me, they loved me, man." He smiled tenderly. It was the smile of a hippie who has been comforted in an endless blanket of free love.

"Yes, man," he said, "yes, they loved me and they showed me the hills."

"What hills?" asked Richard.

"Over there. There are twelve of them."

The hippie's mention of hills would have been lost if Richard had not been listening. The veteran said Jesús the boatman had spoken of a series of pinnacles due west of Shintuya. "They're kind of pyramids," he said, "man-made pyramids."

I would not have paid any attention, but I had read that the Incas built stone pyramids and worshipped the sun from them. So we looked for Jesús to ask him about the pinnacles. He wasn't at home. His wife said he had run off to his mistress's house. "She's a witch," said the woman, "but I don't care. One day he'll come home but I'll be gone. There's a man in Santa Cruz, a good man, who looks at me nicely when I pass his house. He needs a wife. He must do, his house is all messy."

"Do you know about the pinnacles?" I asked.

"Don't believe anything Jesús has to say," she snapped. "He's a fool, a fool with a big dick."

Back in the camp, Darwin had gathered up his belongings and disappeared on a canoe filled with bananas in search of the cannibal monks. I was glad to be rid of him. We strolled up to Gloria's veranda and inspected the map in its shade. About twelve miles due

116

west, up the winding Inchipata river, there was a curious series of what looked like hillocks, jagged with contours, like the grooves of a saw. It was impossible to say if they were man-made or not, but they were mysterious. My mind filled with the image of an Inca priest, slitting llamas' throats in honour of the sun.

The only way to know something for sure is to go there yourself, so we set about hiring men and mounting a reconnaissance trip to the so-called pinnacles. It was a good way of testing the equipment. Gloria said she would look after the luggage we did not need.

"Get your porters from Panataua, Hector's village," she said. "You don't want men from Shintuya, they're lazy and weak."

We crossed the river and marched over to Panataua. The headman was blowing cigarette smoke into his infant daughter's hair in the hope of killing the lice.

"We need to hire some porters," I said.

"*¿Cuántos necesitas?* How many do you need?"

"Fifteen at the most."

"Wait here until dusk."

Passing time in a Peruvian hamlet can drive a reasonable man berserk. The village was thin on entertainment. There was no electricity, so no television, and no theatres, or shops, or anything to help pass the time; nothing except a church. As we soon found, it was the one attraction, patronized energetically by every member of the community. It was a bright, whitewashed building, set at the far end of the village in a thicket of breadfruit trees. Open-sided, with

117

a sloping tin roof, there was a space under the floor where feral dogs took dust baths and fought.

Twice a day the entire village donned their best clothes and tramped into the church to pledge their love to God. Most of them carried oversized Bibles wherever they went. While we were waiting, I asked the headman about Hector. "If anyone knows about Paititi, it is Hector," he said. "He is trusted by the Machiguenga. They tell him things. They come to his house and whisper to him."

"He is a bridge between our world and the world of the natives," I said.

"*¡Si! El puente*, the bridge."

That evening, when dusk had turned into darkness, and the air was filled with the rustling of cicada wings, ten men arrived at the headman's shack. Most of them were farmers, earning a meagre living by growing bananas and *yuka* for Cusco. They were all clutching well-thumbed Bibles, dressed in their best clothes, ready for church. None looked at all strong. They looked like preachers.

"How many pounds can you carry?" I asked them.

"Eighty," said a very short, feeble man. "We can carry eighty pounds at least."

Boris, who had served as a conscript in the Bulgarian military, weighed out eighty pounds, and stuffed it into a kit-bag. I marked out a distance of a hundred yards through the village. The first puny man stepped up, wrestled to pick up the pack, and staggered ahead for a few feet, before dropping it. Behind him, the other young farmers looked sheepish. We cut the weight by half. The farmers still found it a struggle. I asked how many of them would come with us for fifteen *soles* a day. They all put up their hands. I fished out a bottle of Peruvian grape brandy from the supplies. "We don't drink," said the feeblest of them all. "We are Adventists."

"Fuckin' girlies," said Richard. "I've never heard of such a thing."

We planned to leave Shintuya at dawn the day after next. The Adventists' frailty meant we would have to deposit the bulk of our equipment at Gloria's shop.

After I forbade him to prepare hallucinogens, Rodrigo turned his shamanic hands to cooking, and became quite an accomplished chef. Everything he served up from his magic cauldron was wonderful, not least of all his *pont-neuf* potatoes. That evening, after the pot had been scraped clean, he went down to the river to drink his last batch of *ayahuasca*. He said it was to search for Paititi.

It rained all night, a torrential downpour that found crevices in the tarpaulin, soaking us as we slept. When we woke at about six, we found the river had encroached all around us, turning our sandbank into a miniature island. The equipment was drenched. Three hours of hauling the gear up to higher ground followed. At the end of it, Rodrigo seemed to have something to say.

"*La muerte nos espera más adelante*, death is waiting upriver," he said, through a grin of broken teeth.

"The Curse Lines?"

"*Sí, una pared de energía*, a wall of energy, of power, a power of death. Touch it and you will die." Nothing pleased Rodrigo so much as the prospect of misery being visited on his friends. "The only way through it is to burrow under it, like dogs. After that is a stone wall, eight hundred metres tall, covered in vines."

"Like the wall of Sachsayhuaman?"

Rodrigo didn't reply to the question.

"*Después de la pared hay un lago*, after the wall is a lake," he said, "it's very deep, like an ocean, and filled with dolphins with fangs. If they smell your fat, they will eat you. Beyond the lake is another wall. It's made of gold. And after that is Paititi. It is waiting, eager for visitors."

"That's excellent," I said.

The shaman regarded me with a poisonous glance. "It's waiting for visitors," he repeated, "*entonces los podrá matar*, so it can kill them."

CHAPTER
EIGHT

Bones
Another remarkable substitute for firewood is bones;
a fact which Mr Darwin was, I believe, the first to
mention. The bones of an animal, when freshly killed,
make good fuel; and even those of cooked meat, and
such as have been exposed to the air for some days,
will greatly increase the heat of a scanty fire.

The Art of Travel

Rodrigo was the first to succumb to madness. At six
thirty that evening, after scrubbing his cauldron clean,
he grabbed a cooking knife and held it at arm's length
at the film crew. He didn't say anything at first. His eyes
seemed clouded, and his mouth was dry. His long
tongue poked out from between his teeth at intervals,
like a viper tasting the air. I called Richard. He came
over to see what the fuss was about.

"I'm going to kill you," said Rodrigo, jabbing the
knife at me.

"What's wrong with you?" I said sternly.

"The potatoes! You are forcing me to cook potatoes.
I am a shaman, not a chef."

I had not imagined Rodrigo could make such a
protest; until then he had never raised his voice. Leon
begged him to put the knife down.

"We're not *forcing* you to do anything," he said, "but the hallucinogens are destabilizing Richard, and he's frightening when he's unstable."

Richard strode over and grabbed the knife. "Pull yourself together!" he shouted at Rodrigo. "Or I'll kick your ass all the way back to Iquitos."

"I'm going back to Iquitos anyway," replied the shaman. "I don't need a knife to kill you. I'll do it with a curse."

With that, Rodrigo stood up, took up his wet cauldron and his cloth bag, and walked away into the night.

"Shall we go after him?" I asked.

"Fuckin' phoney," barked Richard. "Let him rot in Hell!"

We never saw the shaman again.

Next morning, disbanding the camp did much to boost morale. The tarpaulin was removed from its frame and furled up like a bedsheet. The film crew insisted on bringing most of their equipment, which piqued my anger and caused me to shake my fist. The porters were too feeble to carry much, even though we were taking only a fraction of the equipment with us. We agreed that if we did find ruins, I would send some of the men back to ferry the rest of the gear up there. The porters didn't turn up until noon. They said they had been in church, praying for our souls. I lined them up and paced up and down like a sergeant inspecting his troops.

"From this moment forward," I said, "if there's any praying to be done, it has to be done in your own time."

The men didn't say anything. They just looked at their bare feet timidly.

"Don't any of you own shoes?"

Again, they strained to look meek. Marco fished out the kit-bag full of rubber boots, and handed them out. I had learned years before that the majority of Peruvians have wide Central Asian feet, and most take size-nine boots. Their universal foot-size is a legacy of their ancestors who crossed the frozen Bering Straits from Asia twenty thousand years ago.

Then the packs were divided and we moved on out, with Richard in the lead. For the first time he seemed revitalized. I wondered if it had anything to do with Rodrigo's sudden departure, or with the large quid of coca leaves pressed tightly into his cheek. He was dressed in his usual camouflage fatigues, the Ninja singlet, and a bandana tied over his head. Across his chest was the Brazilian riot shotgun, loaded, he said, with buckshot. The weapon took seven cartridges, and could spray fire across forty-five degrees.

"Any trouble with these kids," he said acerbically, "and it'll be showtime."

The procession moved in single file, heading due west through low jungle. Words cannot describe my elation at moving. Venture to a remote corner of a faraway land and, from the moment you get there, every person and every thing becomes an obstacle, designed to entrap you, to stop you proceeding on your way. The crew were documenting the momentous departure, which slowed us down considerably. It took them precious time to get out the cameras and put them away once they were finished.

I watched the path before me like a hawk. One moment it was as level as a bowling green, the next it had become an acute wall of mud and roots and, beyond that, a downhill slope. The mud was terrible. It came up to our thighs in places. Dodging round it was difficult because of the weight of our packs. Shift the weight too much in one direction and you could snap an ankle.

Over the first three miles we made good progress, having essentially followed the course of the river back down to near the porters' village at Panataua. The men moaned from time to time about their burdens, but the sight of Richard's riot shotgun muted their protests. We crossed the river in relays, taking our chances in the unsteady hollowed-out canoes. Then, after regrouping on the other side, we cut a path due west so as to bisect the Rio Inchipata.

Ten minutes after entering the forest, the men put down their packs and sat on them. They did this simultaneously, without the faintest whisper between them. It was as if each man had an identical threshold of imagined discomfort.

"What's the matter?

"*Es trabajo duro*, it's hard work," said the farmers. "We don't like walking like this."

Richard cocked a cartridge into the chamber of his weapon.

124

"Force is not the way," I said to him. "If any man wants to leave, let him leave right now."

The farmers looked at one another tautly.

"Does anyone want to go back?" I asked again.

The smallest of the porters, a slender wisp of bone, called Máximo, stood up as their leader. "We will not be threatened by the American," he said. "If you want us to walk hard you have to feed us well."

"There's good food," I told him, "food from England. It's special food called Pot Noodle."

The men seemed pleased for a moment.

"Pota Noodel?" said Máximo.

"Yes. It will make you feel stronger than you have ever felt before."

"Does Pota Noodel make you strong down there?" Máximo jabbed a finger between his legs.

"Yes!" I smirked. "Your wife will boast that you are a king of kings!"

The men cackled, took up their packs and strode ahead through the mud. There were sometimes paths in the undergrowth when we neared a village. The advantage was that the *macheteros* did not need to do so much chopping, except where the path had been reclaimed by the jungle. The drawback was the glutinous mud that took us constantly by surprise, sucking the men down to within an inch of their lives.

By late afternoon, we reached the Inchipata river. I had planned to float the old rubber boat, but the water was no more than ankle deep. A tense moment passed, during which the farmers realized they would have to carry their loads the entire way. Again, Richard brandished his weapon menacingly, as if ready to dispatch a band of Vietcong lurking between the trees.

"We will camp here for the night," I said.

The first camp took a long while to build, there being no routine. We erected two tarpaulins, one for us and one for the men. They had put down their loads and were waiting for Pot Noodles, and for someone else to prepare the camp. I gave a volley of orders: collect firewood, secure the gear, put up the tarps. Máximo shook his head, smiling the smile of an obsequious salesman who thinks he knows best. He took off his boots and lay back.

"We are praying," he said.

"No work, no Pot Noodles," I responded.

The farmers were galvanized into action, even though they had still to taste the exotic English dish.

I had known from the start that I could not expect a local team to be charged with the insatiable enthusiasm that drove me on. As I saw it, the single objective was to keep going. Anything that did not aid this goal was against me and against us all. Running an expedition can bring out the worst in a man. It can make you a power-crazed monster. Even if you keep hold of your senses, you find those under your command detest you from the start. When I read in historical memoirs how a commander was adored by his troops, I take it with a pinch of salt. For if the commander pushed his troops through landscapes of unendurable hardship, they would have no choice but to despise him.

I took comfort in the expeditions of the great Victorian explorers. Their methods were at best ruthless, at worst criminal. But men like Stanley, Livingstone and Samuel Baker could maintain movement for months, even years. I had to respect them for that whatever their methods.

The farmers said prayers before dinner, each reading a passage aloud from his Bible. Then they ate their Pot Noodles in silence, as if they were a religious symbol of some kind, a jungle Eucharist. Rogerio, the most sullen of the men, was overcome with pleasure. He said he could feel blood gushing like a waterfall into his underpants. "*Un afrodisíaco*," he said, gloating.

"*¡Si!*" exclaimed the others, "*¡un afrodisíaco!*"

On the first night, I lay on my back wrapped in my sleeping-bag, my head propped up with a tangle of wet clothes. If I looked out from the end of the makeshift tent, I could see the stars. They were like a million fragments of chalk dust blown across a sheet of black card. I gazed at them, adoring them, worshipping them. The air was still, motionless, punctuated from time to time by the sound of one creature caught by another, the chorus of death.

The film crew lay still, lined up like anchovies in a can. Richard was sitting up at the far end of the tent, smoking Marlboros and chewing coca leaves. Like me, I think he appreciated the calm. It reminded him of Vietnam. Then, from the distance, my ears registered a faint sound. It was the sound of a man groaning, a man in pain. It grew louder and louder, as if the pain was increasing. I sat up. "What's that?"

"Nothing to worry about," said Richard.

"It sounds serious."

"Go back to sleep."

"But what is it?"

The veteran exhaled a cloud of smoke. "It's just the farm boys buggering each other," he said.

We walked all next day, the porters groaning about their packs, and the smirking of other wounds, fresh from the night. Morale was tremendously low, pathetically low, considering we had covered little ground and endured nothing in the way of real hardship. The jungle grew very thick, a snarled mess of *paka*, fine thorny bamboo; brush against it and it lacerated your skin. The undergrowth was too thick to traverse with machetes, so we marched up the river in a line, slipping on the flat round stones on the bottom. The new danger was the sudden dips, which took us by surprise. A misplaced foot, and you were underwater, pulled down by your pack, struggling to get upright, flailing like a drowning man.

Sometimes there was a slender strand of silt that formed a beach along which we could walk. The difficulty of walking on wet sand was tremendous. From time to time it was dotted with the haphazard tracks of a large quadruped.

"*Sachavaca*, giant tapir," said Richard. "Good meat if you can catch it."

The farmers squirmed and moaned with every step, like schoolboys lost on a cross-country run. The film crew and I were carrying the same weight; we found we could endure our packs with comfort.

"I've been around," Richard explained menacingly, "and I've never seen a bunch of sissies like this. If we were in the army, I'd get physical with 'em, beat the shit out of 'em."

Then, as the Inchipata veered north-west, we caught the first glimpse of the mountain ridge, on the windward side of which the pinnacles were said to lie. The farmers stopped trudging as soon as they caught sight of the ridge. They took out their Bibles and held an impromptu prayer session.

At four that afternoon we made camp. Richard had found some "magic" psilocybe mushrooms and planned to chew them once it was dark. He had been performing well since Rodrigo's departure, so for once I didn't berate him for giving in to his addiction.

"It's medicine," he said, under his breath.

That night I gave the order for some spaghetti to be cooked with two cans of sardines. I wanted to keep the aphrodisiac out of the farmers' blood. They ate heartily, gorging themselves on the food. Later they prayed long and hard, until the full moon was high above the camp, hanging there like a disc of antique ivory.

Richard took his military hammock, a candle and a machete, and went to be alone. He climbed up into the undergrowth and made a simple camp, slinging the hammock between a pair of kapok trees. Then he lit the candle and, I assume, he chewed his magic mushrooms. The film crew didn't say it, but I knew they were now fearful of the veteran soldier. In the four years since he and I had worked together, his mind had become eroded, damaged by the constant stream of nerve agents and, perhaps, by the jungle itself. We were all part of the same unit, the same team, but somehow Richard saw us as a threat.

I stumbled down to the water's edge to fill my canteen. The moon's platinum light reflected off the river, as if the surface had been burnished in some way. I stood there for many minutes, staring out over the silhouette of trees, wondering about Richard, the film crew, the porters and Paititi. I wondered, too, why I find it so necessary to set myself impossible quests. It would be far easier to stay at home and get more gainful employment.

Then I turned back towards the pair of tarpaulin canopies. Beyond them I caught a glimpse of Richard's candle, its wick flickering between the intertwined foliage. Very silently, I crept over. Richard was standing naked, a bandanna tied tight around his scalp, a machete in his hands. He was stoned out of his mind, dancing in slow motion round the candle, like a man who had been separated from his sanity. It was so easy to pity him, to see he had been betrayed by his people. He was adrift, clinging to a frail memory, a memory of the time that had both created and destroyed him.

My eagerness for an early start was never fulfilled. The porters started praying an hour before breakfast. They then insisted on eating a vast amount of fish soup, which the cook had brewed up. While eating, they moaned and groaned about the pain of the straps, which they said cut into their shoulders. It was almost eleven a.m. before we were once again wading through the river.

The chief danger of late morning was the stingrays, which liked the warm shallow water close to the banks. Most of us cut bamboo staves and stabbed them ahead of our feet. Richard looked very off-colour, as if he had been up all night. He didn't utter a word all day, to the thrill of the Swedes. They were distressed that their bags were being drenched in the river, hour after hour. Then in the afternoon, the Arriflex's lens fogged up. They had to get the generator going, and use the hairdryer to warm the glass.

We walked for four hours, bursts of movement punctured by regular breaks for rest and prayer. By the late afternoon we were being plagued by sweat bees. The vile nature of those creatures is indescribable. They swarmed over us, silently sipping the sweat from our faces, hair and arms. As soon as we removed our packs, they flocked to the damp patches where the packs had pressed up to our shirts. I tried removing my shirt entirely, but my skin was soon covered with a thick layer of ecstatic bees.

The river zigzagged to the west, doubling back on itself every mile or two. The only compensation was that the current was slow: walking upstream would have been much harder work in heavy water. From time to time we cut a trail through the jungle where the river formed a horseshoe. The porters liked to stop in the forest, take off their packs and gather wild berries. It was at one of these berry breaks that we learned of the cook's obsession.

He was called Roberto, a young man of no more than about nineteen, with close-cropped hair, and a youthful cleanliness. His skin was fresh and undamaged by hardship, his hands smooth, his voice feminine and soft. The porters were eating the berries they had collected, giggling and poking fun at Roberto. It was gentle fun, like women playing in a harem. I asked them for the joke.

"It's Roberto," said one of the others. "*Él está enamorado de* Richard, he's in love with Richard."

That night, when the sun had set and the moon ascended to its full height, Roberto plucked up the courage to sneak from the porters' tent to Richard's alcove in the jungle. I was almost asleep but, through half-open eyes, I saw a slender shadow move across the beach and into the undergrowth. A minute went by. It was followed by a high-pitched, terrifying shriek of fear, and the sound of the cook's bare feet tearing back to bed.

Richard had mistaken the naked young suitor as a predator, and had lashed out with his machete. By a great stroke of good fortune, the blade had missed the boy's throat.

The routine of wading through the river continued for three more days. The porters whinged about the pain at every opportunity, scowling at me as if I had murdered their families in the night. So great was their anger that the Swedes suggested I sleep with a machete under the knot of clothes I used as a pillow. They said it was just a question of who snapped first: the porters or Richard.

The men might have reviled me as their tormentor, but Richard's condition was far graver. From the moment Roberto had sought to attract his affections, Richard had been behaving very oddly indeed. He stopped talking, plugged his ears with candle wax, and if anyone addressed him, he would tremble uncontrollably. We tried to stay out of his way, fearful that his withdrawal symptoms might be reaching a climax. The focus of my overriding concern was the shotgun, designed to bring down a maximum number of people in the least time. His hands were always moulded around it as he walked. It had become an extension of his body, just as the M16 must have been in Vietnam.

Every so often I went to Richard to make reconciliations. But he stared through me, as he did with all the other men. The only one he struggled to focus on was the cook. He watched the boy like a hawk, as if waiting for the right moment to kill him. Worse still was that the more threatening Richard's gaze became, the more Roberto adored it.

As much as I disliked the porters, I went to them after their early-evening prayer session, and advised them in the strongest terms to rein in Roberto. "If he carries on like this," I said coldly, "the gun will claim its first victim."

Máximo spoke for them all: "*Le advertimos, también*, we have warned him, too," he said, "but Roberto has the fire of a woman who has been rejected. It cannot be put out, but must blaze on and on. My friend," he continued, with increased drama, "*este es el fuego del verdadero amor*, this is the fire of *true* love."

133

In the evening Richard made his usual modest camp in the forest, built a campfire, and sharpened his machete on a stone. We could hear the blade rasping up and down, again and again, like the sound of the sea breaking over rocks. Roberto was looking on in the darkness, timid and bewildered. He had removed his clothes and was crouching low. For a moment, in the silver light, I thought I saw him clench his knees as if he was ready to hurl himself upon his true love. It would, of course, have been suicide.

At 10.24a.m. on the fifth day, we spotted the so-called pinnacles. It was hard to make them out at first, as they were densely covered in trees and shrubs, lying in the shadow of the low ridge. They didn't look like pinnacles or pyramids at all. From the first moment I saw them, I knew the journey had been a waste of time, that the pinnacles were no more connected to Paititi than anything else. They were certainly not man-made.

The porters took one look and refused to go another step. They stripped down to their underpants, sprawled out on the warm sun-baked rocks, and were soon covered from head to toe in sweat bees. If I had been Stanley, I would have resorted to corporal punishment — but, I reflected, a great explorer such as he would never have hired such a pathetic bunch of men in the first place. "What's the matter with you all?" I shouted.

"*Es demasiado caluroso*, it's too hot," said one.

"Our backs are hurting us," said another.

"The devil is up there on the pinnacles," said a third.

134

"*¡Sí, el diablo!* Yes, the devil! The devil!" cried the others.

With the porters almost naked and on the point of mutiny, I invited the film crew to carry on with me, on a reconnaissance expedition. We took two climbing ropes and left most of the other gear and food beside the river. I was concerned that the farmers might pilfer the supplies, then mutiny. And so, before we left for the recon mission, I made them give me their boots and the Bibles just in case. We hid them in the jungle a few hundred yards away. Most jungle porters would happily have walked barefoot, but not these softies.

After following the watercourse for days, it was a wonderful feeling to climb above it. Within an hour of slashing and traipsing through undergrowth, we reached a natural *mirador*. From there we got a good look at the pinnacles. There were about a dozen, all odd angular shapes, probably having fallen away from the ridge in ancient times. To get to them, we had to cut a trail in an arc, veering down to the south. Without the porters, and the equipment they bore so unhappily, we made fast progress.

Three hours after setting out, we had managed to climb one of the structures. As we ascended, the vegetation quickly changed, from trees and bamboo to ferns and other higher-altitude flora. There were orchids now, and bromeliads, and every branch and twig was encrusted with green-grey lichens. The temperature fell sharply, too. It was as if we had crossed an invisible barrier, a divide between one realm and the next.

135

Despite the coolness of the air, we sweated uncontrollably from exertion, and were caked with sweat bees and small black flies. They crawled over our skin and clothes, desperate to suck liquid from our dry mouths and from our eyes. With the river so close, I couldn't understand why their thirst was so great.

Near to the top of the pinnacle, we were forced to haul ourselves up over decomposing vegetation. The granite base was lost beneath many layers of dead branches and fallen trees. We used one of the static ropes, but it wasn't much good. The amateur climbers for whom they were made rarely have the inconvenience of such a deluge of roots and twisted stems.

Finally we made it to the top and surveyed the area. It was a place of astonishing natural beauty, and of some secrecy. But it lacked a key ingredient: enchantment. The Incas would have liked it there, I thought, as we went down, but they would never have constructed Paititi in such an obvious place. For them nothing was quite so important as a landscape in which they felt the enduring presence of their god.

CHAPTER
NINE

Warm Carcasses
In Napoleon's retreat, after his campaign in Russia, many a soldier saved or prolonged his life by creeping within the warm and reeking carcass of a horse that had died by the way.

The Art of Travel

We arrived back at the camp at twilight. The temperature had continued to fall through the afternoon and the air was now filled with a sinister calm, the kind that can only lead to a massive, unrelenting downpour of rain. The porters were snuggled up together, some naked, others not. Richard was sitting alone by the river. He didn't say a word when we got back. He was shaking, rocking back and forth, as if he was very, very cold indeed.

The porters were reluctant to talk to me, and when they did it was only to say that Richard had been acting strangely all day. They said he had urinated into a cup and stared into the liquid for an hour or more; and that he had wept uncontrollably while they were praying after lunch.

"What's the matter with him?" asked Roberto. "*¿Qué pasa con mi amor?* What's the matter with my true love?"

137

I said that I didn't know, but that I was frightened.

"He has been trained to kill people," I told them, "so we must forget our differences and protect each other."

I would have devised a plan to wrestle the shotgun away from Richard, but feared it would enrage him further. In any case, a man like that, I reflected, could kill us all with his bare hands. He was a killing machine.

Roberto got up in the night and made a secret meal for the old warrior. He took it to him in his lair in the forest. I don't know what he was expecting, or hoping, but he was chased away, yelping like a small dog that had been kicked hard by an unkind man.

At about two a.m. the temperature cooled a fraction of a degree, a rustle of wind streamed over our faces and it began to pour. The rain of Madre de Dios is similar to that of the Amazon, but there is a petrifying aspect to it, as if it seeks to wound rather than to nurture. It rips down in sheets, with anger, with hatred. We lay in our sleeping-bags hoping desperately, as always, that the water would stay out. But, as always, it found its path in, and was soon being sponged up by our bedding.

The rain continued to fall. It fell through the remainder of the night, all the next morning, through the next day and the following night. All the while, the river rose, inch by inch, until it was ten feet from our camp. We had the option of moving, pitching again in the forest, but the farmers didn't want to budge. They said that the rain would stop . . . and, sure enough, it did. It was how the world must have been in the wake of the biblical flood. Birds were seen twittering in the *chonta* palms, bright sunshine spilling between the fronds.

The river, which so recently had been little more than a creek, was now a surging body of water. Transformed from innocence to maturity, it was now our greatest foe. The current was so tremendous that we could not get across, let alone wade down it.

That morning the porters were slower than usual. At eight a.m. they were still cuddled up with each other beneath their long green tarpaulin.

"What's the matter with you?" I shouted.

"*Es sábado*, it's Saturday," said Máximo. "Seventh Day Adventists don't do anything on Saturday."

So they lay there all day. Their only breaks were to eat a meal of roasted fish heads and *yuka*, and to pray.

The next day, the river was still far too high for wading. There was only one solution: to blow life into the rubber boat. Máximo and Rogerio took out the Zodiac and unfurled it. Since I had purchased the boat, from a used-car salesman in London's East End, it had remained untested. Now was the chance to impress the locals, I thought. The porters gathered round. Their amazement lasted until the fragile foot-pump had begun to work. It was soon apparent that the craft was riddled with holes, twenty-three of them.

Marco, the Russian banker, got to work with a repair kit. He glued and glued, until the boat was covered in patches. The problem was that in addition to the holes, the wooden floor was about to fall out, as the seams were in a terrible state. We decided to use it only for luggage, which would be placed on a platform above the waterline.

As the gluing was in progress, the farmers went out into the forest and hacked down a thicket of balsa trees. They felled about eighteen in all. Within an hour or two, they had stripped the bark of the smooth trunks and nailed them together, using pins made from *chonta* wood, the same wood that the Machiguenga used for their bows. Their skill and speed in making the rafts astonished me. Until that moment I had regarded them as good for nothing.

The equipment was packed on to the rafts and wrapped twice in polythene. Then they were launched, along with the antique Zodiac, and we set off back to Panataua.

The pinnacles might have been a disappointment but, as I saw it, there is nothing like testing equipment and men. As my grandfather would always say: "Time spent on reconnaissance is seldom wasted."

The Zodiac took in water the moment it was eased into the raging current. The balsa rafts fared much better: unlike the rubber boat, floating came naturally to them. Their other great advantage was their strength: they could be hauled effortlessly over the sharpest rocks.

It took only two days to retrace our route down the Inchipata. The farmers were thrilled at the prospect of returning to their homes. I longed to get to Panataua so I could talk Hector into setting out with us. If the porters from his village were the best around, I had no idea how we would ever transport our gear on a larger scale journey.

For the moment the greatest concern was Richard. He lay on one of the rafts, outstretched and delirious, trembling with fever. At first I thought he was putting it on, that it was a bizarre act, perhaps to pull out of the main expedition. But as time wore on, I began to wonder if he was genuinely ill. The Richard Fowler we all knew and endured would have torn your head off for making fun of his past. But now he put up with the porters' taunts, and even allowed Roberto to stroke his thighs — until I ordered the young cook to move away. It seemed unfair to allow him to caress a man incapable of defending himself.

At Panataua, the porters lined up to be paid. They looked like a concert party about to put on a performance, rather than serious jungle porters. I counted out a wad of notes for each and forced myself to shake their hands.

"*Nunca encontrarás* Paititi, you will never find Paititi," said Máximo, when his turn came.

"Why do you say that?"

"Because you do not have Jesus in your heart."

I thanked him for his observation and handed him his money. Rogerio was next. He asked me if he and the other men could be given a Pot Noodle as a bonus. I said that none of them deserved a bonus but, as a gesture of goodwill, they would each be presented with one of the tasty dehydrated meals. They thanked me.

"You know, they are not to fill our stomachs," said Máximo darkly, "*para satisfacer a nuestras mujeres,* they are to satisfy our wives."

It took me a moment to make the connection. He had referred to the supposed aphrodisiacal properties of the white plastic pots.

When the men had been given their Pot Noodles, we received word from Hector that we should come to his shack. I didn't know what to do with all the gear, so I coaxed the farmers to ferry it to his part of the village as their gesture of goodwill. Hector was standing under a *wayuru* tree, waiting for us. It was good to see him again. He was smiling, his mouth framed with white beard, a baseball cap pulled down tight on his head. "I see that you survived the jokers," he said.

"What do you mean?"

"The farm boys, *eran débiles como los niños,* they're as weak as children."

"Why didn't you warn me?"

The old man laughed ominously. "If you really want to find Paititi," he replied, "you have to learn how to choose a team. Without the right people you will never succeed."

Hector owned two modest wooden shacks. The one on the right was used for cooking and eating; there was an antechamber filled with general bric-à-brac and week-old chicks. The other building was larger. It consisted of a small sitting area open to the elements, a storeroom, and a room in which Hector, his wife, daughter and son slept. The shacks were surrounded by a mud garden. The arrangement was as primitive as one

142

could imagine. Hector had come from the big city of Arequipa eighteen years before, but had not bothered to build a more permanent home. There was no running water, no lavatory or stove and, of course, no electricity. The family relied on candlelight, cooked on an open fire and washed at the stream like everyone else in the village.

The old man took one look at Richard, who was barely able to stand, and shook his head. "You must all stay here with us," he said. "This man is in a bad condition, and he should not be moved."

"He's used to a diet of hallucinogens," I responded, "but he can't get them. So he's getting weaker and weaker."

El Maestro helped the old soldier to lie down on a bench in the shade. "There is only one thing that can save him," he said, "*el amor de Jesús*, the love of Jesus."

With that, Hector ushered us in to eat. His wife, Doris, was cooking a meal in the cramped kitchen. She was a short woman, hunched from years of stooping at the hearth, her head crowned with dull grey hair, her childlike eyes reflecting the flames.

We told Hector about the pinnacles, the porters, and what we had learned. I declared that the journey had been a waste of time.

"No, it certainly was not," said Hector. "It was the beginning of your preparation."

We sat at the rough table and held hands in prayer. The old man's son, Paolo, said grace. He was about twelve, with the face of an angel, a complexion so delicate that we all gazed at it. The food was brought in by Mariella, the teenage daughter we had met at the *chacra*. There were wide enamel bowls filled with creamy maize porridge, and boiled *yuka* on a bed of rice.

We ate in silence, and when the meal was over, Hector thanked Jesus on behalf of us all for providing the food. At first I felt I ought to confess my aversion to missionaries. Then I realized Hector might find it necessary to convert me. I asked the Swedes what to do. They talked animatedly in Swedish for a minute or two.

"Don't confess anything," they said. "It'll blow our cover."

So we all agreed to endure the message of Adventism as best we could. After lunch Doris spoon-fed Richard a bowl of chicken broth. His eyes had rolled up in an alarming way. I thought he might die. Hector was cordial, but wouldn't approach the sick soldier. He disliked even looking at him. "He is filled with bitterness, with evil," he declared, slapping his hands together. "Only a diet of prayer can return his health. *Este hombre le ha dado la espalda a Dios*, this man has turned his back on God."

"He's here to protect us," I said, in a moment of enthusiasm.

Hector peered down at the outstretched figure, regarding him with absolute loathing. "My friend," he said, "this man here could not protect anyone from anything. But let us pray for a miracle."

We held hands and formed a circle around Richard: Hector, Doris, Paolo and Mariella, Leon and David,

144

Marco, Boris and myself. It was as if we were attempting to will life into the body of a dead man. Hector led the prayers, beseeching Jesus to give Richard another chance.

"He will be born again!" he cried. "And will learn to walk and talk, and will be your child. He will love you, oh, Jesus, he will be your son."

The film crew and I exchanged troubled glances. We were all concerned for our host. He was a religious maniac, but at the same time he was our best hope of finding the ruins.

That evening we sat on home-made benches on Hector's verandah. The candle wicks were long, their flames fanned by a gentle breeze from the west. Richard hadn't moved since we had arrived at the shack. He was still lying on the bench, his military clothing soaked with sweat. From time to time he would stir, ranting as if he was looking death in the eye.

Hector thrived in the darkness, when the candles were burning, projecting shadows across the walls like phantoms. He sat back, rubbed his beard and conjured his own world with words: "*Tienes que venir con el espíritu limpio*, you have to come with a clean spirit," he said softly. "It must be like a child who has not lost his innocence. To gain that purity you must cleanse your soul."

"But how do we find Paititi?" I asked.

"I told you," he said. "The only way to find it is not to look for it at all. Only a man who has no greed, no avarice, can succeed. When you find Paititi you can take

145

nothing from it. Touch anything at all and you will go blind." Hector paused, picked up his tattered Bible, and pressed the soft leather cover to his lips in a kiss. "If you do find Paititi," he continued, "you will have to repay the earth. *How do you do that?* Well, if you find a few ruins you will have to kill something small, a dog, perhaps. But if the ruins are great, you will have to kill something far larger." Again Hector paused, but this time he looked at me through the ochre light. "*Si las ruinas fueran grandes*, if the ruins are great," he repeated, "*tendrás que matar un hombre*, you will have to kill a man."

Hector walked the tightrope between lunacy and genius. Like everyone else, I was drawn in, willing to suspend judgement, for the Maestro mesmerized his audience, daring them to believe.

Before we knew it a week had passed, each day filled with a rigid routine of prayer, and sermons on how one might find Paititi. It felt as if we were growing roots, planting ourselves on the mud floor of Hector's home. Richard barely moved. He grew increasingly frail, and swore in a whisper at anyone who spoke to him. An attractive young nurse came from the village to examine him. In more usual circumstances, the veteran would have been all over her, but he was broken.

"What's the matter with him?" I asked her.

"*Es un resfrío*, it's nothing but a cold," she said. "Please try to make sure he washes. He smells very bad!"

146

Before she left, the nurse enquired about the strong medicine I had brought from my home country.

"The painkillers?"

"No, Señor," she said, holding a hand over her mouth as if she was about to utter an obscenity. "*Los afrodisíacos*, the aphrodisiacs."

I squinted in confusion, then remembered the potent medication.

"Women all over the village are asking me for the medicine," she said. "They have heard it makes a man fiery, passionate."

I handed her a Pot Noodle. "It's a special new kind of drug from Europe," I said. "You take it orally."

Every day Hector's harangues grew longer, and wilder, and every day I sensed that we were farther from reaching our goal, Paititi. The scruff of white beard that hid his mouth and quivered when he spoke gave our host an aura of sophistication. And when he spoke, those around him listened. You couldn't help yourself. You were drawn in, like a swarm of insects desperate to touch a flame on a tropical night. Hector would speak of veiled evil on a Biblical scale, hinting of curses and *brujería* and ferocious, diabolical forces lurking between the trees, and in the mists of the waterfalls.

One night, he claimed to have seen a UFO. He said it wasn't a "normal" extraterrestrial, but was created by sorcerers upriver: the very same place to which we were planning to travel.

"*Era una bola de luz*, it was a ball of light," he said, "a sphere burning brilliantly like phosphorus. It glided through the sky, and down, down, down over the trees. Then, when it reached the river, it dived into the water."

"Weren't you fearful?" I asked.

"No," El Maestro replied stolidly, "we had no fear, because we have Jesus."

On the eighth day Hector had a visitor, a man we had not met before. He was wearing a simple uniform, part military, part civilian, and was called Señor Franco. He was tall and had an uninteresting face; the kind of man your eyes would not pick out in a crowd. He walked with a dead straight back and chewed the corner of his mouth between sentences. The frosty reception put on by Hector and his family indicated their feelings for him. It turned out that he worked for the government and he had not come to speak to Hector but to us.

"If you go to look for Paititi," he said, in a clear, practised voice, "we will have you arrested and incarcerated."

"Paititi? What's Paititi?" I asked flippantly.

"You heard what I said," he riposted. "I am waiting for you. I am watching you."

When he was gone, Hector warned us of the authorities. "There is a layer of bad men plundering our country's wealth," he said. "It's big business, the business of a few."

"Is Señor Franco one of them?"

"No, no, he's low down in the chain of command," Hector replied. "He's employed by the government, but is really working for the oil company."

148

★ ★ ★

A second week slipped by and, with each day, it was as if our roots anchored us a little more firmly to Hector's shack. He was now saying there was no point in leaving for the lost city before the next year. He had crops to plant, and money to repay. Again and again he declared that we were still not pure, our souls were not yet cleansed.

"Will we ever be ready to search for the ruins of the Incas?" I shouted in despair.

"*Quizás no*, perhaps not," was his reply.

Meanwhile, Richard grew ever weaker. The villagers would troop in from time to time and look at him slouched in his camouflage hammock. Some would stretch out their arms and poke him, as if jabbing a strange animal to see if it was alive. They all had the same diagnosis: that the Vietnam veteran had descended into Hell and turned his back on Jesus. They were praying for his soul, they said coyly.

But then, one morning, Richard was standing up outside the house. We rushed over. He was smiling. We applauded. No one had seen him smiling in a very long time.

"I'm better," he said angrily.

Hector praised Jesus for the miracle.

We must have been at the house too long, for we prayed to the Lord and were happy to do so.

"What's wrong with you?" Richard snapped at me. "You gone all fuckin' religious or something?"

It was a great moment. The soldier was back to his old self. We were a team again. I went up and hugged him. "It's good to have you back," I said.

149

"Yeah, well, get me some chow, will ya?"

Doris piled a plate high with roasted *yuka* and handed it to Richard as if her prodigal son had returned. Then, after the meal, we sat in the sunshine and Richard told tales of the wild times of his youth.

David was the one to stir the memories from him. "What about Vietnam?" he said.

To us it was a single word, the name of a place, but to Richard it was a word whose intensity he had never found elsewhere. Like so many veterans, he relived it in his mind every day.

"Vietnam?" said Richard, drawing deep on his Marlboro. "I'll tell you about Vietnam. Sure it was ugly, it was fucking obscene. But I had a ball down there. I'd be camped out in the jungle, inserted behind enemy lines and all that shit you see in the movies. If I got bored, and you did get bored, I could call in a fuckin' airstrike. There I was, a kid of nineteen, calling in a two-hundred-and-fifty-thousand-dollar airstrike. It blew your mind."

"What about the killing?"

"Yeah, there was killing and death and plenty of it," said Richard. "They called our platoon the Widow Makers, and there was a reason for it. When you were new what they'd do was to take you out on a trail with an experienced guy. All your life you're taught that killing is wrong, and all that Christian shit. But now you're out there, trained to do the shit. It's like cowboys and Indians when you were a kid. You're with these guys and they set you up. They put you in the bushes and you're sitting there watching, waiting. All of a

150

sudden you see part of a guy and he's lookin' around and he's coming along . . . and now you're getting ready to kill him. He could have a wife but you don't think about that kind of shit. You got your weapon on automatic 'cos you're new to the game. You raise it up and lock on to the body. You let out a burst . . . *Brrrrr!* Then you take off, running like a madman up the trail.

"After a while, when you're more experienced, you get cool at it, and you can kill with one or two rounds. Then you got people saying to you, '*Way to go, man! You rock! You finally got yourself a gook!*' You get a case of beer and they're shaking your hand and you get this kinda sick fucking feeling. To do your job is one thing, but all of a sudden you've crossed the line with these guys and you're one of them. You've been initiated."

Richard's illness had destabilized us all. I think it was because we feared he might kill us in the night. That evening, as I struggled to sleep, I thanked Jesus for bringing him back to us intact.

CHAPTER
TEN

Porters for Delicate Instruments Entrust surveying
instruments and fragile articles to some respectable
old savage, whose infirmities compel him to walk
steadily. He will be delighted at the prospect of
picking up a living by such easy service.

The Art of Travel

Life at Hector's shack continued as a routine of prayer,
sleep and mental preparation. Days drifted by and, as
they did so, I felt myself losing grasp of the expedition.
Sometimes it seemed as though Hector had us there
like captive animals in a strange menagerie. We would
listen to his stories, his warnings of what lay upriver. It
was crazed talk but it relieved the boredom.

The routine began with hymns. They were sung at
five each morning, usually led by Paolo, whose voice
had not yet broken. Then we would saunter off into the
woods and wash down by the stream. After that, Doris
would provide some rice and roasted chicken for
breakfast. Then the harangues would begin. Hector
could sit at the kitchen table for six hours or more.
With narrowed eyes and flailing arms, he conjured a
realm of terrifying danger.

"We will pass through a vast chasm filled with
rapids," he said one morning. "We will know it because

the walls will be so steep that merely looking upon them will send shocks of electricity pulsing down our spines. After that will come three more *pongos*, great rapids. It will be impossible to use boats or rafts. You have no idea how hard it will be!"

Hector cut himself short. He was about to continue, but for some reason he sat in silence, slid his fingertips over each other and prayed to Jesus. Doris looked on from the kitchen area. "*Espíritu santo*," she whispered, "the sacred spirit."

"Is there a problem?" I asked.

"*Sí, muchos problemas*, yes, many problems," said the Maestro. "If you knew the hazards that lie between us and Paititi, your hair would turn white in a moment, just like my own."

"What problems lie ahead?"

Hector peered down at the worn table, blew a spider from its surface, and said: "After the fourth *pongo* we will come to a place of negative energy. It will affect us all, turning friends into enemies and enemies into friends. The compass will spin round and round, and we will lose all orientation."

"But we have the river," I interjected.

"*Ah, sí, el río*," said Hector, disdainfully. "The river is the greatest enemy of all. It will try to drown us, sucking us into an underwater world of spirits and demons."

There was a point in all Hector's rants at which he crossed a dividing line. It separated two worlds: one of questionable but interesting possibility, the other in which his fantasy ran amok. I would always notice the

153

dividing line approaching and seek to halt the conversation before we crossed the threshold.

"Underground tunnels connect Paititi with other places," he exclaimed, in one such tirade. "You may laugh at me, but Paititi is linked with the lost continents of Atlantis and Mu."

The film crew and I regarded each other with disappointment. Our host had descended once again into the twilight zone of his own imagination.

One way to deflect Hector's attention away from the fantasy, back into the natural world, was to mention the name of the Machiguenga tribe. He despised them, although he would never admit it. In his eyes they were not noble savages but a barbaric, atheist people. "The time for conversion will come," he would say grandly. "It's time for them to grow up, to taste the Word of God on their tongues."

It was at one such debate about Paititi, the tribe and the Word of Jesus, that we first heard of Pancho. Hector uttered the name in passing, as part of another tale.

"Who's Pancho?" I asked.

Hector inhaled a deep breath of air, and let it out gently, in a prolonged sigh.

"Pancho," he said, "is the man you will need if you want to find Paititi," he said.

"Why? What does he know?"

The old man caught my eye. It was like a paralysed man signalling to me, signalling a grave danger and a secret solution.

"Pancho has seen the ruins of Paititi, *con sus propios ojos*, with his own eyes," he said calmly.

I wanted to slap Hector on the back and curse him for not telling us before. But he must have had reasons not to reveal Pancho until then.

"As a young man seeking new hunting grounds," said Hector, "Pancho spotted a big wall deep in the jungle. It was overgrown with creepers and vines. Nearby he found another, and then another. He realized that it was a series of vast ruins, from the time of the Incas. He saw something poking out from beneath a big stone, so he dug with his hands and discovered a hatchet, its blade adorned with gold. He was very excited, so he took the thing to his father, who was then head of the tribe. But his father grew very angry. He shouted at the boy, ordering him to return the hatchet at once and to forget about the ruins . . . for fear of activating the curse, the curse of Paititi."

Again Hector paused, this time to heighten the dramatic effect. "Pancho returned the hatchet, but . . ." he said slowly ". . . *pero él nunca podría olvidar*, but he could not forget."

"Where did he find the ruins?"

"Only Pancho knows exactly," Hector replied. "*Sólo él puede llevarnos allá*, only he can take us there."

"Let's go and meet him now. Let's beg him," I said. "Surely there's something he wants in return."

"You are not ready yet," he responded. "You are not cleansed of your sins."

Hector stood up, put on his clean white shirt and went to church to pray. As far as he was concerned, we ought to have been living in the church: it was the best route to Paititi. I was buoyed by Pancho's story, but

155

until I heard it from his own lips, I suspected it was just another tale from the dark side of the old man's mind.

Another week drifted by. We hardly saw Richard in that time. He would get up at night and walk round the village, scurrying from one shadow to the next. He never turned up for meals, and refused to pray.

"*El hombre que no reza*, a man who does not pray," said Hector one morning, "*es un hombre que tiene el alma envenenada*, is a man who has a poisoned soul."

He didn't say so, but I knew he was referring to the Vietnam veteran. Word spread in the village that Richard was in league with the devil. The headman said he had seen him jumping on chickens, ripping off their heads and drinking the blood. And Hector's neighbour, a kind woman with gold front teeth called Dolores, said she had seen the veteran "raping the pigs". Richard and I might have been at each other's throats much of the time, but I had to protest at the allegation. Even he, I felt, would have drawn a line at bestiality.

Then, one morning, Richard approached us as we sat in the shade studying the maps. He was chewing a big quid of coca leaves. I noticed that his jungle boots were laced, as if he was ready to set out on a journey. I asked him what was going on.

"I'm leaving," he said, "pulling out."

We all showed surprise.

"Yeah, well, just remember," he said "that I'm no pussy cat. I got friends, people of influence. Mess me around and the Lima police will be buggering you before you know it."

156

Hector and his family got wind of the departure and fled to the church to pray for Richard's poisoned soul. They said later that they didn't want to say farewell. It was left to the film crew and me to walk him down to the river to begin his long journey back to Iquitos.

A moment before he stepped on to the rickety hollowed-out canoe to cross the Madre de Dios river, Richard shouted back, "You'll be hearing from me."

Sure enough we did hear from him a few days later, through a middleman. The communication came via the film crew's satellite telephone. A voice at the other end was asking for twenty-five thousand dollars in used fifty-dollar bills. "It's for the tapes," said the voice. "Take down this number and call me at dusk."

A sick, panicked feeling washed over us all. David and Leon ran to their camera bags and counted their videotapes. Twenty-five hours' worth of material was missing. The two Swedes huddled in a corner for a long time, chattering in their native tongue. At first they seemed in the depths of despair. But then their voices strengthened. They stopped talking and came to where the rest of us were sitting.

"How can we ever raise that much money?" I asked.

"We don't have to," said David.

"What do you mean? Shall we call the police?"

"We've decided not even to return the call," said Leon. "It's like kidnapping a man who no one wants. We'll shoot more film. It's as easy as that."

The next day Hector was up as usual at five a.m. But that morning he did not sing hymns. Instead he had taken out his rubber hunting boots and his best machete. He was sharpening the knife on a block of oiled granite.

"No hymns?" I said quizzically.

"No *hay tiempo para canciones*, no time for songs," he replied.

"But what has changed?"

Hector, El Maestro, looked at me down the razor-sharp blade of his machete.

"The wickedness that cloaked you has vanished," he said. "*Estamos listos para partir*, we are ready to leave."

As if he had been listening from behind a tree, the Peruvian official Señor Franco appeared from nowhere. He said he was passing and merely wanted to remind us of the danger of breaking sanctioned boundaries. It was obvious that Richard had tipped him off on his way back to civilization.

Hector said we would need to spend a little time getting a good group of porters together, and making contact with Pancho. "You need chainsaw men," he said, slapping his biceps, "not feeble farm boys. You need men who can uproot trees with their bare hands, and live on raw jungle meat if they have to."

"Do such men exist around here?" I asked.

"Of course," the Maestro replied, "but they're deep in the forest cutting down trees. You have no idea how many trees there are to be felled. I will call for them."

The next problem to overcome was Pancho. Although he supposedly knew where the ruins lay, he had refused to return to them. He was not so fearful of activating the curse as he was of his own tribe. They had threatened to burn down his hut if he even talked

158

of Paititi. I begged Hector to think of something that might tempt Pancho into taking us. Surely there was something we could give him worth more than his wattle-and-daub *maloca*, and the land it was on.

"There is something that Pancho wants very, very much," Hector replied. "He would risk everything he had on it."

"What is it?"

"He wants to go to Cusco."

"We can arrange that," I said. "We can take him."

Hector smiled softly. Then his look of pleasure turned to one of contempt.

"It is worse than that," he said. "You see, Pancho wants to go to a brothel with 'high class' women, with big breasts, and he wants to go dancing in a discothèque."

I looked at the Swedes. They looked at me. We all looked at Hector, and said together, "We can arrange that."

With the Maestro fighting us every inch of the way, we marched out of Panataua and up along the jungle route to the Machiguenga village at Mantacolla. Our visit coincided with their annual carnival. Rather than being linked in any way to the tribe's culture or heritage, it was centred around their unremitting desire to get extremely drunk on *masato*, the manioc-root beer.

By the time we got to the village, the festivities had been going on for about three days. Many tribesmen were so drunk they couldn't stand. In our society a person may have a few drinks in the evening. But in

159

Machiguenga culture, a man will drink all day and all night for days on end, with short periods of stupor-like sleep in between. The sight of fifty inebriated men and women was made all the stranger by the fact that most of them were painted fuchsia pink. Those who could stand were dancing around a tree in ankle-deep mud, swiping at its trunk with axes and singing.

Hector forbade us to mention the name of the lost city to any of them. Do so, he said sternly, and they might kill us, so strong was their fear of the curse. I asked him to go and find Pancho. Two hours passed, and Hector returned. He said he had found his friend, who had agreed to come to Lima. "Pancho's very happy," he said, "but he won't go now, because everyone is watching. The tribe have told him they'll kill him if he breaks the bond of secrecy."

We stayed at the carnival for two days, in the hope of befriending the tribe. They were suspicious, and only began to warm to us when they saw us drinking their unpleasant saliva-fermented beer. They sat in the middle of the village, watching the sun go down, a glorious backdrop against which the theatre of the Machiguenga carnival was played out. As we sat there, drinking the vile *masato*, declaring how delicious we found it, I reflected.

Pancho's ambition was the mirror image of my own. I yearned to find a *lost* city, all overgrown and deserted, while Pancho dreamed of a *live* city, bustling with people and traffic. Taking a Peruvian tribesman from the jungle to the city was certainly not a politically correct thing to do, but I didn't see that I had much choice. Pancho was the only man who could lead me to Paititi . . . or was he? I asked Hector.

"His brother knows the location of the ruins as well," he replied. "He is called Javier, and he lives upriver at Aboroa."

"Do you know him?"

"*Sí, por supuesto*, yes, of course I do," said Hector. "I've known them both since they were young men."

With the Machiguenga festivities in full swing, it seemed as if the carnival might last many days longer. Hector said they would celebrate until no one had the strength to stand. "In some ways it's a good thing," he said. "They go crazy from time to time and get it out of their system, then they go back to their ordinary lives."

Hector was careful not to condemn the tribe, a people whose souls he obviously regarded as damned. They all knew him, from the old crones to the strapping young warriors who wore bands of black toucan feathers across their brows. They would offer him a bowl of warm *masato* or try to rub fuchsia dye on his face. Hector would simply smile, thank them for thinking of him, and shy back into the shadows.

Before we left Mantacolla to walk back to Panataua, Hector pointed to a glade that lay between the village and the forest. He seemed overcome for a moment, as if a higher power were signalling to him. "That would be a lovely place to build a church," he said.

That night Doris served stewed bananas. They were lightly salted, sitting on a bed of macaroni. Since Richard's departure, Hector's wife had been filled with

161

an intense energy. She said it was the soul of Jesus filling her veins. You could see it in her eyes, in her manner. She no longer stooped, but swaggered around the shack, singing, laughing.

"*El diablo estaba acá*, there was evil here," she said, "*pero ahora él se ha ido*, but now the evil has gone."

Hector was equally buoyant. He was ready for the journey, and spent all the next morning looking at the map. What surprised me was his lack of knowledge of the great jungle that lay west of the village. But no one else in Panataua knew any more than he: only the Machiguenga had explored the wilderness of Madre de Dios. As far as everyone else was concerned, the jungle was a place where blood-drinking phantoms lurked, a place to be avoided at all costs.

Just before lunch a squat, crag-faced man in blue denim shorts came to the house. We had often seen him stalking us as we wandered through the village. Hector had once said that this man, who was called Francisco, had killed his wife but that no one could prove it. The woman had disappeared one night, fifteen years before, after a night of rain. Rather than show remorse, Francisco had been seen dancing drunk in his shack. He was universally despised for being a busybody. I was taken aback to find Hector welcoming him into his home. "Francisco will be coming with us on the journey," he said.

The crag face lit up for a moment, before its mouth barked, "Well, you'd better give me enough food, or you will see my anger!"

162

I regarded Hector incredulously. Francisco shook our hands and stumbled away into the bright light.

"What do you mean?" I asked, once Crag-face had gone. "He's terrible. He can't come with us. Everyone hates him. He is an enemy, not a friend!"

"Precisely!" said the Maestro. "I told you . . . we will reach a place of negative energy, *hará amigos a los enemigos y enemigos a los amigos*, it will turn friends into enemies, and enemies into friends." He paused to allow the warped logic to sink in. As he saw it, we would have to take along an enemy who would ultimately become a friend. "On the journey to find Paititi," he said, "you have to prepare, and use your mind. Francisco is indeed my enemy, we loathe each other, and as my enemy he could be the one man to save our expedition."

"But why didn't you want Richard to come on the trip, then?"

The old man looked at me hard, blinked, and said, "Because there is a difference between an enemy and the devil."

Hector could see I was worried. We might have had a mountain of Pot Noodles to feed our porters, but we still didn't have any porters, except the village busybody whom no one could stand. We had a map with gaping white spaces across it, Peruvian officials snapping at our heels, and the one man who could take us to the ruins, Pancho, was too fearful to join us.

"Put your trust in Jesus, and clear your mind," Hector counselled. "The problems will melt like butter on the desert sand."

"When will the porters get here?"

Hector looked at his wristwatch. It ran two hours slow, but in the jungle precision timing was not important. "They should be here in a few minutes," he said.

Sure enough, the sound of men in rubber boots was heard soon after, stomping across the baked-mud path. I opened the door and peered out. Even through the twilight it was instantly clear that they were not farm boys but chainsaw men. There were fifteen of them. Their arms were bulky and over-developed, part attractive, part grotesque. They walked with confidence, purpose, as if they knew where they were going, and they had no fear of the destination. Best of all, they were not carrying Bibles.

Hector nudged me as they approached. "These men don't need aphrodisiacs," he said.

When they had greeted the old man, I asked them if they would work as porters, for eight dollars per man per day. They did not show much excitement about the wage. But Hector said it was merely their manner, confident yet reserved. The porters agreed to carry as much as they could for as long as the journey took. I asked whether they were frightened of the jungle. The men showed humour for the first time, laughing until their eyes were glazed with tears.

"We have no fear of the jungle," said one man, "but it is terrified of us, because we are the chainsaw gang."

* * *

The day before leaving upriver, Boris, the Bulgarian film student, woke up in the night. He ran out of the dining shack, where the five of us were sleeping in a line on the floor. We found him in the morning, crouching on the path outside. He was gripping his belly. Leon asked what was wrong, if he had stomach problems.

"The spirits entered me through my dreams," he said. "I can feel them in there."

Until that morning Boris had seemed to me an intelligent young man, not the type you would expect to believe in such nonsense. I warned him not to mention the dream or the spirits to Hector and Doris. But, unfortunately, they had overheard the conversation. They rushed out of the shack with an oversized Bible.

"*Los espíritus*, the spirits," said Doris darkly, "they are battling for Boris's soul. We must take him to church at once."

The expedition was put on hold as Hector led the Bulgarian to the wooden church at the edge of the village. They stayed there all day, praying, beseeching Jesus to cast out the malevolent forces from Boris's intestines. Two further days of praying followed. The rest of the film crew and I went mad with waiting, but there was no alternative. Then, on the morning of the fourth day, Hector said that Boris was healed. We could leave at once.

CHAPTER
ELEVEN

Wasp and Scorpion Stings The oil scraped out of a tobacco-pipe is a good application; should the scorpion be large, his sting must be treated like a snake-bite.

The Art of Travel

The full moon reflected off the surface of the river, glinting, teasing, luring us upstream. It was as if an unseen force had lit a beacon to light the way. Hector insisted that we leave his village at midnight to avoid the penetrating eye of Señor Franco. In the hours before our departure, he had spread a rumour through the community that we were heading to another river, the Rio Negro, in search of *boutou*, pink dolphins. The rumour wasn't strictly necessary, as I had already bribed the villagers with a promise to buy a new Bible for every man, woman and child if they pointed the official in the wrong direction.

To make faster progress, we had hired a pair of clinker-built boats to navigate the course as far as the western mouth of the Palatoa river. Shortly before midnight, the chainsaw gang heaved the mass of equipment and food down to the water and stowed it in the boats. They were moored to the bank of a rivulet, which fed into the Madre de Dios. The water was low there, the moonlight shaded by tall kapok trees.

There is no feeling quite like the nocturnal commencement to a journey. It was a rich blend of anticipation and secrecy, as if we were a part of something devious and depraved.

The one major setback had come at dusk when we had done a full inventory of equipment. Richard had not only taken the video cassettes but had stolen our entire stock of morphine as well. He was planning, no doubt, to use it for recreational purposes. It was too late to replenish our supply, so we would have to head into the jungle without it. It would be needed, though, if a man snapped an ankle on the slippery stones that lined the river.

From the start the crag-faced Francisco was irate. He didn't approve of leaving in the middle of the night. Late nights, he said, gave him a migraine, and migraines made him very angry indeed.

Hector simply laughed at the protestations. "Think of it like this," he whispered, as we covered the bags with tarpaulins, "the greater his fury now, the greater his friendship later."

Just before we pushed off, Hector's young son, Paolo, hurried through the jungle and called to us: "Señor Franco knows you are leaving," he said. "He's at the main branch of the river with his launch, flashlights and six of his men."

Francisco cackled bitterly, insisting we should turn ourselves in or, better still, go back to the village and call off the trip. His expression was sour, as if he had

167

sucked down a plate of limes, his cheeks pulled back to the ears, all stretched and tight.

But Hector had already come up with a plan. "It's too risky for so many of us to travel past Franco with the boats," he said. "He will know we are up to something. We will walk through the forest and meet the boats at the second bend."

Hector said he was concerned about the boats. They were so heavy that they were terribly low in the water. While they often ventured downstream fully laden with *yuka* and bananas, they rarely went upriver with a load. The cargo was covered first with our tarpaulins, and second, with ragged sackcloth sheets, forming a primitive disguise. Unlike the tarps, the sacking did not reflect the moonlight.

The film crew were unhappy at being separated from their precious camera equipment. I had little sympathy because they had not heeded my pleas to cut down their gear. Film may look far grander than video, but the film cans were bulky and an awful nuisance.

One minute before one a.m. we tramped into the forest, moving in single file. Hector and the other locals knew the path so well they needed no light. The film crew and I had more difficulty: the trail ascended and descended sharply without warning, there were roots and armadillo holes to catch our feet, and a mesh of low branches that whipped us in the face every few feet. We walked in silence, the ghostly curve of the moon breaking through the trees from time to time.

In the distance we could hear the faint grumble of the engines, the boatmen forcing their craft against the fast current of the Madre de Dios. With hidden boulders so common, even the most experienced pilot risked much by navigating the river at night. Franco was certainly aware of the danger. His curiosity would surely have been piqued by a pair of craft pushing upstream in the middle of the night.

We walked due north for two hours. In that time not a word was spoken, yet we were deafened by the din of the jungle. Insects with wings no bigger than postage stamps created a sound as loud and piercing as a siren; their noise was drowned out in turn by the chorus of tree frogs, and the clamour of barking rats.

The men were unladen but I could sense their strength and eagerness. As we pushed on, I considered the importance of enthusiasm: with an enthusiastic team you can achieve virtually anything. When I am selecting people with whom to work, it is the one quality I look for. I don't care if someone doesn't have a specific skill, they can learn it. With enthusiasm, a man can overcome his limitations; without it, he is a dead weight.

Suddenly my train of thought shifted. I realized that Hector and most of the chainsaw gang were armed with machetes. We had been parted from our equipment, were walking through the jungle at night, and no one but they knew where we were heading. They could have slit our throats, hacked up our bodies and grabbed the boatloads of gear without a second thought. Within a few days the jungle fauna would have consumed us, and we would be a memory, a cautionary tale, like the Nichols expedition had become.

I was about to urge the film crew to be vigilant for signs of imminent execution, but Hector spoke first: "Can you see the river down there?" he said, pointing through the trees. "It looks as if we're ahead of the boats."

I glanced down to the water's mirrored surface, a scene of absolute peace, in stark contrast to the undergrowth. The river moved with an angelic ease. On either side of it, the grey-green foliage was charged with life, the savage fauna within it feeding on itself and on intruders. My legs were running with blood, released by an army of microscopic insect teeth. In more usual circumstances I would have complained, but I noticed that everyone else was affected in a similar way.

We crouched there, mopping our shins, waiting for the rumble of the *peki-peki* engines. They didn't come.

"We have not yet passed into the restricted area," Hector said quietly, "so Señor Franco cannot confiscate the equipment."

"But he can cause trouble," I said.

"*Sí*," said the Maestro, with a deep sigh. "That man can cause trouble."

Another hour passed. Hector was going to send one of the men to spy on the official's position but just before he dispatched him I made out the faintest murmur of mechanical sound. It was low, rhythmic and consistent, and was getting louder, increasing in echo and pitch. Hector slapped his palms together. "Here are the boats," he said.

They pulled up a few minutes later. We stayed in the shadows lest Señor Franco had come upriver as well, but there was no sign of him. The boatmen reported that the official had swung a bright searchlight across their bows, but the boats had carried on without stopping.

"There must be so much oil up there," said Hector. "I cannot believe that a place so beautiful can shelter a commodity so wicked."

"Is it safe for us to travel on the boats?"

"Climb aboard," said the old man. "Franco won't bother us now. He has to check in with Cusco every morning at six."

We lay outstretched over the packed boats, which moved in fits and starts against the current. The moon had gone, replaced by a blush of pink in the east. I stared up at the sky, my eyes picking out the last trace of stars.

It was eight thirty when I was wakened, forced with the others to jump into the water and ease the boats through the shallows. The payloads were pressing the craft deep, and the boatmen were becoming bitter. They said they would charge us if their boats were damaged on the rocks and, if we didn't pay up, they would report us to Señor Franco.

My temper almost got the better of me, but Hector cautioned me: "Let them shout like children," he said. "There are bigger problems to take our attention."

He was right. Fifty yards ahead a throng of Machiguenga warriors were waiting on the shore, many armed with bows and elongated arrows. There must have been about forty men, women and children.

171

Twenty more were squatting on homemade rafts. It was obvious that they were not out fishing.

"They want money for passing through their stretch of river," said Hector calmly. "We must talk to them. They'll kill us if we trespass."

The boats struggled over to the huddle of Indians. They greeted us nervously, suspiciously, as if they had thought up a devious plan.

Hector jumped out and waded ashore. The tribe knew him and, although they did not share his belief in Christianity, they liked the old man, and he made an effort to be liked. The rest of us sat in the boats, waiting for Hector's command. In such circumstances your trump card is the man with experience. He chatted with them, sharing jokes, lifting the atmosphere. He knew as well as they that money was the only subject of discussion, but he eased the conversation along, warming it, readying it for the matter at hand.

Eventually the dialogue of negotiation began. Numbers were called out in Machiguenga and Spanish, fingers counting sums. After a long while, Hector approached the boat in which I was sitting. "Shall I give them some alcohol?" I asked.

"No no, that will make them even greedier," said Hector, "and they are far too greedy already. They have nothing to use this money on — they don't even know the value of it — but the missionaries have told them to demand currency."

"How much do they want?"

"*Cincuenta mil soles*, fifty thousand *soles*," he replied.

"That's four thousand dollars! It's nothing short of piracy."

"Of course it is," said Hector. "Most of them have never even seen a shop."

I sent the Maestro back to get the price down, or to offer them some equipment after the expedition. Two hours of discussion followed. At the end of it, gourds of warm bubbling *masato* were served up and the warriors were grinning. "I've offered them your rubber boat and five hundred dollars," said Hector. "Regard it as the value of our lives."

By dusk, the boatmen were seething with anger. They had been enraged for a good long while, surpassed only by Francisco, who was driving us all mad. He moaned about anything and everything, from the condition of the boats to the sound of their engines to the scent of the air. Whenever he heard Crag-face's reprimands, Hector would exclaim how fortunate we were to have him along, and how valuable he would be once we reached the zone of negative energy.

We had seen no houses on the shore since leaving Panataua, except for two or three at the tribe's village. In the Upper Amazon, communities were much more common along the rivers, but the Madre de Dios jungle is higher and sustains far fewer animals, and therefore fewer people.

Venus was visible, and I spotted a triangle of bamboo *malocas* three hundred yards ahead. At first it was an unnerving sight; I feared more Machiguenga wanting yet more money. But Hector's spirits were boosted at

173

the sight. "It's Aboroa," he said, "the home of Pancho's mother, and her other son, Javier."

"The one who also knows the location of the ruins?"

"*Sí, sí,*" he replied. "*Él puede ayudarnos,* he can help us."

The boatmen put us ashore and fled back downriver. They were both incandescent with rage. It seemed miraculous that they had taken us as far as Aboroa. All around the water was filled with boulders, rising up like miniature black icebergs. I was sorry to see the craft retreat; it meant that we would be carrying the luggage from then on.

Before we could ask about Pancho's brother, we greeted his mother. She was a wizened woman with a bald head, twig-like limbs and a mouth naked of teeth. I am uncertain of her name, as I never heard it spoken. Hector and the others called her Tia, aunt. He hugged her, and she rewarded him with half a gallon of *masato*, its raw ingredient chewed by her gums.

When we had all greeted the old woman, and drunk a similar quantity of the wretched beverage, Hector asked her about Javier.

"He's gone upriver to trap parrots and hunt tapir," she said. "Go up there and you will find him." She made it sound so easy, as if we would spot him straight away among a million trees.

We pitched a camp beside her shack, and she presented us with a male curassow. One of the porters tore off the bird's head and the jet-black feathers; he said he was very hungry. We had brought a large amount of *yuka*. It was boiled up as well. The roots

174

were so heavy that I was keen for them to be eaten, rather than carry them. I strained a little of the starchy water from the pan and poured it into a Chicken and Mushroom Pot Noodle for the old woman. She took a nibble with her gums and grimaced.

"It tastes like *pacamama*," she said.

"What's *pacamama*?" I asked.

"It's bamboo rat," said Hector.

Tia fed the Pot Noodle to a cluster of chicks that she kept as pets. She had woven them a kind of wicker nest; it was an impressive example of craftsmanship. Her home was awash with jungle animals — there was a clutch of *matamata* turtles, a spider monkey, four toucans and a pair of young anteaters. It was like a zoo without cages, but it was clear that all the creatures were being raised for the table. The Machiguenga regarded the jungle as a giant larder that is always stocked. If they needed something to eat, they looked around for an animal to catch. If they saw one, they killed it. They never hunted for sport, and always ate what they killed.

The porters were eager to try the Pot Noodles for themselves. Since our trip to the pinnacles, word had spread about the additive-rich snacks brought from far away. Their leader was a strong-willed man called Julio, whose chest was ribbed with muscle; he begged me to let him try a mouthful.

"Is it true that one Pot Noodle can make a man potent all night long?" he asked, when there was a pause in conversation.

"*Si,si,*" said another, "I have heard that you can satisfy six women and still not get tired!"

I warned the men against believing misinformation. Do so, I said, and our expedition's success would be plunged into danger.

Pancho's mother had much to say on the subject of danger. When she had heard of my mission to discover Paititi, she declared simply that we would all perish on the trip: "*El río los tragará*, the river will drink you up," she said.

We came across remarkably few people in the jungle. But all of them, without exception, foresaw disaster. Some said that a giant serpent would rise up from the river and drown us, others that a storm would slay us with lightning, or that El Tigre would pounce, and swallow us while we slept.

We found one of Tia's old neighbours pilfering our supplies that night. He took one look at me and shouted something.

"What did he say?"

Julio seemed anxious. I repeated the question.

"*Él dijo que eras un hombre malvado*, he said you are an evil man," he replied.

Perhaps the warnings were expressed because of the wretchedness of our equipment; after all, most other expeditions must have seemed far more glamorous. But, looking back, I assume our gear had nothing to do with their reasoning. As far as the tribe was concerned, any outsiders — by that they meant non-Machiguenga — were intruders. To them intruders had the power to trigger the wrath of the jungle. They regarded the cloud-forest as a single being, a creature, an animate object capable of thought. They believed that the jungle could be made happy, just as it could become enraged.

I took the cautions of danger lightly. They flooded in from all sides, most strongly from Hector. He ranted on all the time about wild renegade warriors lurking in the undergrowth. He said they carried special arrows designed to pass straight through a man's chest. It seemed ludicrous that he believed in such hazard; but danger, or the myth of it, was his own twisted currency. Like Tia and everyone else we met, the idea of sinister forces waiting to prey on our feebleness fed his mind and gave him strength.

My concern was that the men were listening to the tales of impending disaster, and they were believing what their ears took in. The more they heard, the more they chattered together in the darkness; and the more they chattered, the more fiercely they regarded me each morning. Sometimes they would approach me in ones and twos, hoping to discuss the risk. I knew that I had to keep them moving at all costs. There was no time to speculate on phantom predators, and no sense in it. Speculation was perhaps the most dangerous enemy of all.

Hector might have been the originator of many rumours and legends, but I was realizing his great value. He charged the men with fear, but he motivated them at the same time. I wondered if the talk of terror was in fact a tool by which he sought to control others. The porters looked up to him as a kind of superhuman. As far as they were concerned, he was a man in tune with the mortal and spiritual dimensions. Unlike the previous team of porters, the new group were not Adventists, although they were Christians.

The day after arriving at Aboroa, we left it. I was pleased to have escaped Tia's unending supply of *masato*. The first dose had given me a bad stomach, which was to plague me for weeks. The film crew were equally affected, all except Boris, the Bulgarian, who became strangely addicted to the saliva-based alcohol. He couldn't drink enough to satisfy his thirst.

We had spent the morning building a pair of balsa rafts, and swapped some *yuka* for a large raft owned by Pancho's mother. The dilapidated rubber boat was inflated, much to the Machiguenga's amusement. By the late morning we were on the move again.

Heading upstream without even the feeble *peki-peki* engines to propel us forwards was gruelling beyond belief. The water was high, the current fast, the rapids endless. With hindsight I can say that it was impossible, but I was unaware of that then so I drove the men on. The previous porters would have mutinied in the first hour, but the chainsaw gang thrived on the physical pain. We tied the long climbing ropes to the rafts and to the Zodiac, and split into teams, four men to a craft, two pushing, two pulling. The ropes were paid out a hundred yards or more. The longer the distance between the boat and the pulling team, the faster the progress.

A week of routine passed, during which we covered no more than a mile or two a day. It was an absurdly slow advance but, as I saw it, any advance was good going in such intolerable conditions.

We would begin at nine a.m., after a meal of fish stew and rice. The team would pull like mad for two hours, break for raisins, and pull again for three hours. By mid-afternoon they were too exhausted to continue. I would start scouting for a suitable place to camp. Fortunately the river was teeming with fish, which allowed us to conserve the precious supply of Pot Noodles.

Only one thing can maintain the stamina of hard-worked men: an unending supply of hot food. For this reason, I encouraged the porters to fish from the moment camp was struck until we sat for the evening meal. Others would go into the jungle and search for roots and for *chonta* palm, the heart of which is a rather bland delicacy. Sometimes Julio and his friend Alfonso would shoot a bird with their old shotgun. Whatever was caught was skinned and tossed into the pot.

After a handful of days in the fast current, we had all sustained terrible injuries to our feet. The sand in the river eroded the skin between the toes, and eventually stripped it away completely. Constant immersion prevented new skin becoming hard. The damage was severe, irrespective of the quality of one's boots.

Each evening after the meal I would sit on a rock and tend my wounds. The only way of preventing our feet rotting was to lubricate them morning and night with petroleum jelly. Feet were not the only cause of discomfort. An expedition on the move sustains all manner of minor injuries. If not treated, they quickly escalate. While making the rafts, one man's forearm was slashed with a machete and another lost a considerable amount of blood from a knife wound on his hand. Every inch of every man was pocked with insect bites and bee stings. We were all stung so frequently that no one bothered mentioning the pain. My own face was badly swollen — I was stung more than thirty times when I walked face first into a wasps' nest. I thanked God that my eyes had been spared.

The stones became more slippery with each mile we covered, adding to my fear of snapped ankles.

None of us mentioned Richard, except to voice our delight at his departure. Hector was the veteran's loudest critic. "*Él es un hombre sin alma*, he is a man with no soul," he barked one morning, "and a man with no soul is empty, like a corked bottle adrift on the ocean."

"But Vietnam damaged his mind."

"*Mi amigo*," he said solemnly, "*no hay palabras suficientes para excusarse de tanta debilidad*, my friend, no words are sufficient to excuse such weakness."

CHAPTER
TWELVE

Drowning
A half-drowned man must be put to bed in dry, heated clothes, hot stones placed against the feet, and his head must be raised moderately. Human warmth is excellent, such as that of two men made to lie close up against him, one on each side.

The Art of Travel

On the morning of the eighth day from Aboroa, Francisco, the crag-faced enemy of us all, spotted a thin plume of smoke rising up from a pile of banana leaves on the far bank of the river. Near to it was a severe rapid, and a series of natural caves carved by the river in ancient times. As we approached, it became clear that the banana leaves formed a primitive dwelling. The earth around it was scuffed up, as if a commotion had recently taken place. Other than the smoke, there was no sign of life.

Hector clapped his hands, whistled, and clapped again. Still no one came. "This place is Pusharo," he said ominously. "That must be Javier's camp."

"Pancho's brother?"

The Maestro ducked his head in a nod. A second or two after that, a squat, wispy figure climbed out from the shelter and peered over at our group. He studied us

181

cautiously, his weight balanced as if to take immediate flight if required. Hector called again. The figure stooped a fraction, then stood tall.

"It's Javier," Hector said.

"Call him over."

"He won't come. He has no curiosity."

"But we have to talk to him, to ask him about the ruins."

Hector slunk away to be alone on the rough, stony beach. He had a curious manner of hunting down a contact, getting very close to it, then drifting off, as if he were fearful of something. I went over and asked what was the matter.

"You can't ask Javier about the ruins," he said. "Do so and he may kill us."

"But he's your friend," I said.

"I know, but we are nearing the place of negative energy. I can no longer trust my friends. We are nearing Paititi now," he said.

"Are you sure?"

He blinked in confirmation and rapped his palm over the rock on which he sat. "*Míralo*, look at it," he said.

The block was about three feet by two, with straight edges, carved from a slate-grey stone.

"Hand-cut . . . by the Incas," he said.

Again, I pleaded with the old man to invite Javier for some food. At last he agreed, as long as the film crew and I conceded to more mental preparation. In turn we agreed, and Hector called to Pancho's brother.

A great deal of negotiation followed, loud shouts across the boiling rush of water. Eventually, the nimble figure was lured over to our side with a labelless plastic bottle filled with clear liquid. If hot food is the key to maintaining an expedition's stamina, then low grade gut-rot alcohol is the key to sustaining its sense of pleasure.

As soon as Javier set eyes on the bottle, he appeared more energetic. Without wasting a fraction of a second, he ran upstream, and dived into the foaming river above the rapids. For thirty seconds we all focused on the miniature head bobbing among the white curl of waves.

"He will drown," I said. But I was wrong. Javier clambered out of the water, naked but for a band of toucan feathers on his brow, and a pair of tattered underpants. He was five foot tall at the most, his lean frame glistening in the bright jungle light. We welcomed him, oozing with friendliness. He had a kind face, quite round, muscular and smooth. There was the faintest hint of hair on his chin, and a look of innocence in his eye, as if he had never seen a bad deed done. He grew anxious when the Swedes began documenting the scene, with Boris the Bulgarian filming them.

Hector handed him an enamel cup half filled with *pisco*, Peruvian grape brandy. He smiled, sniggered, and pressed the rim of the cup to the bridge of his nose. In a moment the liquid was gone. More laughter followed, and another cup of the intoxicating drink.

We made camp, clearing the rocks away from an area of beach. There were many hand-cut blocks of stone; I counted about forty. It looked as if they had been washed downriver. They were so large in size that it was

183

improbable they could have been carried far, even by the most turbulent water.

That evening, I tended the men's wounds as usual. Their feet were getting worse. I had no choice but to call a two-day halt to allow our feet to harden. At the same time, I urged Hector to interrogate Javier, but he held an index finger to his lips. "You do not eat an apple until it's ripe," he said.

So we waited, all of us drying our feet round the campfire. At dusk Javier passed out; and I reprimanded Hector for feeding him so much *pisco*. It was like offering cigarettes to children.

"You are the one who needs purifying," he said sharply, "not Javier."

Before turning in for the night, the Maestro lit three candles, and waxed them on to one of the hand-carved blocks of stone as a simple altar. He said a prayer, then reminded us of the danger. "We are near the place of negative energy now," he said, the candlelight washing his face with colour. "We need to remain strong, and stay together. You will soon be at each other's throats, fighting like dogs. But resist, resist!"

He paused to look me in the eye. I could feel the warmth of his presence, his charisma.

"Remember what I told you before," he said. "To find Paititi you must not look for it, and if you do find it, you will have to repay the earth. Do not look for the ruins, but let them look for you."

The Maestro paused once again, this time to blow out the candles. "To have a hope of success, you must clear your mind," he whispered, "wipe it clean, forget

184

your family, your life, your world ... and prepare to enter the Gateway to Paititi."

The sound of Hector's low, sleek voice affected all who listened, charging the audience with energy. You could fight it, but were powerless to prevent it seeping in. The old man was attentive in locating flaws in the psychology of the team, but it was for his own sanity that I was growing increasingly alarmed. The further we progressed up the Palatoa, the more he ranted on about witches and extraterrestrial forces. I was surprised that a Seventh Day Adventist would believe in magic at all, or would resort to his own particular blend of witchcraft to confront the supernatural. After his long harangue, he ordered us to strip to the waists and rub ash from the fire into each other's chests. I was about to reverse the command, the words were on my lips, but I halted. If the ritual gave the Maestro comfort, I thought, then let him enact it.

I slept soundly that night, until I felt someone tug at my arm. I squinted at my watch. It was a few minutes before three. Hector was standing over me. "Javier wants to show us something," he said.

The warrior had come to, and was brandishing a burning branch. It was crackling furiously, giving off a good light. Javier was smiling now, his almond eyes glowing.

"What is happening?"

"Let's follow him," Hector replied.

We walked a few paces into the foliage which ran along the margin of the beach. I smelt the fragrance of passion fruit, and was deafened by the piercing chorus of cicada wings. Javier was leading the way, with Hector in his footsteps and I in his. We climbed over a fallen tree trunk, then another, and rounded a bend. The torch flames spat in the breeze as if to warn of a conspiracy. A moment later the undergrowth ended.

Before us was a massive granite rockface. It stood like a curtain in the jungle. As we drew nearer, I saw that its surface was etched with symbols and signs — labyrinths and serpents, faces and suns. "What is this?" I asked, in a whisper.

Hector ran his hand across an icon of a face: two holes for eyes and the curve of a mouth. "*Es la llave hacia* Paititi, it is the key to Paititi," he said.

The sun rose in an arc above Pusharo and dried the porters' feet. I had forbidden them to go near the water, an order that brought much pleasure. They sat together powdering each other's toes, boasting of the levels of pain they could endure. After breakfast I returned to the wall and showed its petroglyphs to the film crew. Marco, the banker, said he had seen similar symbols in his childhood, scored into a cave wall in the Urals. "They are very, very ancient," he said sombrely.

"Older than the Incas?"

"For certain they are," he replied.

We stared at them, trying desperately to unlock the puzzle. Most of the petroglyphs were within the height of a man; but a few were considerably higher on the wall, as if one man had stood on another to reach. I dug down with a spade, to see if any more symbols were

186

hiding below the surface of the ground. The wall continued very far down. The effort of digging was rewarded with a dozen more petroglyphs: faces, the outline of men, birds and other mysterious signs. The most alluring of all of them was a serpent. It ran horizontally at the right of the wall, etched deep into the granite, a zigzag body ending in a diamond-shaped head.

Hector was sure the serpent depicted the route to Paititi. He believed we were poised on the creature's tail, struggling to reach the ruins at its head. The river was the body, he said, running jagged through canyons, gushing down from the headwaters in the Andes. The Maestro regarded Pusharo and its petroglyphs with awe, and said the place was a source of energy, of magic. I had to agree. There was a sense that ancient man had worshipped there, and the legacy of signs was certainly puzzling. But if the symbols had been carved before the Incas, how could they have a connection with Paititi? Hector said the link was obvious. He declared that Paititi was built on a pre-Inca site. It was the first sensible thing he had said for a long time, and sounded plausible. The Incas had established a society based on overrunning others, and converting conquered assets into their own.

I explored the area to the right of the main granite rockface, climbing on to a narrow ledge. There I found more petroglyphs, including one that depicted a warrior in what seemed to be a feathered robe. It reminded me of the intricate textile designs from Nazca, and helped to support the link to a pre-Incan people.

I had not wanted the porters to see the petroglyphs, for fear they would become alarmed and decide to retreat. Some of the men asked me to allow them to go hunting. I was against the slaughter of wildlife but it provided food for the pot, which meant our dried rations would last longer, so I sent them off. Javier led them into the forest. The hunting also kept the men away from the wall. Francisco was the only one with curiosity. He followed me behind the screen of foliage during the afternoon. When he saw it, he shielded his eyes with his hands. The wall was impressive, but his reaction was over the top.

"They are pre-Incan, I think," I said.

Crag-face was shaken: he fell to his knees and prayed silently, his lips flickering with words. When he had finished, I asked him for his impressions.

"Can't you hear them speaking?" he said.

"No."

Francisco led me by the hand to the rockface. He motioned to one of the smiling faces. "*Pon tu oreja en la boca,* put your ear to the mouth."

I did as he requested. I could not hear a thing, except for the beating of cicada wings in the trees.

"Listen harder!"

Still I could hear nothing.

Suddenly Crag-face was overcome with rage. He pushed me away from the wall. "*Estúpido,* you fool!" he bellowed. "Why do you endanger the lives of so many men?"

With that, he ran back to the camp, where he sat alone in the shade of a *cashapona* palm. I was unsure of the reason for his outburst, but he was becoming more disturbed all the time. In the late afternoon I noticed him at the far end of the beach, where the smooth pebbles gave way to sand. He had stripped off his clothes, and was performing what looked like exercises. The Swedes saw him too, and asked me what he was doing. I said I had no idea, but in truth I thought the river was tipping the balance of his mind.

As dusk fell, Javier led the porters back to the camp. The hunting party had been successful, bagging seven or eight scrawny birds. They were plucked, gutted, and flung into a pot of cold river water. But the last bird was not cooked immediately. The team clustered round it, marvelling. I went over to inspect. It was the size of a grouse, clad in royal-blue feathers, and had a dainty crest, similar to that of a peacock. But the most curious thing about it was the tube of miniature feathers hanging down from the throat. Javier, who had lived in the jungle all his life, had never seen such a bird before.

"*Es lindo*, it's nice," he said, grinning broadly, then stripped away the feathers and tossing the naked bird in with the others.

We spent a second night at Pusharo. The Maestro wrapped himself in a blanket cocoon and went to bed before everyone else. The porters' morale had been boosted by the rare flesh of the blue bird. They said it tasted like the meat from a hoatzin's breast.

"I have never eaten that," I said, rather gladly.

Giovanni, the cook, looked at me with wide eyes. "*Entonces nunca has vivido*, then you have never lived," he said.

I lay awake on the second night, weighed down with worry. A mist had rolled in and made it difficult to breathe. At about four a.m. Hector unfurled himself from his cocoon, fumbled for a torch, and crept out from the tarpaulin. It looked as if he was making his way to the rockface. I pulled on my boots and followed, leaving the distance between us long enough so as not to arouse his suspicion. The path was moist with dew, the air heavy and white with the mist. The Maestro had a long stride and reached the petroglyphs quickly. I stayed well back, watching through a gap in the undergrowth.

He had switched on the torch and was arching its yellow beam over the symbols as if he was looking for something. I would have approached and asked what he was up to, but thought it wiser to leave him alone. For fifteen minutes he swung the light, skimming it over the contours of rugged stone. Then he put it down, thrust out his hands before him and rubbed them over one of the petroglyphs. I could not see clearly, but realized next morning it had been the symbol of the snake. He pushed against it with all his strength, as if struggling to hold up the wall. I could hear him wheezing, then he fell to the ground, exhausted.

In the morning, Hector did not eat with the rest of us. He had a distant look in his eye, and seemed tremendously sad. I half expected him to fall away, as Rodrigo and Richard had done. I went over to him with an enamel mug of weak black coffee, with four

190

tablespoons of sugar, just how he liked it. He took it, glancing up in thanks. But our eyes did not meet.

"We must question Javier about the ruins," I said.

"He knows but he will not take us," Hector said gently.

"Can we at least talk to him?"

The old man gazed out at the raging water, and swivelled round to look me in the eye. "All right," he said. "We will talk to Javier."

An hour later, the tribesman was back in our camp, with a mug of *pisco* in his hand. I had dug out a few postcards showing the giant stone walls at Sachsayhuaman. I passed them to him. "That's what we are looking for," I said.

Hector put his arm round the warrior's shoulders and swung him to face me. But Javier tried to shy away, shifting his weight on to his back foot. "*Mira*, look," Hector said. "Look at these pictures."

Nervously, the warrior squinted at them. He said nothing.

"Have you seen this?" Hector urged.

Still Javier said nothing.

"He knows, I'm sure he knows," said the old man, "but he's frightened. You cannot imagine the depth of his fear. Outsiders are not supposed to go there."

I was irritated that Hector would work against me. He was the one man who had the tribe's respect, yet he would never press them for answers.

A moment later my irritation turned to dismay. The Maestro called together the film crew and me. "We cannot go any further," he said.

I was too struck, too angry to answer at first.

"What is the problem?" asked the banker.

"There are many problems," he replied. "The rapids are so perilous that we will drown, and if we do get ahead, the savage tribe upriver will slit our throats. But, worst of all, the spirits are waiting."

The leader of an expedition has two responsibilities. The first is to solve problems, and the second is to drag his team ahead, whether they like it or not. I brooded in silence, waiting for Hector to finish. Condemning him as a coward would have served no purpose, for he was our link with the tribe. But then, as I saw it, the tribe were next to no good at all. For all his grand talk about Paititi, Hector was proving himself a dreamer — a strong man, but a dreamer none the less.

The sun was not yet hovering above the trees. It was still early.

"We will leave in an hour," I said. "There is no point wasting time with Javier, at least until we have forded the rapids. We will move on with the gear, then send a team back to talk him into coming."

The film crew went to gather their equipment together. Hector and I were left alone.

"*No tienes temor, mi amigo*, you have no fear, my friend," he said, with a wry smile.

"My ignorance protects me."

Search for a lost city and you need heroes. They provide solace in the days of miserable rain, illness and fatigue, and are a beacon of hope at times when the only certainty is failure. On hard journeys, as I huddle

192

in the tent waiting for sleep and the wretched night to pass, I find myself standing before my pantheon of heroes. They sit in judgement, peering down at me in the dock. They are all in shadow, except one whose face I see quite clearly. Each night the face is different. Sometimes it speaks, urging advice, or simply leers down, as if to remind me of its triumph over adversity.

The face that I was to see most often was that of Hiram Bingham, the American explorer celebrated for discovering Machu Picchu in 1911. For any man on the quest of Paititi, Bingham is the example of excellence. At thirty-six, he was the same age as I was then when he found Machu Picchu. The portrait I would see of him in my mind was the one so often presented in history books: Bingham the glorious, posing before his canvas tent, dressed in safari jacket, puttee leggings, stout walking shoes and grey trilby. Glorious he might have been, but his expression was almost sullen, as if he was not quite content with his achievement.

Bingham was a scholar and an expert on Incan history. He was associated with Yale University, which funded his expedition, and was a man who pursued his goals with single-minded determination. He scanned the historical treatises for clues and quizzed the local people, but his success was largely a result of good calculation and time spent on the ground. On 24 July 1911, he reached Machu Picchu, and first set eyes on the ruins of which he had dreamed for so long. He saw houses, built "of the finest Inca stone work", overgrown with creepers and vines; there were walls of white granite blocks, funerary caves, flights of stone steps, sacrificial places and, of course, the *intihuatana*, the stone post to which the Incas tied the sun.

Locating Machu Picchu set Bingham up for a life of celebrity, and made him a household name. He mixed with the rich and famous, lectured all over the world, and was even elected to the US Senate.

If Hiram Bingham was to teach me anything it was to keep going, however rotten the conditions, and to drive on the team mercilessly; but, most important of all, Bingham's example taught me never to give up on any account.

We pushed ahead for six more days, enduring miles of rapids. At the time I could not imagine a terrain more terrible. The water cascaded down from the mountains, churning with unimaginable ferocity. It was white, always white, alive, like some horrible creature desperate for revenge. The porters pulled the boats ahead an inch at a time, like an army pitting all in the hope of gaining a few feet of no man's land.

They proved their strength. They heaved at the ropes, until their hands bled and the muscles in their arms were raw. The film crew were forced often to stop filming and help. Every hand was needed to haul at the ropes, to clear away rocks and create an easier passage. Inch by inch, we progressed, but as soon as one rapid ended, another began. I asked for Hector's advice.

"*Estos no son los verdaderos rápidos*, these are not the *real* rapids," he said.

On the third evening a new problem visited the camp: the great fever. We had learned to put up with the guinea worms, which bored out of our thighs. They were alarming, but small. We also endured the other great scourge of the Madre de Dios jungle, the chigger fly, which burrows into the skin and inserts its eggs into a cavity beneath the subcutaneous fat. The chigger fly, known locally as *uta*, has beset jungle explorers for centuries. It plagued our legs, as it must have done those of the *conquistadores* five hundred years before. Once the larvae have hatched, the wounds turn to sores and then go septic. The pain was severe and, as we spent each day in the water, the infected skin could not heal. In the sixties an American socialite traveller in the Amazon, called Nicole Maxwell, discovered that the best way to kill the unhatched larvae was to dab the spot with red nail varnish. Unfortunately we had taken no beauty products with us.

The chiggers grew worse every day, and affected us all. But the new torment to hit us was the fever, which caused the victim to sweat so uncontrollably that the shape of his face changed. I realized, some time later, that it was dengue fever.

The Swedes were the first to go down with it. They lay beneath the tarpaulin, shaking like madmen in a cell. River travel ensured that most of our clothes were always wet, but for them this no longer mattered. Sweat poured from their bodies in astonishing quantities. The rest of us stood and marvelled as they wrung out their shirts.

Hector did not say so, but I knew he wanted to turn back. The Swedes' condition grew worse, as did the pressure on me to call the retreat. The film crew were my friends, but they were there only to document the journey. Stubbornly I ordered the team to continue upriver.

On the afternoon of the fifth day, I felt the air temperature cool a fraction. We were resting, having secured the cargo on the rafts, and rubbing our feet with Vaseline. The chill was followed by a distinctive silence, a calm, an indication of change. I glanced up at the sky, and noticed a faint wisp of cloud in the west. I asked Julio for his opinion.

"It will rain in an hour or so," he said.

"Then we will push on for a little longer."

The chief porter narrowed his eyes.

"*Muy bien*, very well," he said.

In the jungle things can change very fast. We continued hauling the rubber boat and the rafts for thirty minutes. Then, suddenly, darkness fell, and at the same time a storm of demonic proportions descended.

It began with a sprinkling of rain: heavy droplets at first, a messenger of the tempest. We were in the water negotiating an arching staircase of boulders, the river ripping round us like a hurricane. There was no beach on either side, just towering walls of *paka*, thorny bamboo.

With no riverbank, and nowhere to anchor the boats, we had little choice but to continue. Let the craft go, and our precious equipment and supplies would have been dashed on the rocks. We struggled ahead. Then the full force of the storm broke. The rain hurled down in sheets with such force that it bruised our arms. It threatened to drown us right there and then. The water level rose instantly. Within five minutes the river had doubled in its cruelty. After that the wind whipped up, tossing us about like skittles. I called to the porters, but no one could hear me. Each man was fighting to save his raft or boat.

The film crew clutched their black Pelican cases, and wrestled through the waves. We took it in turns to throw ourselves upon the mercy of the riverbank, only to have our hands and faces gashed by the thorns. As if the scene was not bad enough, the darkness was suddenly illuminated by arc lightning, which tore across the sky, claps of thunder fast on its tail. The heavens were lit up for minutes at a time.

My head was forced under the waves, smashing against one boulder and the next, as I was swept away. It was like being flushed down a sewage pipe. My shirt and shorts were ripped off by the current, leaving me naked except for my boots. Instinct told me to count: one, two, three, four . . . I'm not certain why, perhaps it was a countdown to my own death. But the counting suddenly stopped. I had become wedged on my back in a crevice between two boulders. I struggled to thrust my mouth above the surface, and suck in air, glorious air.

I expected to be washed away at any minute. It would have meant certain death. The fury of the water was like when the sluice gates of a dam are flung open wide. All efforts to pull myself round, to sit upright, failed. So I lay there, waiting for the torrential rain to cease, and for the men to spot me.

An hour or so later Francisco arrived. He had been running up and down through the rapids, searching for my remains. I did not see his face at first, just the shadow of a man moving in slow motion through the white water. He struggled over and whistled to the others, sounding the alarm. I was so firmly lodged in the cleft that it took the strength of Francisco and Hector to release me. Crag-face was laughing, the first time I had seen him do so. But there was no smile on Hector's lips: he was stirred with anger. "You will get us all killed," he shouted, against the noise of the water.

The porters were equally enraged. I couldn't understand it. They had tied one of the tarps in a copse of saplings, and were sheltering beneath it like sodden chickens on a roost. I thanked them for their endurance, but the line of their faces scowled back. Julio said he wanted more money, and Oscar snapped that he would slit my throat if he did not get some hot food. Another exclaimed he had been robbed, and accused his best friend of the theft. Then Hector strode up and castigated the men for allowing the supplies to get drenched.

There was only one explanation for the hostility: we must have reached the place of negative energy.

CHAPTER
THIRTEEN

Fever The number of travellers that have fallen victims to fever in certain lands is terrible; it is a matter of serious consideration whether any motives, short of imperious duty, justify a person in braving a fever-ridden country.

The Art of Travel

The storm died as quickly as it had been born. Shortly before midnight, the lightning ceased, as if an enormous electric switch had been turned off. The rain stopped, too, but the river rose all night, ascending to the high ground on which we were camped. I had ordered that some of the valuable kerosene be used to start a fire, and that each man could eat two Pot Noodles. In usual circumstances, they would have responded with cheers, but on that bleak night, they cursed me, and swore that the expedition was a waste of time. They picked fights with each other, like children brawling over toys. No one was unaffected, except Francisco. He scurried from man to man, muttering words of encouragement.

"He is a stupid fool," said Hector, "they're all stupid fools!"

I accosted the old man. "Don't you see what's happening?" I shouted. "We are at the place of negative

199

energy. Friends have turned into enemies, and enemies into friends."

Hector slapped his hands together, grimaced, and stormed off into the rain. The film crew were busy drying out the Arriflex and their other camera equipment. They were all bitter beyond belief. I stood apart from them, for fear of an exchange of anger I might regret. Boris scolded Marco for his clumsiness, and the Russian rebuked the Swedes for nothing at all. They were both very frail, still sweating despite the cold.

By morning, water was lapping around us. We were lucky no one had drowned in the night. I woke at about six to find everything I owned soaked through. The camp was like a scene from a shipwreck. The men were all asleep, except Hector. He was standing in the water, gazing upstream. I called to him, then plodded over. After a long while he turned. "You are right," he said.

"About what?"

"The place of negative energy." He motioned to an old military compass sitting in his palm. "*Mira eso*, look at that," he said.

The needle of the instrument was flitting back and forth. There must have been a scientific reason for it, but at the time it filled me with a terrible haunted sensation, as if we were being watched from the trees. The Maestro had no doubt. As far as he was concerned, the field of energy was part of a divine curse. It had caused the storm and had whipped up hostility between the men. Wait another hour at that place, he said, and no man would escape alive.

We packed up our soaking gear and moved out.

By noon the sky had cleared, and a fresh cool breeze blew in from the west. I didn't subscribe to Hector's belief in witchcraft, but it certainly seemed as if we had crossed a barrier of some kind. The smell of the river had changed, too: it was no longer sour and hard on the nose, it was perfumed with a scent of ripe fruit.

By the afternoon, the place of negative energy, if it had existed at all, was behind us. The current was stronger than ever before, but now the high water helped to ease the boats ahead. We advanced fast, covering four miles or more, the progress boosting the porters' spirits. Their resentment had dissolved, as had Hector's.

That evening, seeing that Francisco was sitting alone, I went over to thank him for saving my life. "Is the earth a better place that you walk upon it?" he asked, and turned away angrily.

When the team had eaten, their feet had been greased and their sores smeared with iodine, I told them we were closing in on Paititi.

"We need a volunteer to go back for Javier," I said. "Without the Machiguenga, we have no hope of finding the ruins."

The porters stared down at their boots, their lips tight shut. I said I would double the pay of the one who escorted Javier upriver to our camp. No one volunteered. I rooted through the small black pouch I carried at my waist. It contained a Leatherman knife, a bottle of alcohol wash, a miniature torch, Vaseline, and a few feet of damp loo paper wrapped twice in plastic. None of the items was of sufficient value to entice the porters to volunteer for the mission. Then I noticed a small white plastic box at the bottom of the pouch. I took it out. The men's eyes followed the object, as I weighed it in my hand. To them, the thin cord contained inside the box was the most useful substance ever devised. They were always asking for a few inches, to sew up their boots, to go fishing, or for hanging the snake-bite antidote *piri-piri* round their necks. It was waxed dental tape.

I offered the entire box to the man who would fetch Javier. All the porters jumped forward, puffing out their chests like sprinters at the finish line.

That night the long, bearded face of the explorer F.A. Mitchell-Hedges appeared in my mind before I slept. All but forgotten now, Mitchell-Hedges discovered the ruined Mayan city of Lubaantun in Belize back in 1924. As well as an explorer, he was a big-game hunter and adventurer, a yachtsman and an amateur archaeologist. The story of his life reads like a *Boy's Own* annual. He claimed to have ridden with Mexico's Pancho Villa, to have sheltered Leon Trotsky for the night, and to have found ruins on a massive scale.

If anyone has ever proved that you need no credentials to be an explorer, it was Mitchell-Hedges. For years he traipsed around the Caribbean and the Pacific with his adopted daughter Sammy in tow. Like many others of the time, he was a master of self-promotion. His *Who's Who* entry of 1928 includes: "Life devoted to exploration and deep-sea research work . . . holds numerous world records for capture of giant fish, penetrated unknown portion of the hinterland of Panama, 1922–3, discovering a new race of people."

Mitchell-Hedges is best remembered not for the great lost city he found, but for owning the finest rock crystal skull in existence, known as the Skull of Doom. He always claimed that his daughter had found it glinting among the ruins of Lubaantun on her seventeenth birthday. The skull, which has a hinged lower jaw and rectangular ocular cavities, has been a centre of attention for the lunatic crystal-believing fringe for decades.

Cast an eye over Mitchell-Hedges' curriculum vitae, and you see light shining through the holes — he massaged the facts or made them up. But to me that was not the point: he was a man whose life was never confined by nine-to-five, never restricted by the opinions of others.

All next day we pushed on, as we did the day after, and the day after that. The team was working together like never before, energized, raring to cover ground. They had become expert at rearranging the stones in the rapids to allow the craft an easier passage. Oscar had gone back for Javier, holding the dental floss high like an Olympic torch. I would have sent two men back, but we needed everyone else on the boats.

Hector counselled me often on the price of doubt. Fail to believe in Paititi strongly enough, he would say, and we had no chance of success. Believe in it, like a sinner touched by God, and, he told me, I would be rewarded. I did believe: I believed that Paititi was there, hidden in the cloud-forest, and I believed that, with Javier's help, we could find it. Every river bend we passed made me more certain that we would triumph, and that locating the ruins without him was impossible.

The routine on the river was matched by the routine on land. We worked together to build a camp each afternoon and to strike it the following morning. We all had duties, including the film crew, who had the added burden of having to clean their equipment each night. They would take immense care to ensure that the damp didn't penetrate the Arriflex and the lenses. Their most valuable tool was the hairdryer. It was powered by the generator, surely the greatest burden of all.

On the fourth day after the great storm, we rose early and prepared to move out. The camp was criss-crossed with the oversized tracks of a *sachavaca*, giant tapir. The footprints were deep in the sand, hinting of the creature's considerable weight. Hector had been up in the night, and appeared depressed and anxious. He was sitting on a stone beside the smouldering fire, his palms pressed over his white beard. I asked what was the matter.

"The energy is becoming stronger," he said.

I was going to beg him to be optimistic, but Marco nudged me. "Hector is a dreamer," he said. "Let him dream."

So I did, and we pushed out into the chill water. One bend followed another, and the jungle came alive with hyacinth macaws, which cluster on the riverbanks to feast on the clay. The Palatoa had long been following a ridge, which ran to the north like an impassable bulwark. It was shrouded in trees. Perspective made them seem like seedlings, but in reality they were a hundred feet high.

A great swarm of sweat bees appeared at about noon. They covered our faces, suffocating us as we struggled ahead. Suddenly the river was swept into a vast chasm. It came with no warning at all. We stood there, up to our chests in water, gaping at the canyon walls. Our gaze descended in unison from the top of the canyon, down across the sheering grey granite walls, to their base. We had been hardened by weeks of river travel, but the sight that greeted us was awful beyond belief. A series of immense rocks had created a *pongo*, rapids, on a grand scale. I could not compare them to anything we had seen. The boulders were shale-black, worn smooth by millennia of turmoil.

"God help us," murmured Julio.

"There is no hope," said another.

"This is the Gateway to Paititi," Hector whispered.

We stood for many minutes, staring as the sea of water raged through the chasm, charging at the walls. If it was the Gateway, then the Gateway was shut. The porters managed to moor the rafts and the old rubber boat. Their morale had been crushed. The Maestro was similarly despondent. I begged him to continue, at least until our lives were in danger. But he warned me: I was becoming overpowered by greed, he said.

I struggled to find a route along the periphery of the gorge. The scant foliage and slimy rocks hindered my efforts. From the corner of my eye, I saw Hector piling up stones, one on another. Perhaps he had a plan. I called: "What are you doing?"

The old man shook his head glumly. "I am building a memorial to the place of your death," he said.

There was no choice but to retreat. Hector said it would be months before the water level was low enough for us to pass through the Gateway. We could wait until later in the year, he said, and next time, he promised, we would return with Pancho as our guide.

In early March I left the cloud-forest and flew back to Europe. It was like exchanging one life for another. Time has never passed so slowly as it did during those five tortuous months in London.

The journey back to Hector's village had ground us down, rubbing in the sense of failure. The only advantage was that we were no longer warring against the current, even though the rapids were still precarious. The old man had no idea what returning to Europe involved. He had suggested it as if it was nothing more than a stroll from one village to the next. The journey from the Gateway of Paititi to my London apartment took more than three weeks. It entailed wading through rivers, and travelling by dugout canoe, tractor and truck, by bus, taxi and aeroplane.

The film crew came with me. On the way home I went down with dengue fever, the "broken bone" disease. My wife found me collapsed on the doorstep, sweating buckets, ranting about ruins, warrior tribes and curses. I had lost a third of my body weight, was covered from head to toe in septic insect bites and sores. "Thank God you are home," she said. I looked at her hard, my eyes burning into hers. I didn't have the heart to tell her I was going back.

I stayed in bed for a week, sweating, raving, calling commands to the porters in the night. My home was a palace of comfort, yet I was an outsider there. I had dreamed of its luxuries while deep in the jungle, now they frightened me. My life had been stripped down to the bare mettle, trained to survive, to progress upriver.

On the ninth day, I met the film crew in a dismal café. We hugged each other, and felt a bond, the bond of shared anguish. I remember that meeting so well. We sat there with cups of tepid coffee on our laps, staring at one another, not needing to speak. It was enough that we were together again. Marco had contracted the fever as well. He mopped his brow with a monogrammed handkerchief, and looked close to death.

In the second week, I received a call out of the blue. The voice was gritty and cold, like the sound of footsteps on broken glass. It said that I would fail, that I had no hope. "Fail at what?" I asked. The man didn't reply, then he hung up. I tried to trace the call, but without success. The week after, I had lunch with an old school-friend who was working in the oil business.

When I mentioned the name of the oil firm prospecting in Madre de Dios, he told me they were rotten to the core. "Beware of them," he said.

The next day I was invited to talk about exploration on the radio. I got in a fast jab against the oil company, without naming it exactly. To my surprise, the gritty voice called again late that night. My wife picked up the telephone and passed it to me.

"Do not go back to Peru," said the voice.

"Who are you?"

Again, the caller hung up.

Another week slipped by. I stocked up with more provisions, and ordered a pair of new Zodiacs. Although I had promised it to the tribe, I had not yet given them the antique rubber inflatable, so on the return trip we would have three boats. The balsa rafts had proved themselves extremely durable, and they were free, but I wanted to be ready for any conditions that lay beyond the Gateway. The added expenses, and the cost of the second trip to Peru, put me in debt. But I was lured back by the thought of Pancho, and by Hector's promise: that the tribesman would guide me when I returned.

For five months I lived in limbo, unable to think of anything but going back to the Madre de Dios jungle and progressing beyond the great *pongo*. Every day I waited, other expeditions were preparing themselves, gearing up and moving out. I stopped buying newspapers or watching television for fear of hearing that a rival expedition had located the ruins of Paititi. Friends would invite me to their houses, expecting a dependable entertainer at the dinner table. But my animation, my zeal for the exotic, was dead. I would sit in a corner, numbed by my distance from the jungle. Everyone wanted soundbites of expedition life, but I shunned their requests. How could they begin to understand the depth of our experience?

Each night the jungle tormented me in dream: the sound of macaws flying overhead in pairs, the clatter of rain on the river, the smell of termites rubbed into one's skin. But it was the river itself that beckoned most strongly. It was calling me, urging like a siren, goading me to return, to continue the search.

In early August I kissed my wife and our little daughter goodbye, and boarded a flight back to Lima. As before the film crew were in tow. Our dynamic was still the same: they leeching off Marco, the banker, and I freeloading off them.

I had sent the two new Zodiacs and many more Pot Noodles by air cargo, having done a deal with an airline. Marco's platinum credit card had paid for everything late one evening when he was in high spirits. It had been a valuable session, which earned us all new jungle boots and wristwatches with electronic compasses built in.

I spent three days begging Lima's cargo office to give me the boats. They had evolved a system of red tape that surpassed even Indian bureaucracy in its ruthlessness. Forms had to be filled out in quadruplicate, stamped in pink, then blue, then black, signed once and signed again. I queued for the stamps, then to pay, and again to collect my change. Finally, after three days of wasted time, the boats were expelled from the great bureaucratic machine.

That night Leon unwrapped one, and discovered it had been slashed open on the left side. We checked the second. It, too, had been damaged, then rewrapped. I suspected the evil hand of Paititi saboteurs.

The manager of our hotel, lost in the war-lands of downtown Lima, was a short Japanese Peruvian, named Señor Kanagawa. He had made a career of telling people what he thought they should know. He already knew about our expedition. I dragged one of the Zodiacs down to Reception and asked for his advice. The manager pulled off his bifocals to get a better look at the damage. "You are not the only people searching for *el gran* Paititi," he said. "To you the search is an entertainment, but to others it's big business." Señor Kanagawa ran the tip of his index finger down the gash in the boat. "If I were you," he said softly, "I would be careful to avoid treading on tall men's toes."

The night before, I had read a far-fetched newspaper piece that claimed Sendero Luminoso, the infamous Shining Path, might be searching for Paititi. The article said that the Marxist organization would use the lost city's gold to relaunch itself. I asked the manager for his opinion.

"It's not their style," he replied, "and in any case their leader, Abimael Guzman, is locked up in jail. But there are equally powerful people in this country, and abroad, who want to get to Paititi before you."

"Then whom should we fear most?"

210

Señor Kanagawa thought for a moment, and pressed his hands down on his desk. "You should fear each other," he said.

A week later we arrived by bus at Cusco, dusty and cold. Our spirits were high, even though winter had descended on the Andean town. On every street corner young boys were touting alpaca sweaters, embroidered with vistas of the mountains. The alleyways behind Plaza de Armas were teeming as always with backpackers, walking softly with a glint in their eye.

We spent two days in the town, stocking up on fresh provisions and morsels of cheap equipment that we really didn't need. Marco managed to get the Zodiacs repaired by an army of mechanics. Their workshop was oily and overlooked, the kind of place normal people crossed the street to avoid. The workers took a liking to the banker, and invited him to drink beer with them while the adhesive dried. When they heard he was going to Madre de Dios, they were all overcome with fear. "¡El Tigre!" one had shouted. "He will gobble you up."

"He will bite off your face," said another.

"¡No!" exclaimed a third. "He'll suck out your blood and *then* he will bite off your face!"

On the morning of our departure, I went to buy some vials of morphine at a clinic off Avenida del Sol. A doctor in a filthy white medical coat asked me why I needed so much of the drug. I explained our mission, saying that this was our second trip to find Paititi.

"When you came before," he said, "did you have a sickly-looking American man with you?"

I replied that we did. "He was a Vietnam veteran," I said, tapping my brow, "all messed up in the head. Do you know him?"

"I treated him."

"For fever?"

"No, no," said the physician, "for chronic venereal disease."

The bus to the edge of the jungle was seven hours late. When it finally rolled up, its driver jumped down and threw up in the gutter. He was a broad man, with a neck as wide as an elephant's foot, and dark, bloodied knuckles. He stank of alcohol. We stowed the cartons of Pot Noodles and the rubber boats in the hold, and climbed up. The driver hardly waited for the passengers to take their places. He jumped into his seat, spewed beer and half-digested chicken over the dashboard, then shouted, ¡"Déjanos comenzar nuestro largo viaje al infierno! Let us begin our long journey to Hell!"

The driver's inebriated condition and the poor state of the road made for slow, painful progress. The vehicle rumbled out over the *altiplano*, and began the descent down into the forest. I can hardly describe the joy that welled inside me. Returning after five months had strengthened us, filling each man with the highest expectations. The ruins continued to elude our competitors, a point that energized me beyond all else. As the mist filtered through the web of trees, I

212

counselled myself to be strong, to stop at nothing until we had found Paititi.

In the middle of the night we arrived at Pillcopata. The sky was lined with stormclouds, darker than on any night I can remember, the air silent and chilled. As soon as the bus pulled up, a pack of the town's most savage dogs surrounded it, circling like sharks round a bleeding whale. We spent the remainder of the night at the only hotel. The owner, Walter, remembered me from before. At breakfast he sat on the slim veranda, smoking an Inca brand cigarette, pondering the future.

I asked him for the latest news on the Paititi-hunters. He wiped a rag over his bronzed face. "There are French and Americans, Chileans and Peruvians all looking for it now," he said buoyantly. "Someone will find the ruins any day. This time next year Pillcopata will be a boom town."

We made a grotesque heap of our bags, boxes and packs in the middle of the town, and waited, and waited. There was no transport heading towards Hector's village. There was no transport heading anywhere on account of the torrential rain. Walter screwed up his face when he saw us trying to hitchhike in the rain with so much gear.

"All the other expeditions have their own transport," he said. "Some have helicopters as well."

Two days later we were still poised in the middle of town, ready for immediate evacuation, but no vehicles had come or gone in that time. The ferocious dogs no longer baited us: they reserved their energy for fresh

213

targets who were filled with the great fear they so enjoyed.

In the afternoon of the fourth day, a high-sided truck stopped near the hotel. The driver said he was going to the end of the road at Shintuya. He could take us. I didn't want to alert the official at Santa Cruz, Señor Franco, that we were back in the area so we decided to alight at the hamlet of José Olaya and take a dugout canoe from there.

By evening, we had crossed the Madre de Dios. In the five months we had been away, it had transformed from a massive waterway with entire trees coursing down it to a modest river with a near glassy surface. Paddling across in dugouts was easy, even when they were laden with the gear.

An hour later, at about eight p.m., the film crew and I staggered up the steep mud bank into Panataua, and made our way to Hector's shack. We could hear singing from a distance, muffled by kapok trees. It was Paolo's voice, perfect and innocent. We stood at the empty window waiting for the family to see us. Nothing had changed. The Maestro was poring over his Bible, and Doris was sitting over a tray of beans, picking out the rotten ones. The dining area was illuminated by three or four candle stubs, long wicks feeding the flames. It was like looking back in time at a place far away.

I said Hector's name. He looked up, startled. Then he smiled. "*El* Señor Paititi *ha regresado*, Señor Paititi is back," he said.

214

We lined up to hug the old man. There was a remote look in his eyes, as if he had seen something he had not wanted to see, like death.

No one in the village could understand the great distances we had travelled since leaving for Europe. Except when venturing to their farmsteads, none of the villagers, Hector included, ever left the area. For them, travel was one of the many pointless activities with which we fill our lives.

On the night of our arrival I didn't mention the second expedition. I was itching to quiz Hector about Pancho but I knew it was more sensible to wait.

In the morning we had a meeting. I spread out the map on the coarse wooden dining-table, and boasted of our new equipment. I exclaimed that we had two rubber boats, and hundreds more Pot Noodles. Hector did not utter a word, until he was sure I could think of nothing more to say. Then, lowering his head, as if a great weight had been placed on his shoulders, he said: "*Muchos problemas*, many problems."

I pretended not to have heard the remark, but Hector pressed his hand on my arm. "*Escúchame*, listen to me. We will never find Paititi now," he declared.

"Why? What's wrong?"

Hector stared down at the floor. "Pancho is dead," he said.

CHAPTER
FOURTEEN

Good Temper
Tedious journeys are apt to make companions irritable one to another; but under hard circumstances, a traveller does his duty best who doubles his kindliness of manner to those about him, and takes harsh words gently, and without retort.

The Art of Travel

The reunion with Hector was followed by a tide of gloom. There seemed hardly any reason to ask how Pancho had died as it would not bring him back. When I did ask, the Maestro said that Pancho had gone upriver three months earlier and had not returned.

"In his village people are saying El Tigre slayed him," he said, "for offering to be our guide. His wife has run off with another man, and his house has been burned down to the ground. His brother is so ashamed and frightened he'll be next that he is hiding in the forest."

Hector clicked his tongue in remorse. "*El destino es algo terrible*, fate is a terrible thing," he said.

"But if no one has seen a body," I said, "then there's no proof that Pancho is dead."

"Believe me," said the old man coldly, "Pancho is not coming back."

216

We turned to other matters and Hector listed more difficulties. He said my maps were wrong, that there were no men to be porters, and that Señor Franco had put a bounty on our heads.

The film crew and I huddled in the bright afternoon light and tried to formulate a plan. We had travelled half-way round the world and none of us was ready to give in. But Hector seemed to have lost all hope. Perhaps it was because he had lost interest, or that he did not have the energy needed for another hard expedition. I asked him if he would come with us even if we did not have Pancho. "You can count on me, my friend," he said desolately, "but what of the porters? We need the same men as before."

We sent messages to the various logging sites, asking for the men to regroup in Panataua. I knew that if I could get the expedition moving upriver, everything would fall into place. Without Pancho, it was true we had little chance, but I hoped we could find another Machiguenga warrior, as someone else must know where the ruins lay.

A few days passed while we waited to hear from the men. As soon as Hector was busying himself with preparations, his morale picked up. He harangued us, declaring that we had been violated by the depravities of the West, that we could go nowhere without purifying our souls once again. For five days we sang hymns, prayed to Jesus and drank creamy tinned milk, which Doris assured us would chase the devil out from our hearts.

A week after arriving at Hector's home, Julio turned up. He said the old team of porters were ready and willing to leave. They would come at dawn the next morning. We might have not had Pancho as a guide, but I was thrilled that the chainsaw gang was on board.

That night Hector locked his precious Bible into a tin chest, which he kept stowed under his bed, along with a photograph album, his father's dentures and a rat-trap baited with a piece of dried fruit. I asked him what he was doing.

"*Llamaré a los espíritus*, I will call the spirits," he said.

"But why lock up your Bible?"

"There are some things Jesus should not see," he replied.

The Maestro lit as many candle stubs as he could find, placing them at equal spaces in diagonal lines across the dining-table. There must have been twenty of them, none more than an inch in height. The flames cast shadows across the bamboo walls like a warlock's den. Outside, the long grass and shrubs rustled with cicadas.

Doris locked Paolo and her daughter into the family's bedroom. She was fuming that her husband would invite dark forces into their home. "He is a damn fool, that man!" she shouted, then joined her children.

The Swedes, Boris, Marco and I sat at the table, waiting for Hector. The moment he had locked away the Bible his character changed. Gone were his constant references to Jesus, replaced by more sinister subject matter, talk of phantoms, curses and witchcraft.

218

His eyes had become frozen with a kind of wickedness, his expression switching from one of benevolence to one brooding with mistrust. We sat waiting while he prepared himself in the kitchen.

After a long delay, the Maestro swept into the room. He was wearing his best cotton shirt, and had wetted his hair, as if he had been getting ready for church. I asked some unnecessary question, but he waved it aside and took his usual seat at the head of the table.

"*¡O espíritus sagrados!* O sacred spirit!" he called, gazing at the shadows playing across the cobwebbed rafters. "Visit us, you are most welcome, visit us here."

There was no reply, of course, except for the sound of bats in the trees and a lone bamboo rat far away. Again, Hector called: "O sacred spirit, talk to us!"

I felt the old man had been trapped for far too long in the inflexible regime of Adventism. It was clear that he would rather have been a high priest of the witches. I made a mental note to discuss the matter with him later, but he had more to say: "Spirits, tell us where Paititi lies, where the ruins of the great city are hidden. Tell us and we *will* protect the secret!"

The candles began to burn down, smoke, and then extinguish themselves one by one. Hector called to the spirits one last time, but still there was no reply. He undid the top button of his shirt, signifying an end to the rite, and laughed at his own foolishness. "Why should the spirits reveal anything to a stupid old man like me?" he said.

We moved the dining-table aside, unfurled our sleeping-bags and the film crew and I lay down on the floor in our usual positions. As I lay there, trying to make sense of the old man's ceremony, I understood his motives. Hector had long begged Jesus to take him to Paititi. He was a dreamer, but a believer. He knew very well that locating the lost city would transform his fortunes, and would save his face. In the years Hector had lived at Panataua, Jesus had not been forthcoming with the co-ordinates of Paititi. His desire was now so great that he was willing to conspire with the forces of darkness to get results.

The porters arrived at dawn, just as Julio had said they would. It was good to see their faces, all smiling and cheery like children home from school. Their memories of the previous journey had transformed into a picture of perfection, glazed over and false. They regarded the film crew and me as wise men, saviours from the routine of their everyday lives. I warned them that hardship and danger awaited us beyond the Gateway to Paititi. They could stay in the village and dream, I said boldly, or join the expedition and learn the truth. A roar of delight surged through their ranks, and they lined up to shake my hand and pat me on the back. For a brief moment, I felt like a hero. Only Francisco remained reserved. He stood behind the others, staring at me like a man with cruel intentions. I greeted him, saying how good it was to look at him again. He screwed up his face and let out a high-pitched sigh. Julio begged me to leave Crag-face behind but, as I reminded him, the village busybody had saved me from drowning in the place of negative energy.

As always, there were problems to be addressed. The first was getting to the mouth of the Rio Palatoa. The Madre de Dios river was so much lower than before that it was no longer passable in *peki-pekis*. We would be forced to use rafts, the Zodiacs, and to carry much of the equipment.

The greater problem was the official, Señor Franco. For five months he had been awaiting my return. His superiors in Cusco had recently commended him for catching a team of Spanish Paititi-hunters. Rumour said they had been deported, and Franco had been presented with a pension direct from the oil company. Hector said that Franco's elevated status had boosted his confidence, and heightened his desire to catch others sneaking into the restricted zone. Someone had apparently informed him that we had returned.

Since our arrival in Peru a few days previously, the newspapers had been filled with stories about the government's wish to exploit national oil reserves. The multinational petroleum firm with interests in the jungle was being heralded as the potential saviour of the country. The authorities would surely now be policing the restricted area more fervently than ever.

My fear, of course, was that Franco would come after us. His recent success would have enlarged the resources at his disposal, perhaps including military assistance. There was no point in continuing upriver if Señor Franco and his cronies were going to follow. I spread the map on the cracked mud outside Hector's shack, and had a good look. The Madre de Dios river ran north-south, with a dog's leg bend between

221

Shintuya and another community, a gold-mining area named Bonanza. The Palatoa ran to the west, uniting with another branch of the Madre de Dios near Aboroa. The only road was the one running from Pillcopata down to Shintuya.

As the film crew divided up their gear, I stared at the network of rivers and contours against a backdrop of green. Even though there were blank areas all over the map further up the Palatoa, there was good detail on the main branch of the Madre de Dios. I stared and stared, hoping a plan would emerge. Gradually an outline took shape.

For Señor Franco to be assured we were not heading into the restricted area, he would have to see us travelling in another direction. My plan was to send the porters with Hector and the gear upstream, towards the mouth of the Palatoa. They would wait for us in the shaded rushes where the Rio Negro flowed out into the Madre de Dios. Meanwhile, the film crew and I would travel downstream in a rented boat. We would make efforts to be seen by the officials, and would then backtrack, and rendezvous with the others.

I explained the ruse to the film crew, Hector and the men. None seemed convinced, except Francisco. He thought it was an excellent idea, a bad omen by any standards.

The previous journey upriver had taught me the value of continuity of orders. To gain this sense of continuity, you need one man giving the instructions, just as in the military you must have a clear chain of command. The man in charge may make blunders or

222

miscalculate from time to time, but at least he is consistent. The more time I spent in charge of the expedition, the better I understood the workings of a military machine. We were faced with a similar range of problems: transporting large amounts of equipment, feeding the men, keeping morale high and staving off illness. The only way to function with any degree of efficiency was for me to dish out the orders and to assume full responsibility for the misery they caused.

I instructed the porters to haul the gear through the undergrowth as far as the second bend. There, they were to inflate the three rubber boats, and to construct a pair of rafts if they could find enough balsa trees. After that, they were to look out for Franco's spies and, if the coast was clear, they could continue up to the rendezvous point.

Hector set out with the men, leaving Julio to guide us downriver. The water beyond Panataua was sufficiently high for *peki-pekis* so we hired two. I had brought fifteen woven nylon laundry sacks from England to give away as gifts. We filled them with inflated garbage bags, and stowed them on the boats. They looked suitably burdensome. Then, we pushed away.

The grind of the primitive engines announced action on the river. As the boats rounded the bend near Santa Cruz, I saw a tall, straight-backed figure on the shore. He was squinting at us through field glasses, jolting them left and right. Then he let them swing down on their strap and shouted:"¡Hola! ¡Hola!" I ordered the *motoristas* to steer us into the shore. They arced to the right, but drew short of the bank, idling in the shallows.

I called out enthusiastic greetings to Señor Franco. He was dripping with sweat, almost overcome by the sight of us.

"Where are you going?" he asked, obviously surprised at our direction.

"To Bonanza," I said, "to look at the gold mines."

The official glanced an eye over the laundry bags. I thought it unlikely he would request to see inside them. Instead he asked how long we were expecting to remain downstream.

"We're planning to build rafts there and sail all the way down to Puerto Maldonado," I lied.

"Where is your friend Hector?"

I shrugged. "Haven't a clue," I said, tapping the *motorista* on the shoulder. A moment later we were cruising back into the middle of the waterway.

We stopped a few miles later, and camped for the night. It was hard to put myself in Franco's mind, but I felt as if he believed the cover story. At least, there was no way for him to call Bonanza, as they did not have a radio at the outpost, which was why Hector had suggested it in the first place.

At first light we deflated the garbage sacks and set off upstream. Everyone who had ever crossed paths with Señor Franco despised him, and the *motoristas* were only too happy to conspire against him. They said he was always giving them trouble about permits. "One day," said the elder of the boatmen, "someone will tie a big stone to his ankles and throw him in the river. Each morning when I get up I wonder if that glorious day has at last come."

As we neared Santa Cruz, we lay down in the boats, and covered ourselves with rotting sacking sheets. They ran wild with wolf spiders and stank of decomposing life. Minutes later we were heaving upriver towards the meeting point. I had expected the water to be too shallow for the boats, but the *motoristas* made good progress, easing their craft from one pool of deep water to the next. It was a fine day, the sky abundant with cumulus clouds, the sunlight dazzling as it reflected off the water's surface.

A dozen Machiguenga tribesmen were waiting for us at Mantacolla, armed with their short *chonta* bows and elongated arrows. They had seen the porters ferrying the equipment to the place of rendezvous, and knew instantly that a debt had been incurred. The tribesmen were restrained in their greetings; the eldest warrior grimaced when I ducked my head politely. He was frail and oyster-white, the tips of his fingers pale blue, as if he was about to expire. Unlike the others, he spoke good Spanish.

This time our mutual friend, Hector, was not present. I feared that negotiating without him would lead to us being overcharged, and forced to drink gallons of the wretched *masato*. I explained that we still intended to give them a rubber boat once we had finished with it, but that they would have to wait. The warriors didn't like waiting. They mistrusted matters relating to the future.

While in Cusco I had managed to get fifty dollars converted into the smallest Peruvian coin. I had thousands of them, heavy and jingling in a bag. I handed them over. The warriors shuffled forwards like cattle advancing to be fed. They seemed pleased.

"*Dinero metálico*, metal money," said the elder.

I nodded.

"*Bueno*," he said, spreading the neck of the bag to peer in. "*Mejor que el papel*, much better than paper." The others crowded around and cackled.

I said it would be easier for them to divide the money as it was in small denominations.

"Yes," said the elder, "and it is more useful than that paper you gave us last time. We used it to light a fire, but it was soon gone . . . These little pieces of metal, they have a hundred uses."

I was going to ask about Pancho's death, or express my condolences, but something held me back. In Hector's absence I didn't want to make a *faux pas*, or say something that might endanger us. I bowed again, and cued the film crew to show the same respect. Ducking our heads and smiling obsequiously, we walked backwards to the boats, leaving the tribesmen to their chips of metal.

At the bend following Mantacolla, the water was no more than three feet deep. We were forced to jump out and walk the remaining few miles. I was filled with new energy, and was anxious to begin the trek beyond the great *pongo*. The only question was, who would be our guide? My plan of action was to petition Pancho's mother to tell us what she knew. She must surely have had an inkling of where the ruins lay.

At five that afternoon, we arrived at the designated meeting point. Hector and the porters were waiting, their shirts soaked with sweat. I used the opportunity to chastise the film crew for their ridiculous amount of luggage. Then I singled out Marco. Hoping to make an example of him I emptied his bag. The hardship of the previous expedition had encouraged him to pack a few extra luxuries. These included an unopened box of Montecristo No. 5 cigars, a monogrammed bathrobe, a pair of black velvet bedroom slippers, and a bottle of vintage Armagnac. The porters looked on in wonder. None of them had brought anything except a change of shorts.

Hector cautioned us. He said that Señor Franco had a sixth sense, that he would soon work out the ruse and come after us. We had to make fast progress, he said, and get beyond the great rapids. Even then, Franco could search for us in a military helicopter, although the noise of its rotor blades would give us time to hide.

We camped for the night beneath the branches of a magnificent mahogany tree. Morale was high, the men ready and willing for the big push. I rewarded them with Kendal Mint Cake. I had bought a huge quantity of it cheaply in London, as it had long passed its sell-by date. They loved it.

That night, the flames flickered like orange ribbons touched by a breeze, sparks spitting into the darkness. I found myself reflecting on my life, my good fortune in being able to follow a path of my choosing. The porters told me they dreamed of travelling the world, but they had no documents or money to do so. I thought of my friends in Europe: they had the funds and permits to travel, but were trapped in comfortable lives.

Hector seemed to have pulled himself out of his melancholic state. I didn't want to quiz him on the plan until we were further from his village. The same went for the porters: push them too hard at the outset of the journey and they were liable to scurry home at first light. I handed out more Mint Cake and droned on about how happy I was with their work.

They sat on their haunches, chewing the peppermint squares. Sometimes they would talk about me after dinner, when they were alone. I could understand little of their conversations, as they tended to speak in their native Quechua, the language of the mountains. From what I could make out, they called me El Tormentoso, The Tormentor, and they referred to the mission to find Paititi as El Loco, The Madness.

I rose early, and sat on a stone beside the smouldering fire, worrying. An expedition to find a lost city can fill its leader with terror: the terror of sickness and of injured men, of running out of food, of getting lost, of failure.

Giovanni was up before the others. He stewed a dead bird, cooked some rice, and boiled some *peekhwaya*, a fibrous savoury jungle fruit. Out of all the porters, Giovanni was one of the best, always brimming with enthusiasm. "*Será un buen día*, it will be a good day," he said, smiling, an honest smile.

"I hope so," I said.

"Oh, yes," he replied. "With weather so fine only good things are possible."

I didn't reply, but stared into the spiral of grey smoke, fretting to myself about the passage beyond the *pongo*. God knows how we're going to pull this off, I thought. I took a deep breath, and was about to release it in a sigh, when I noticed a figure walking towards the camp through the water. It was a man, striding slowly against a curtain of morning light. He was dressed in a black T-shirt and torn blue shorts. In his hands he was carrying a bow and long arrows, preferred weaponry of the Machiguenga. I squinted hard. He looked familiar, his face vacant of expression.

Giovanni had seen him too, and was also squinting in the man's direction.

"I hope it's not the Machiguenga wanting more money," I said.

A moment passed. There was silence. The figure drew closer, his stout form now silhouetted against the river's brilliant surface. Giovanni held a hand above his eyes and strained forward.

"My God," he said. "It's Pancho."

CHAPTER
FIFTEEN

Pitching A Tent
A tent should never be pitched in a slovenly way: it
is so far more roomy, secure and pretty, when
tightly stretched out, that no pains should be spared
in drilling the men to do it well.

The Art of Travel

We rolled out the red carpet for the warrior, and
showered him with gifts. He was presented with a pair
of sturdy walking-boots, an electric lantern and clothes,
a digital watch, sewing kit, cigarettes and a big stiff
drink. I even tied his shoelaces. The very sight of
Pancho had boosted our spirits beyond all imagination.
He crouched on the upturned cooking-pot, grinning.

"We thought you were dead," I said.

The warrior took a deep swig of *pisco* and grinned
even wider than before.

"The villagers said you had run away," said Oscar.

"They said you'd been eaten by El Tigre."

Pancho slapped his knee to kill a wasp.

"They are bad people," he replied. "They chased me
away, said I should have stolen your bags. My wife went
to another man. The people burned down my house."

I apologized that our arrival had led to so much
turmoil. The tribesman glanced adoringly at his lantern

and asked to be shown how it worked. I flicked on the switch. "I have been waiting for you to come back," he said, "because I have not forgotten your promise."

"Will you now take us to Paititi?" I asked.

"*Sí*," he replied.

"And we will take you to the city," I said.

We shook hands, and grinned at each other like Cheshire cats, each delighted with his side of the bargain. I knew that if I could keep Pancho on board we had a real chance of victory. The warrior's well-being became my obsession. There was little I would not have given him to keep him happy. But Pancho's requests were modest. He asked if he might look through the Arriflex's lens, and smell the strange white powder that Marco frequently rubbed under his arms; and he asked if he could have a few feet of 16mm celluloid film. Leon gave him as much of this as he wanted, and he tied it round his neck in a crude necklace.

"*Voy a mantener El Tigre lejos*, I will keep El Tigre away," he said.

Hector found a grove of balsa trees set back from the water. The men chopped them down for rafts. As members of the chainsaw gang, nothing gave them more pleasure than hacking down healthy trees. I sometimes felt that, if they had their way, they would have felled the entire jungle for firewood.

By late morning, the expedition was on the move again, pushing through the low water with tremendous difficulty. In the five months since we had been away, the river had lost more than fifteen feet in depth.

231

Hector said it was still falling, and by our return it would be lower still. I dreaded the thought. From time to time, we were forced to unload the Zodiacs and the rafts, and heave them up over rocks. It made for a punishing routine. As before, the great advantage of rafts was that they could be slid over sharp surfaces without any damage.

It took two days to reach Aboroa, the home of Pancho's mother. She seemed pleased to see her son. The tribe had told her he was dead. In the West, she might have displayed a riot of emotion, but she merely laughed, and passed him a gourd of *masato* to drink.

"The villagers are bad," she said. "They will all die of *chamaga*."

I asked Pancho what she was referring to. He pointed to his genitals. "Sífilis," he said.

For eleven days we pushed on, fighting to cover the same ground as before. Our supplies and equipment were drenched in the river by day, and our makeshift camps were lashed by storms at night. Our feet had healed during our months of luxury in Europe, but the repair was quickly undone. Within days of our return, all of us were lame. I had anticipated the problem, bringing a jar of petroleum jelly for each man. At every rest break, the entire team would pull off their boots and grease their feet. I had presented Pancho with a tub of Vaseline, but he didn't use it for the intended purpose. Instead, Giovanni found him eating it with a plastic spoon.

Each morning the first thing I did was to look around to see if the tribesman was still in the camp. He had no idea of the effect his presence had on me and the team. But the porters did not share my fear that he would abandon us: they had other worries, most notably of El Tigre. That old anxiety had resurfaced on the eighth day upriver.

It had been a full moon, silver light charging the air with an eerie electricity. None of us could sleep, not even Hector, the soundest sleeper of all. There was a sense that something sinister, something wicked, was about to take place, like the second before a murder in a low-budget Hollywood film. I opened my mouth a fraction, to help me hear, and held my breath. In the distance there was a faint sound of branches breaking, of feet moving, a sound of fear. I sat upright. The noise was getting louder, smashing and crashing through the trees. Within a moment the entire team was awake, poised for flight. Then came the moment of death: an animal struggling from a predator, wrestling, clawing for life.

"What is it?" I whispered.

To the porters it was an inane question. They all knew what it was: El Tigre, the ghost of the jungle.

The cloud-forest had a powerful effect. It could bring happiness, a relief from society, but it could also fill ordinary men with unspeakable terror. The porters had spent most of their lives traipsing in and out of the jungle, but they were traumatized by it. They would never admit it, but their fear ran deep, like the hanging roots of a banyan grove. Hector was the only one who would speak of the hazards. He thrived on the subject, tantalizing the others with his lust for the supernatural. I asked him repeatedly to cease reminding the men of imagined danger, but he couldn't help himself. The porters would gather round, their jaws locked with fright, their faces frozen, as the Maestro revealed the limit of his fantasy.

By the time we reached Pusharo, and its wall of petroglyphs, the men were in a bad state. They might have been bristling with muscles, but they were jelly inside. I pleaded with Hector to refrain from telling ghost stories at night.

"They are not *ghost stories*," he snapped. "They are the world around us."

My concern that Pancho would leave was now compounded with worry that the porters might mutiny. I didn't know what to do. I tried sycophantic kindness, oozing praise and offering double rations to anyone who admitted aloud that El Tigre didn't exist. But no one took up the offer. They were too scared. So I tried a harsher approach, calling them sissies. They didn't like that at all. Latin men loathe having their sense of machismo dented.

Marco rambled on about fear and the havoc it can reek. He told me of the days when the KGB roamed the streets in his home town of Kiev, hauling away innocent men. "The fear was terrible," he said. "Your father might go out for some milk for the tea, and never come back."

"How did you cope?"

Marco sucked at a long, thin Cuban cigar and winced as the smoke swirled into his eyes. "We used to buy as much vodka as we could afford," he said, "and get so drunk that we passed out."

"How often did you do that?"

The Russian narrowed his eyes and pulled at the panatella. "Every night," he said.

I knew that beyond Pusharo the water would be too low to continue with the Zodiacs and the rafts. We would have to resort to carrying the equipment and supplies. Again I implored the film crew to cut down their gear, calculating that they could easily shed two hundred pounds and not feel the difference. They went through their endless Pelican cases and bags, and separated out a handful of odds and ends. They disliked cutting down, and regarded me as a spoilsport for hounding them. Setting an example, I reduced my backpack's contents by three-quarters. Then I went through the food supplies, weeding out the tin cans and anything too heavy to be taken upriver. There was no point in bringing the alcohol either, as it was so heavy. We had about five gallons of it, gut-rot *pisco*, distilled grape juice. The porters adored it, so I let them drink it all, hoping it might stave off their fear.

Giovanni opened the cans and tossed their contents into the big metal pot, along with a few bony *sabalo* fish, and a couple of ripe-smelling birds. He poured in a bucket of river water, and boiled until the stew was thick like tar scraped from the hull of an ocean-going ship. The men gorged themselves until their eyes bulged with excess. I passed out the enamel mugs and filled each one to the brim with the firewater. By the second mug the men were drunk like sailors on shore leave; and by the third they had all passed out.

Hector had crept off to be alone at the petroglyphs. When he returned, the team were lying sprawled on the ground.

"It is medicine," I said.

"*Pisco* is strong stuff," he replied, "but it cannot lessen the fear of frightened men."

Next morning the porters were still lying where they had fallen. They looked like soldiers slain in battle. I hid the rest of the alcohol in the undergrowth, along with much of my gear, and the deflated Zodiacs. Then I walked back to the camp and was about to write my journal when I saw three people approaching. They were not tribesmen, but were dressed in Western clothes, with smart khaki safari shirts and black Stetsons. I rubbed my eyes, astonished that there should be any other foreigners in the area. They were travelling light, no more than ten or fifteen pounds per man, and were moving quickly along the far riverbank. I pointed them out to Hector, who had just woken up.

"They are the competition," he said.

"Looking for Paititi?"

"*Sí.*"

They did not stop but crept nimbly past. Like a stealth force on a mission through enemy territory, they moved swiftly, with nothing more than bare necessities. When they had rounded the bend and were out of sight, I surveyed our camp. The ground was littered with the porters and mounds of luggage. I shouted for the men to get up, but no one responded. They were still too drunk to stand.

I cursed them with a deafening exclamation of fury. But, as Hector reminded me timidly, it had been I who had served up the alcohol. He tapped his hand on a stone block, inviting me to sit. "Don't be in too great a hurry," he counselled. "Haste is the enemy of success."

I might have been guilty of plying the men with *pisco*, but it was a tonic to quell their fear. I could not restrain myself from feeling bitter at their weakness. My anger towards them was matched only by my resentment of the film crew. They had volunteered to document the expedition, but their presence was now affecting its progress. I had slimmed down my personal gear to a fraction of what I needed; and the porters carried next to nothing in the way of personal effects. The food and basic equipment were bulky, but that weight was exceeded many times by the possessions of the crew.

Whenever I looked round, they were amusing themselves with new trifles, new gadgets pulled from their bags. I would pounce, ordering them to leave the luxuries behind. But they would respond sharply, declaring the devices were for the film. Sometimes I would see them pressed tight, hiding together in the bushes, gorging themselves on sweetmeats from Marco's pack. I sensed their shame, and it fanned my anger.

The day after the porters' drinking session, we moved no more than a mile upriver. I kept an eye open for the foreigners, but assumed they were way ahead by now. There was no sign of anyone at all. Pancho said his brother had probably scaled the ridge on the western bank of the river in search of monkeys to eat. It was like a mountain chain, a granite spine, enveloped in dense forest. I couldn't imagine how a man would ever enter it and hope to come out alive.

That night, as we sat in silence around the fire, I quizzed Pancho about the ruins he claimed to have seen. He grew nervous when I eased into the interview, offering him a cup of tepid tea, and praising his strength. The air was cooler than it had been for a long time, and was thick with insects, attracted by our lanterns. We sat together awkwardly, as I wondered how best to draw the truth from the warrior's mind.

In our world a simple question is so often answered with an equally simple answer. We have a tradition of asking and replying, and have rigid divides between fact and fiction, legend and reality. Anyone who blends the two beyond an acceptable point is regarded as a liar, or a madman. But the world of the Machiguenga has developed a curious hybrid of fact and fantasy, a world in which they are one and the same.

The first time I realized the extent of the blurred dividing line was that night when I spoke to Pancho. I asked him if the tribe feared the jungle. He did not seem to understand the question. Hector, who was sitting with us, explained it to him. The warrior pulled his arms into his chest, covered his mouth with his hands, and smiled apprehensively.

"*El Tigre está allá*," he said, in a muffled voice. "The tiger is there." "Where?"

Pancho drew a circle with his finger in the air. "Everywhere."

"Why do the tribe fear the ruins?" I asked.

Again, Pancho seemed reluctant to speak and, again, Hector coaxed him. "*Hay peligro*, there is danger," he said.

"At the ruins?"

"*Sí.*"

"What kind of danger?"

Pancho said nothing. He closed his eyes and seemed hardly to be breathing. I repeated the question once, and then again. "What is the danger?"

"Pai-ti-ti," he said.

"You fear it?"

The tribesman nodded. "*Muy peligroso*, much danger," he whispered.

I asked him about the ruins he had seen. Could he describe them? I yearned for him to recount the tale, but it was like getting blood out of a stone. "Have you seen the ruins yourself?"

"*Sí.*"

"Were there stone walls?" I asked.

"*Sí.*"

"Can you tell me what they looked like?" Silence.

"Did you find a hatchet with gold on it?"

"*Sí.*"

"Were the walls made of big blocks of stone?"

More silence. Hector helped me, working to extract the details. "*Las ruinas*," he said, motioning with his hands, "what did they look like?"

As before, Pancho closed his eyes, but this time he let silence be his answer. I built up the fire, so that it would burn all night and ward off El Tigre, then I crept into the tent. Hector and the film crew had already turned in for the night, and were snoring loudly. I could just make out their calm, satisfied expressions — freed from the discomfort of consciousness. As I followed them into dream-state, I saw Colonel Percy Fawcett glowering down at me. He was dressed in tweeds, layers of heavy cloth with a necktie tight round his throat. His face was bearded and serious, the stem of a briar pipe poking from the corner of his mouth. Fawcett has been a hero to many before me. He is not famous for ever locating the great lost city of gold, a place he called Z, but is remembered for disappearing without trace while on the quest. God knows what terror he witnessed or how he died, but to anyone searching for Paititi, Colonel Fawcett holds a special place. He vanished at his height, and his disappearance is almost as great a mystery as Paititi itself.

The Colonel's deep-set eyes regarded me studiously. He looked down at my filthy clothes, my sunburnt face and wounded feet. Then, in a raspy voice, he ordered me to get rid of half my men, and to keep tighter control of those I retained.

"But who will carry all the gear?" I asked.

Colonel Fawcett stiffened his back, narrowed his eyes, and barked:

"Throw it on the fire!"

With so much equipment, we were forced to leapfrog forwards, the men struggling under the tremendous weight. The only path was the river itself; walking through it fully laden was extremely precarious. It was paved with slippery rocks and abounded with hidden dips and holes. The current stirred up the water, making it impossible to see one's feet. I dreaded the advance, and constantly expected to hear the cry of an injured man. But good fortune was watching over our haphazard column.

The chainsaw gang proved their ability to endure hardship, if ever I needed proof, and exhaustion appeared to assuage their fear of El Tigre. They held off talking of it for three days.

We pushed on, each mile an achievement in itself. Morale was neither high nor low. The men were too tired to consider their feelings. Their hands were now as raw as their feet, and their legs were covered with suppurating sores. They lived from one stride to the next, unable to think of anything but food and sleep. I ordered Giovanni to dish up extra rations at every meal. The men had earned it. There were always real concerns about our supplies, but hot food was the single element that could instantly raise morale. Every two days we would pause for half a day to allow time for rest, and to butcher a new selection of endangered animals.

Early one morning, one of the porters, Pepe, spotted a pair of vultures circling above our camp. He pointed them out to the others and, before I could protest, a plan was hatched to trap one. Unfortunately I had translated a passage from Galton's *The Art of Travel* a few days previously. It explained exactly how to catch a condor or a vulture. The method was to spread out a raw ox-hide on the ground. A man lies under it, armed with some cord to tie the bird's feet, with another two men ready nearby to leap out. We didn't have a raw ox-hide, so the porters hacked up the rear end of an agouti they had caught, and laid it out on my green military poncho. Julio crawled beneath it. The men waited in the bushes, ready to jump out. An hour passed, and then another. I whispered disparaging remarks from the shade but at that moment one of the great birds swooped down to feast. Julio thrust his arms up and wrestled with the vulture's wings. The porters jumped out and broke the poor creature's neck. They plucked it immediately and revelled in their success. I was shocked that they would eat a vulture's meat, but they were delighted by it.

I see now why hunting has been so popular a pastime throughout history. It allows a man to exercise his body and mind with a chance of filling his stomach at the end of it. Alfonso had brought with him a decrepit sixteen-gauge shotgun. He and the others took it in turns to stalk through the jungle in search of prey. They knew how I detested them executing innocent animals, but the more I condemned them, the greater their slaughter became.

242

One afternoon, we had been walking almost without pause when Hector called me to the front of the procession. He said that Pancho had drifted away from the river and was climbing into the trees. "He said there are ruins!" the old man exclaimed.

My heart raced. I gave the order to stop and rest. Pancho! Where was Pancho? I ran to the embankment and peered up into the forest. He was standing at the foot of a high granite rockface, about forty feet away. I clambered up, ran towards him, and made a quick inspection of the natural wall.

"These are the first ruins," said Pancho, wide-eyed.

I looked back at the wall. It was hanging with liana, jagged and oblique. Half-way up there was a very large hornet's nest, vigorous with life. But there were no carvings or petroglyphs. It was clear the wall had nothing to do with the Incas.

"This is a natural wall," I said.

Pancho seemed not to have heard my remark. He pointed a thumb at the rock. "*Las ruinas*," he said.

I am rarely gripped by violent rage, but I felt my veins swell with anger. For Pancho the journey upriver was a jaunt, a pleasure trip; for the rest of us it was an experience charged with responsibility. The warrior moved away from the granite and gazed into my eyes, one of the first and only times we ever achieved full eye-contact. It was as if he was laughing at me inside.

Back at the river the men were lolling about, wondering what was going on. Hector took Pancho aside and enticed him to reveal the truth.

"He says these are the small ruins," said Hector later. "The great set of ruins is upriver."

But when I asked Pancho again if he could take us to them, he jolted his head to the left, and then the right. In a whisper so faint as to be barely audible, he said he did not know where the ruins of the lost city lay. If he did, he said, he would gladly take me.

We pressed on, although I no longer knew why we bothered. The expedition had developed a pace of its own, moving ahead through inertia alone. I fell into a state of deep despair, unable to go on. I sat on a stone and could not lift myself up. There was no point in advancing any further, but I was too fearful to turn back. The Swedes filmed me, bent down, broken with dejection. It was good material for them: an explorer shattered by the experience of exploration. They seemed revitalized by my gloom, as did the porters. They headed off hunting in a pack, and killed an endangered *sachavaca*, a giant tapir.

The animal was as large as a small donkey, with a long snout and speckled coat of grey-brown hair. Julio used a machete to chop off its head and limbs. Then he cleaved steaks from its thighs. The meat was flame-scarlet, shining as if it had been lacquered. Pancho spent two days smoking it over a burning termite nest. He said the roasted termites gave it flavour. The animal was cooked until it was so hard as to be almost indigestible. The porters said that only a madman would eat a tapir rare because of the worms.

244

The Swedes were delighted with the meat. It reminded them of elk steaks from Lapland. I did not have the stomach for overdone tapir, so I sat by myself away from the others. Hector patted me on the back. "*No te preocupes,* don't worry," he declared. "*Paititi está allá arriba,* Paititi is up there."

"My belief is flagging," I said.

"Pancho is playing with you," he replied. "He is playing with your mind."

Again, the old man cautioned me on the price of doubt. It could cost us everything, he warned. The only way to succeed was to believe, and to keep moving upriver.

Hector's steadfast belief, that Pancho *did* know where the lost city lay, made me realize how short-sighted I had been. I kicked myself for doubting: how could I expect to succeed if I had any doubt? I took Hector's advice, placed total belief in Pancho and vowed to go on until we found the ruins of Paititi, or until we met disaster.

The cloak of despair was suddenly lifted, and I awoke the next morning feeling like a new man. The porters were in high spirits, too, having feasted on huge quantities of tapir meat. They had picked the animal clean, and had even roasted its bones for the marrow.

Two days later we were at the place of negative energy once again. Despite witnessing the curious atmosphere of the zone on the previous trip, I put down any bad feeling to coincidence. Hector lined up the porters at the start of the day and told them they would soon be fighting like dogs. "You will feel discouraged and tired," he said, "and will gladly tear at each other with your bare hands — but resist!"

The warning, quite obviously, seeded animosity in their minds. We hadn't gone a mile when the first fight broke out. Oscar accused his best friend, Carlos, of trying to trip him up. They started punching each other. Then Julio spat insults at Boris. This time even Francisco did not escape the zone of negativity. He attacked me, declaring I was paying extra low wages and forcing the men to work in impossible conditions. Hector called the busybody to heel.

As before, I was certain the tension was nothing more than fluke. The burden of such a colossal amount of equipment was quite sufficient to turn inseparable friends into enemies. Two miles on, and the men appeared to be back to normal, if there was any normality in the wretchedness. But it was now Hector who was causing alarm. He was talking about witches and wickedness again, hinting that the spirit of the jungle would bear down upon us and consume us all.

"It is written in the Old Testament," he said. "The jungle shall rise up and slay each man who walks upon it."

Unable to remember any mention of cloud-forest in the Bible, I begged him to resist the urge to frighten the porters. His belief in Paititi was a driving force, but it was outweighed by the talk of imminent disaster. That night, as a shark-grey eddy of cloud pushed across the crescent moon, Hector addressed the men once again. They sat at his feet, like the disciples of a guru, on the riverbank. A light breeze cut through the valley,

246

sweeping his tirade downstream. From time to time the wind changed direction, and I caught the odd word: "terror", "diabolical", "revenge". The porters were crouching low, like tigers waiting to pounce on a gazelle. When Hector had finished his harangue, he slunk under the canopy, where I was scratching out my notes.

He glanced at the men, who were now whispering to one another, like convicts on a chain-gang. Then he looked over at me. His characteristic air of humility was gone; he seemed visibly shaken, as if an unbearable secret had been confided to him.

"What's wrong?" I asked.

The old Maestro pressed the tip of his index finger to his mouth, holding back the secret. I repeated my question.

"*No te puedo decir*, I cannot say," he replied.

"Tell me."

The Maestro bit his upper lip in shame. "The porters will return home at dawn," he said.

CHAPTER
SIXTEEN

Portable Food
The kinds of food that are the most portable in the ordinary sense of the term are: Pemmican; meat-biscuit; dried meat; dried fish; wheat flour; biscuit; oatmeal; barley; peas; cheese; sugar; preserved potatoes; and Chollet's compressed vegetables.

The Art of Travel

A journey of considerable hardship requires a strong team, a team with the physical strength to persevere in dreadful conditions, and the mental stability with which to stare danger in the eye. Years of sawing down the jungle had given the porters muscles that would put body-builders to shame, but their reserves of mental strength were pathetically lean. Before the night had been tinged with the subtle blush of first light, I crawled out of my moist sleeping-bag to confront the men. Their spirit was broken, shattered by the fantasy conjured up by Hector.

Giovanni was stewing up the last of the tapir, along with an agouti he had found dead on the forest floor. He would not look at me. When I approached, he pretended to be inspecting the sores on his feet. I had always been touched by Giovanni's humour, his honesty. If any man would tell the truth, I felt it would be he.

"If we push hard," I said, "we will reach the Gateway to Paititi by late afternoon."

The cook did not look up. He was poking at a slender white worm issuing from his thigh.

"Please make sure the men eat well, and fast," I added.

Giovanni swallowed hard, his face tilting down. "We are going back," he said.

"We are going upriver," I snapped.

"You are," he retorted. "We are not."

A moment later the men were gathered around Giovanni, standing shoulder to shoulder like planks in a fence. They were not smiling, and when I took a step forward, they shuffled back as if I would harm them. I didn't know what to do, what to say. Ordinarily I might have turned to Hector for his advice, but it had been he who had fanned the flames of mutiny.

I ranted on for a time about dreams and aspirations, preaching a sermon that a man must follow what is in his heart. The porters' heads were low and their spirits not bolstered by my discourse. I said that Paititi was the magic wand that could transform our lives. It was there, I exclaimed, to test us, to unite us towards a greater glory. The porters stood motionless as I raged with an invented philosophy. I threw my arms heavenward and promised them that the invisible, all-seeing force of nature was looking over us.

"It will kill us," Julio quipped.

"El Tigre," muttered Oscar.

"*No somos estúpidos,* we are not stupid," said another.

I turned to gaze upriver, taking in the screen of *chonta* palms perched at the next bend. Six pairs of green macaws flew overhead, wings flapping, beaks tweeting as they went.

"What do you want to change your minds?" I asked.

The men looked at each other, swapping quizzical side-glances.

"There is one thing that will make us happier," said Julio.

I readied myself for an appeal for more money or increased rations. "What is it?"

"*Queremos tener una ceremonia,* we want a ceremony."

The ritual was a crutch by which the porters could prop up their floundering spirits. I did not condone it, but if that was what it took to continue, I was powerless to stand in their way.

Hector flew into a rage when he heard the team's demand. "It is the phantoms inside them," he shouted. "Don't you see it?!"

"Let them have a ceremony," I said, "if it will keep them with us."

It had been the Maestro who had worked them up into such a state and now I was justifying the remedy. I strode over to where the porters were huddled, all cosy and warm, beneath shreds of coarse blanket. "You can have a ceremony," I told them virtuously, "as long as you are ready to move out first thing in the morning."

There were no smiles, no glimmers of cheer, just a gallery of scowls. I went back to my nest of damp clothing and attended to my feet. The full day of rest would allow me to dry out the rotting skin between the toes. Meanwhile, the diet of Pot Noodles and bad jungle meat had given me terrible constipation. In recent days I had become obsessed by bowel movements. I had once read that Livingstone was similarly preoccupied, and had been plagued by bad bowels throughout his great African journeys. In my diaries I noted each movement in increasing detail, with estimations of weight, notes on firmness and colour. It seems like a sordid pre-occupation to mention, but in the jungle, close inspection of one's stools makes for valuable research.

The day progressed with little sound from the porters. They lazed about, leading me to suspect that the ceremony was merely a stalling device. But then, as the half-light of dusk turned into night, their ritual began.

Oscar had trapped a black pig-like creature in a net. From a distance, it looked like a *paca*, a solitary nocturnal rodent that was always a welcome addition to the evening pot. The others had cut one of the blankets into thin strips, put them into enamel mess mugs, poured in a little kerosene and set them alight. The effect was of a dozen impressive torches, blazing with secret light. Once the mess mugs were burning, the porters called me over. They had gathered in a circle, stripped to the waist, their torsos washed in yellow and orange, their faces haunted by charcoal shadows.

Carlos rapped the back of a spoon against a metal bowl, in a sharp Morse code. The rhythm rang out across the veil of trees, warding away the spirits and luring the attentions of superstitious men.

Hector, Pancho and the film crew watched from a distance. I was planning to do the same, but Julio pulled me from the sidelines. "This ceremony is for you as well," he said.

The first phase continued for an hour. The spoon-rapping was joined by a chorus of grunts, the kind a rugby team makes before a match. Then a sharp knife glinted in the moonlight, and the *paca*'s life ended. Its blood was drained into a Pot Noodle tub, which was passed round. We each rinsed our faces in the crimson liquid. Then Juan hacked off the creature's feet. These were passed around as the blood had been. In the uncertain atmosphere, the men spent a moment or two sucking a foot, before passing it on. I cannot accurately describe the sensation of sucking a rodent's foot. I wondered who had thought up the ceremony and how it could have anything to do with the placation of evil. Once the sucking was at an end, and our faces had been daubed with blood a second time, the men squatted on the riverbank and whined like sows being led to slaughter. I followed their example, for fear of being ostracized.

It was at that point that Francisco told me to go back and sit with Hector. I walked over to the tent and watched from a distance. The ritual continued for another hour, with each man addressing the others in a peculiar high-pitched tone. Then, each one threw

252

something into a low fire, burning between a tripod of stones.

"What are they burning?" I wondered aloud.

"*Su honor*, their honour," replied Hector, "*y su dignidad*, and their dignity."

Next morning we rose early, packed up the camp, and set off before anyone could protest. It had not rained, but the river had risen mysteriously during the night, most probably caused by rain falling on the leeward slope of the ridge further upstream. The porters' faces were rusty brown with dried blood, and their hair was curiously matted. I had not stayed awake to watch them, but Marco told me they had continued long into the night. The ritual, he said, had involved rubbing silt from the river into each other's scalps. Whatever the details, the ceremony seemed to have had the desired effect. The men were moving upriver.

We walked all morning, and through the first part of the afternoon, carrying the equipment up one set of rapids after another. There was no more talk of ghosts. The porters fell into a fine routine, relaying their burdens a few hundred yards at a time. In the many weeks we spent in the jungle, I cannot remember a day with less moaning and groaning, and less dissent. Even Hector noticed the change of heart. "The spirits are resting," he said smugly.

"I don't believe in that rubbish," I replied, as we greased our feet.

Hector reached out to grasp my arm. He held it tight, crushing the bones together. "You will condemn us to death," he said.

By late afternoon I spotted a wide bend in the river, a signal that the chasm was close. Despite the team's exhaustion, I pressed them to continue until we had reached the Gateway. That night we camped on the rocks above the gorge. In retrospect it was a foolish choice. A downpour upstream would have flooded the river and we would have drowned, unable to escape. The water flowing through the chasm was much lower than before, but it was a treacherous passage none the less. To get to the other side, we would have to negotiate a three-hundred-yard trench of white water and rocks.

After the usual Pot Noodle appetizer and the main course of suspect stew at dinner, I rallied the team, thanked them for keeping the faith and staying with me. They pressed around me, their meek faces reflecting the candlelight, like a choir at evensong.

"Tomorrow we will pass through the Gateway," I said, "and we will walk into the future, with our heads held high. Paititi is close now."

The men might not have been impressed by the speech, but I raised morale by promising double wages for every day we spent beyond the great chasm. Julio led the others in a round of applause, and they broke into spontaneous laughter. Much had changed in a single day. The porters were back on my side, and we had reached the new ground. It seemed as if, once again, the expedition had a future.

★ ★ ★

Passing through the chasm required bravery and folly in equal measure. Looking back is easy, and of little help. If we had known the price of the toll, we might never have journeyed through the Gateway at all. We began at dawn, our minds lulled by a night of sound sleep, our bodies energized by a hot breakfast of roasted *caramacha* fish. I harangued the men for a few moments as they loaded up like pack mules. Most had bandaged their hands with tough white tape and some had wound bandages tightly round their knees. They said it helped them deal with the strain.

The procession left camp on the dot of nine, snaking its way through the pouring rain up to the rim of the chasm. I was somewhere in the middle, enveloped in a green British army poncho, which did little to keep out the water.

Hector was at the front, as always setting an example to the others by carrying an impossible load. Pancho, who was supposed to be guiding us, was at the rear of the procession. He kept silent all morning, even when he walked into a wasps' nest. Like the other local people I had met, he cackled with laughter at the misfortune, and went on.

The best route through the chasm was a point of contention. No one could agree on which way to go, and each man seemed reluctant to trust his life to another's plan. In the end, I overruled everyone, and insisted on the path with the least overt risk. Even then, it was necessary to clamber over a series of grotesquely large rocks, each more slippery than the last. After that

255

we were forced to wade up through the white-water trench.

The ability to tell a good route from a terrible one is a valuable skill when leading an expedition. Unfortunately for us all, it was a skill I did not possess. I had failed to take into account the invisible currents. The first three men who stepped uneasily into the frothing water were instantly carried away, along with their packs. The film crew, whose precious equipment they were transporting, whimpered like distressed damsels, as their exposed film raced downriver towards rocks.

That morning Pancho had been of little use. But as soon as he heard the frenzied shouts, he glanced at the river and took in the situation. His experience of fishing near rapids had taught him the way water flows. Within five seconds, he had ripped down a stave, calculated the route of the flow, barred the way and saved the bags.

For eight hours we persevered through the white water, gaining a few feet an hour. Rarely have I felt so drained, so wretched, as on that day. The torrential rain did not cease for a moment. There was water above, below, and all around us. It shrouded us, froze us, and almost drowned us all.

At the end of the experience there was a beach, no more than a few yards of oily claylike silt. We lay on it outstretched, exhausted, tearful and triumphant. I thanked the men for their endurance, but my words were scant payment for their efforts. They disliked me very much, but we had bonded, whether any of us wanted it or not.

Those who had the strength raised their heads a fraction and peered back at the Gateway. The chaos of rocks, grit and white foam, the waves and the ferocity of nature were overwhelming. I marvelled at it, as perhaps a condemned man might be awed by the workmanship of his noose.

As ever, Hector read my thoughts: "The executioner will get us on our return," he said.

His words were to haunt me over the next weeks: each mile I dragged the team on was a mile further to be covered on the way home. Only God knew how we would ever get through the chasm again. But then, if I was to believe Hector, the Gateway to Paititi was nothing compared to the journey ahead.

That evening, as we all crouched around a great bonfire, set back from the river on a plain of needlegrass, the old man spoke again about the danger. His words drifted into the night with the sparks. "Paititi will rob our souls," he said. "It will feast on our guts, spit them out and laugh at our inanity!"

"We are getting near," I said.

Hector spat into the fire: an unlikely gesture for such a refined man. "What do you know of Paititi?" he snapped.

"That we have a chance at finding it."

"*Huh!*"

"We have Pancho," I said firmly. "He knows, you told me so yourself."

"I said that long ago," Hector replied, "when the river was an angel."

"And now what is it?"

The Maestro wiped a tear from his left eye. "From here on, the river is Death," he said.

The first night beyond the chasm was humid, despite the increased altitude. No one slept well. I heard the men talking to each other, and shouting out in their dreams. I let them lie in until eight, to make up for the hardship of the previous day. They were uneasy at breakfast. I could sense that something was wrong.

"What is it?" I asked Julio.

"Oscar saw a ghost," he said, "in the trees ... It's there whether you like it or not."

"I do *not* like it," I said curtly. "Ignore it!"

We put on our clothes, loaded up and moved out. A tense, anxious air hung over the procession. I would have rallied the team and urged them with words of support, but my rallying talk was spent. I knew that, from that point on, no amount of coaxing would work. If I wanted the men to stay with me, I would have to drag them forward an inch at a time.

The way ahead was a monotony of shallow water, sandbanks and heavy rain. Every tree looked like the one beside it, and every bend like the one before. I marched on without thought. It was the most dangerous way to continue. When I could be bothered I worried about the threat of shattered ankles, but most of the time I didn't waste my energy.

Boris started to moan about deadlines. He said something about having shot enough film. He suggested camping at the edge of the river, and waiting for us until we came back. I wouldn't have it, and forced him to continue. On a harsh expedition there's no space for anyone who does not intend to finish. In the army such men are shot as deserters. I told Boris, jokingly, that I would have him shot. We looked at each other when the threat had passed through the air from my mouth to his ear. The Bulgarian's face was taut. "You would do it, wouldn't you?" he said at length.

"Perhaps," I replied.

We carried on and each day melted into the next. It was a routine of getting up, putting on damp clothing, eating stew, trudging in agony, eating Pot Noodles, more trudging, building camps, sleeping and getting up again. The days were filled with painful movement upriver and the nights with fever.

We all dealt with the hardship in different ways, and clung to obessions, in the hope they would help us through. I sought salvation in preoccupation with my bowels, the Swedes were devoted to keeping the Arriflex dry, and Marco thought of nothing but the well-being of his cigars. As for the porters, they became universally obsessed with collecting the spent Pot Noodle tubs, and invented a thousand ways to use them. Back in England, I had given little thought to the snack's flavours. Most of what I had brought were Chicken and Vegetable, and came in a standard white pot. But a few were spicy curry flavour, called Bombay Bad Boy, and came in a black pot. A black-market developed between the men, in which the rare black tubs were regarded as equal in value to a pair of rubber boots. I would have stamped out the trade, but allowed it to continue because it kept them occupied.

On other journeys I had found myself craving the luxuries of home, but not in the Madre de Dios jungle. I did not miss having clean water to wash in, a flush lavatory or laundered clothes. As time passed, I rarely thought of home, except of my wife and our baby daughter, whose first birthday I had missed.

As time progressed we all developed a crude routine. It enabled us to endure what might normally be considered unendurable. Each morning I would put on my wet clothing just before setting out, and stay wet until breaking for camp each evening. I had become obsessed with keeping a single change of clothes bone dry. I would wrap the sacred dry shirt and shorts in multiple layers of plastic when not in use. I never washed them; clothes hanging out to dry invariably got soaked in an unexpected shower. My dry outfit was black with dirt and it stank.

Personal hygiene was equally hard to maintain. Like most of the men, I washed in the river each afternoon. The cleanliness of the water depended on whether it had rained. If it had, then the river's silt would be swirled up into it like lamb broth, and rinsing yourself did more harm than good.

Despite the Vaseline our feet continued to suffer. To make matters worse, a few of the porters developed alarming sores on their backs. They were as wide as coffee cups, with dead white skin round the edges and shiny pink in the middle, like an exotic species of anemone. I experimented with a range of treatments, but none proved satisfactory. I would have handed out antibiotics, but our stocks had been ruined in the rapids.

Ten days after he had passed through the great chasm, Hector ranted on about a curse. He was always going on about curses and sin, exclaiming how Adventism was a defence against evil, so I didn't take him very seriously. We were traipsing through the river, making adequate headway, Pancho at the rear, Hector somewhere near the front. For once it wasn't raining; the sky was a great canvas of indigo, ribbed with cirrus clouds. Better still, the plague of sweat bees had vanished. I was about to give voice to my satisfaction, but the old man suddenly shouted out from the front: "¡Paren! ¡Paren! Stop! Stop!"

"What is it?"

I ran forward, stumbling across the rocks, and passed the porters, who had come to an abrupt halt. "What is it?" I repeated, in a low voice.

The old man wiped a hand over his mouth. "We cannot go on," he said.

"Of course we can!"

"And risk such danger?"

"*What danger?*"

"*Las líneas maldecidas*, the Curse Lines," he said.

Rodrigo had often taunted me with talk of the lines. He had said that only an embalmed cadaver could reveal the safe path between them. Hector's knowledge of the Curse Lines took me by surprise, for I had thought they were a figment of the shaman's expansive imagination.

My worry was not for Hector and his fears, but for the men. If they got a whiff of the new invisible danger, they would drop everything and run back to their village. Again, I pleaded with the Maestro to keep the hazards to himself.

"If we cross this point," he said, jerking his thumb at the ground, "we may not return here alive."

Danger is the companion of hardship. I was prepared to bear risks, but unwilling to be beaten by hysteria. Hector's greatest strength, his humanity, was now working against me. Whenever he spoke, the porters listened. They trusted his judgement and believed every word that slipped from his lips. But I sensed that his usefulness was coming to an end. He was invaluable, but his ability to incite mutiny made him worthless.

We camped early so that I could quiz Pancho and get the old man back on my side. Some of the men took advantage of the remaining light and went to hunt birds in the marshes that formed a floodplain to the river. They returned with a number of straggly-looking ducks, which they plucked and cooked.

I had stopped eating Giovanni's stews because of the fish bones. A great variety of fish could be found in the high jungle, some of which looked primeval. Their common feature was an astonishing skeleton, fragments of which would tear into your cheeks and gums as you struggled to get at the meat. All the others thought I was mad to pass up the nightly blend of fish, game and rodent.

While the men prepared the camp, I went over to where Pancho was sitting. His expression was calm, like that of a mannequin, neither happy nor sad. He was making flights for his arrows from bristly black feathers. I asked him for his opinion on the Curse Lines. He didn't reply.

"Do you know about them?" I asked, again.

"Sí," he said, at some length.

"Do you believe in them?"

Pancho preened half a feather through his lips. "*No los puedo ver*, I cannot see them," he said.

"But do you fear them?"

The warrior did not answer. In the world of the Machiguenga it was considered polite to ignore a foolish question. After several minutes of silence, he turned to me and, staring out over the river, he said: "*Paititi no existe.* There is no Paititi."

Across from where we were sitting, I could see Hector rallying the men. I could not hear his words, but it was evident that he was whipping up their fears. I rushed over, and took him aside. "We can find Paititi!" I said earnestly. "You must believe . . . If we believe, we will find it!"

The old man shook his head. "No, my friend," he said. "Paititi is a fantasy. It is a dream. It does not exist."

I found myself incensed by Hector's inconsistency. The hardship was dragging him down. He was trying to come up with excuses to pull out, and to take the porters with him. The worst aspect was that we had no idea how far there was still to travel. I started to ration the Pot Noodles, encouraging Giovanni to serve up as much of his devilish stew as possible. There was still enough dried food for a few more days, but I had to take into account the return journey. We had stashed supplies en route, but almost certainly too little.

During the night Oscar jumped up and ran off into the jungle, screaming and waking us all. I thought we were under attack. Before I could give an order or find my lamp, two or three men went after him. I could make out the sound of limbs ripping through the dense undergrowth, of panting, and shouts of desperation. Eventually they brought the boy back. He was sweating, and hyperventilating. There was pasty white spit around his mouth; his eyes were dilated, and he was trembling.

"What is wrong?" I asked sternly.

Oscar's mouth chewed at the air. He swallowed hard.

"He's gone mad," said Francisco.

I asked Oscar again what was the matter. He said nothing. His eyes streamed with tears.

"I am sorry," he said, weeping.

An hour later the disturbance was over and the team were asleep again, but I lay awake, worrying about Pancho, Hector and the men. They were all much stronger than I, much more at home in the jungle, but I had the solemn duty of pulling them all ahead. It brought out the worst in me, and they began to call me El Diablo behind my back.

I didn't like being the brunt of their jokes, the focus of their whining, but as long as they were with me, I didn't care what insults they came out with. The more they jeered in private, the more determined I became to carry them with me to the very end.

CHAPTER
SEVENTEEN

Bivouac

Bivouacking is miserable work in a wet or unhealthy climate, but in a dry and healthy one, there is no question of its superiority over tenting. Men who sleep habitually in the open, breathe fresher air and are far more imbued with the spirit of wild life, than those who pass the night within the stuffy enclosure of a tent.

The Art of Travel

By the next morning a dense fog had descended over the valley. The camp looked like the steam room of a Turkish bath but it was chilled, rather than hot, freezing us all to the bone. Hector didn't comment on the mist. The only things on his mind were the spirits and the Curse Lines. He called out a warning from the other end of the camp, but I pretended not to hear and gave the order to move on out.

We walked for five hours over the familiar terrain of algaeencrusted stones, criss-crossing the river dozens of times. The fog made the going slow and more hazardous than ever. I dared not mention it, but it seemed as if we had entered a new region.

The air was suddenly scented with a pungent citrus smell. At first we inhaled it deep into our lungs and

265

blessed its existence. But as the morning progressed, the pleasure turned to pain. It burned our chests and we found ourselves struggling for breath. I asked Pancho what plant could produce such an aroma. He said it was the scent of *tarapa* flowers.

"I would like to see one," I said. "Can you show me?"

The warrior blinked slowly. "If you look at a *tarapa* flower," he said, "you will go blind."

None of the porters heard Pancho's remark, but its timing was uncanny. That night, as we camped in the blur of mist on a long sandbar, Julio called my name. There was fear in his voice. "*¡Ven, ven!* Come, come!" he shouted.

I rushed over. Francisco was lying on the ground, a rolled-up shirt pushed under his head for a pillow. He was speaking very fast in Quechua.

"What's he saying?" I asked.

"He can't see anything," Julio said.

Francisco said that his lower field of vision had gone black, and then the upper vision had disappeared. That morning he had vomited blood, he said.

"Do you have a headache?" I asked.

"*Sí, muy fuerte,* very strong," he said.

No one much liked the village busybody, but the thought of him going blind was too terrible to bear. I suspected a stroke or cerebral malaria. Hector held a prayer session for Francisco's eyes and I rooted through the medical supplies, but there was nothing to treat the poor man's condition. We wrapped his head in cool, damp cloths, and took turns to sit with him, comforting him. He was calm, but terrified.

The night dragged on, beset with fog and an eerie, low-pitched echo that seeped from between the trees, like the howl of wolves. No one slept. The film crew and I crouched round the campfire reasoning what to do. Getting a blind man back through the chasm would be testing. Taking him ahead was out of the question. Pancho was the only one who was at ease. He caught fireflies in his cupped hands and rubbed them on his cheeks to make them glow. I asked him what the tribe did when a man went blind. He laughed at the question. *"El hombre ciego muere,* blind men die," he said.

All the next day, we delayed at the camp, which was perched on the gritty grey sandbar like the outpost of a vast empire. The fog was dense and seemed to get thicker with every hour. It prowled around us, inspecting our wretched congregation; it was devoid of emotion, and at the same time it was haunting, horrifying. You could taste its moisture on your tongue, feel it in your nose, at the back of your throat and on your chest. Slowly, quite pleasurably, it suffocated us. Maybe, I pondered, Hector was right and the place was cursed.

He curled up under his blanket and read the Old Testament. He said it gave him strength, and made him feel young again. The porters hung around the camp with the fog. They were all ready for the order to retreat, to return to their lives chopping down the

267

jungle. There was longevity in the profession, and they knew it well.

I glanced at the maps. It was a pastime that helped me to remember why our ragtag expedition was there at all. The Palatoa river was now no more than a slim streak of blue running north-west towards the Cordillera. West of it was a solid ridge; the region to the east was a corridor of blank white paper, marked *datos insuficientes*, insufficient data. It seemed ludicrous, as if the authorities were trying to keep people out. The corridor of missing data was about a mile wide and twenty miles long. All around it the detail was accurate. I felt certain that the ruins were in the blank zone, along with the oil.

In the afternoon, I showed the map to Hector, and pointed out the shaft of white. "What do you make of that?" I asked.

The old man looked down at the chart, and shrugged. "What do you want me to say?"

"That you believe in the ruins," I replied.

"*No hay esperanza*, there is no hope," he said dismally.

I slapped my hands together, indignant that the man who had driven away my doubt could not read the signs for himself. "Have you gone blind?" I snapped.

Hector was displeased with my over-familiarity. He inhaled a breath of mist sharply. "*Nos pusimos ciegos*, we have *all* gone blind," he said.

The afternoon became night, somehow bypassing evening altogether. The vapour did not let up for a moment. None of the men asked me, but I could sense they wanted to know the plan. The loss of Francisco's sight had unnerved us all. It had demonstrated to me the fragility of our existence; and it had proved to the men that malicious forces were all around us. I said we could not move until Francisco had rested. It was a weak decision, devised through my own uncertainty.

I suggested that we stay at the camp for two more days. After that, I hoped a natural resolution would rise to the surface. The team agreed that it was best to wait, especially as it would allow their crippled feet to dry out. But then, in the late morning of the next day, Pancho gave voice to his fear. He said a great storm was brewing in the west. He could hear it. We would have to move to higher ground. There was a cave where we could take sanctuary.

"How many miles is it?"

Pancho did not understand miles, yards or feet. He did not think in terms of rigid distance or fixed ideas.

"If we go, we will get there," he said.

We packed up and moved out within the hour. There was a sense of urgency, a sense that Pancho was playing down the gravity of the situation. I gave the order to stow some of the food. It could be collected later and would free us to carry Francisco. Julio wove a stretcher from saplings, spread a blanket over it, and eased the village busybody aboard. The men took it in turns to carry him. I was touched by the way they rallied round and took care of his needs.

We struggled upriver for two hours, with Pancho leading the way. The dense fog hampered progress: if you lost sight of the man ahead, you were damned. One porter would whistle to the next, but their shrill signals struggled to pass through the mist. The litter on which Francisco lay was borne forward at waist height. Behind it were the film crew and most of the porters. I took up the rear, and was the last to know that Pancho had moved away from the river, up a narrow stream. Fifty paces ahead, on higher ground, we reached the cave. Its existence proved to me Pancho's knowledge of the area's geography, and warmed my spirits.

The cave formed a natural canopy against the elements, a magnificent arc of stone, ribbed with algae where moisture ran down the walls. It made for a fine shelter, and smelt of prehistory. If it were not for the approaching storm we might never have known it was there, and would have been poorer for it. The men fetched dry sticks, got a fire going, and others hurried out to catch fish. I asked Pancho when the storm would break. He did not answer at once, but glanced out to the stream. "*Vendrá pronto*, it will come soon," he said.

Fifteen minutes later a spine-chilling breeze ripped in from the west, and dispersed the fog. Every leaf on every tree quivered individually, as if the wind was speaking a language they understood. Then the first droplets hit the earth. They were large but infrequent, and quite genteel: an inaccurate hint of what was to follow. A minute later, the storm arrived. The wind seared through the valley like a djinn released from an eternity of servitude. The trees were bent back by the force, the dust swept into a sandstorm that slashed a path downriver.

270

Howling, whistling, tormenting, the current of air alarmed us: for we all knew it was merely the precursor of the gale. Ten minutes on, rain lashed down more heavily than I had ever thought possible. The force of the downpour was shocking. Anyone caught in it would surely have been killed outright, cloven to pieces by the giant natural scythe.

The porters were fearful beyond words, as was I. Only Pancho grinned, but I believe it was his own expression of terror. I suggested that we sing songs to keep up morale, but the men were uninterested. Against the backdrop of sound — trees crashing down, diabolic wind and thunderous rain — they revealed their fears.

"*La serpiente está en el río*, the serpent is in the river," said Carlos.

"*Ella, es el río*, she *is* river," Pepe corrected.

"We have broken the Curse Lines," Julio stammered, "and will now pay for it, like our friend has already done!"

We all swivelled round to look at Francisco's poor blind crag face. His eyes were open yet ineffective.

"You will see again, I promise you," I said pathetically.

Of course it was an empty oath, and he knew it as well as I.

When eventually we gave in to fatigue and slipped into our damp sleeping-bags, the men fell into a deep slumber. I lay awake for a few minutes, comforted by the apparition of the Victorian explorer Samuel White Baker. My other heroes always appeared to be looming downwards, scowling at my frailty, but Baker approached me and stretched out his hands. His thick-set face, scrubbed clean and pink, was smiling, as if urging me to keep faith. The Victorians were masters of endurance, of succeeding when all hope is gone — none more so than Samuel Baker. If anyone knew about keeping faith and carrying on, it was he.

He never discovered a lost city, but he did find Lake Albert in East Africa, and assisted John Hanning Speke in establishing the source of the Nile. He was set apart from the other great Victorian explorers by his gentlemanliness and courtesy, and was the only explorer to be ennobled as a direct result of his travels.

While on a bear-hunting expedition to Transylvania with the impetuous Maharajah Duleep Singh, Baker attended a Bulgarian slave auction. It was there that he first set eyes on Florence, the most beautiful woman he had ever seen. He bought her, and in time they were married. Florence accompanied Baker on all his major expeditions, to the horror of genteel Victorian society. On one occasion she went down with a terrible fever, became unconscious and her eyes rolled back. A grave was dug outside the camp by one of the servants, but Baker himself kept faith. Within days Florence had made a full recovery.

The storm raged for a day and a night. By the end of it, it seemed as if a lifetime had passed. I had felt gentle sadness, total despair, and every mood between them. I was drained by emotion, cold and numb. I missed my little daughter, the face of my wife, and tried to calculate how long it would take to get to them. *Christ!* I thought, they are a world away. I contemplated giving in, ordering the retreat. I was separated from it by three words: "Let's go back." I sucked air into my chest to make the sounds. But they didn't come out right. Instead, I said: "Let's go on."

The porters choked. They were macho but I could feel their eagerness to weep. I strode out to test the depth of the river. The water was running fast, hurtling down from the ridges with pleasing efficiency. The mist had not returned; I climbed to a vantage-point to gain a better view of the path ahead. The ground was sodden, heavy like lead, the air cool yet clement. From the *mirador* I could see for about half a mile. There were small rapids, but the river was high and it was moving fast, unhindered except where a group of fallen trees had plunged across.

I called to Oscar and asked him to build a raft as quickly as he could. If we wanted to take advantage of the high water, we would have to act fast. He rushed away to find balsa trees. As I was making my way back to the camp, I heard Julio shouting from the cave at the top of his voice. "He can see me!" he was shouting. "He can see me!"

Everyone rushed to where Francisco was lying. He was sitting up a little, squinting through half-open eyes.

"What can you see?" I asked cautiously.

"*Todo*, everything," said the busybody. "I can see you all."

The relief was enormous. I felt as if a great burden had been lifted from my shoulders. The return of

Francisco's sight elevated our communal spirits. Giovanni cooked a special meal in his honour. He went into the forest and gathered herbs and the bark of a raspy russet-coloured vine. He boiled them with five or six extra bony fish and a rank-smelling bird, which had been killed and plucked several days before. Everyone ate mountains of the stew, except me. I kept well away.

The first hint that the dish had been poisonous came at sunrise. Julio and Carlos leaped up and ran into jungle, whimpering. Oscar, Marco, David, Boris and the others followed soon after with similar noises of discomfort. Giovanni was the last to succumb to his own lethal cuisine. When his diarrhoea had abated, the disgraced cook raided what was left of the medical supplies. He handed out a variety of random-coloured pills and the men swigged them down with the green-grey river water.

At least Francisco seemed much better. But I couldn't risk allowing the condition to return, and gave serious thought to the problem. Richard had once told me that in Vietnam a platoon would insert and deploy men as it moved forward. Each unit would keep in contact with the next and, if necessary, supplies and munitions could be easily ferried up the chain. I decided to adopt a similar tactic. Francisco and one man would stay at the cave, along with surplus equipment. Then, as we advanced, other teams would be positioned, with runners passing back and forth.

Hector had again begun to disturb the men. I had no doubt that he was the man to leave with Francisco, for his conversation was now endangering the expedition. I led him aside and asked if he could stay at the cave and nurse the busybody. He agreed without a breath of resentment.

By noon a single balsa raft was ready and waiting. We lashed a load to it, and set off. It was good to be moving again, even though we were now wading in deep water. The storm had caused havoc. Dozens of trees had fallen into the water and many blocked the route. The simplest way to pass was to unload the raft and lift it over the fallen trees, then load it again.

It was strange not to have Hector with us. I felt remarkably free, like an adolescent who had broken away from parental control. The porters trudged on, but I realized they were now suffering from exhaustion. I could see it in their eyes, their hanging, dark-encircled eyes. They hated me. Of course they would not have admitted it, not then, but the sentiment was in them all.

My reaction to their fatigue was to drive them harder than ever before. I was powerless to help myself. Any man who has ever led an army, an expedition, or a group of Boy Scouts has sadism in his bones. My renewed belief in the ruins of Paititi gave me strength. I found myself charging ahead, even though I carried as much weight as any of the men. Unlike them, I was fuelled by an unspeakable anger.

At dusk we camped, ate a little rice in a sour broth, and rinsed our bruised bodies in the current. Pancho managed to catch a giant oval fish even though the water was opaque. It was served up as dessert.

The next day Pepe spotted a faint wisp of smoke curling up from the high ground, far away on the western ridge. The men grew anxious at the sight of it, although I was eager to make contact. Pancho said he knew who had made the fire.

"He is a Machiguenga," he said. "He lives up there with his sons. Sometimes they go downriver and carry away women."

"From your village?"

As usual, the warrior paused before answering. "*A veces*, sometimes," he said.

Later on in the day, I found Pancho entertaining the men with the story of a fabulous land. "The trees are laden with ripe fruit," he said, "and the water is so clear that you can see all the fish at once, and there are delicious animals all around, and flowers that make a musical sound when you smell them."

It sounded like Paradise. The men asked if we could make a detour on the way to the lost city. I asked Pancho if he had ever been to the place. He smiled broadly and coughed into his hand. "*Sí*," he said.

"Is it near to Paititi?"

Pancho flicked his head in a nod. "*Puede ser*, perhaps."

Two days on, I left Carlos and his brother, Ramón, at the second position. The following night the fog descended once again. I detested it because it sucked the little remaining energy from the men. We thrashed about like flies caught in an immense web, making pitiful progress. The terrible conditions forced us to leave the raft and continue lugging the gear on foot. A more sensible leader would have turned back right then, but I had lost my level-headedness long before.

I clung to the faintest glimmer of hope, and pleaded with God to deliver us to Paititi. My request remained unfulfilled, and the misery continued. Our fortunes turned from bad to worse. Four of the men were struck down by fever, and another two developed dreadful black lumps on their thighs. They lay together sullenly like foundlings in the rain. I dismissed the injuries as a passing rash, but privately I was alarmed.

The film crew's health also declined. The Swedes had been plagued by recurrent bouts of fever for weeks, and the septic insect bites on Leon's back were as bad as any I had seen. Marco's hands had swollen, and were round and hard like Seville oranges. He could hardly use them, and had taken to eating his food direct from the bowl.

In the evening we built a tremendous fire. It lit up the fog, causing it to glow like a Japanese lantern. We sat around it, marvelling at the light, eating Pot Noodles and telling tales. The hostility that had developed between the porters and myself had given way to a curious camaraderie. I asked the men about their dreams.

"I'm going to Lima," said Rafael, "and I will marry a beautiful *chica* with long brown hair. She will be rich, with teeth like pearls and eyes the colour of opals."

The others chuckled at the fantasy.

"I will go to the United States of America," said Juan. "I will work hard and buy a big car, and then, maybe, one day, I will be President of Peru."

"What about you, Pancho?" I said.

The tribesman stared into the flames, and peered into the limits of his imagination. "We are going to the city," he said. "Don't you remember?"

"You mean, when you have taken me to Paititi?"

"Sí, sí, when we have been to the ruins," he said.

"Are we near to them, Pancho?"

Pancho looked at me and held my gaze as we peered into each other's minds. It seemed like an eternity before he spoke.

"Sí," he said, very softly, "estamos cerca, we are near."

CHAPTER
EIGHTEEN

Seizing Food
On arriving at an encampment, the natives commonly run away in fright. If you are hungry, or in serious need of anything that they have, go boldly into their huts, take just what you want, and leave fully adequate payment. It is absurd to be over-scrupulous in these cases.

The Art of Travel

Spend sixteen weeks in the jungle and you begin to question your own sanity, especially when you are the one goading everyone else ahead. I believed that the ruins were in there, somewhere; I had arrived at a mindset in which there was no doubt. It was just a matter of time before Pancho lifted the veil on the greatest lost city on earth.

To Hollywood, the idea of ruins obscured in an abyss of trees and overgrown with vines is a glamorous prospect. The man who goes in search of such a place is portrayed as a hero, bold and gallant beyond words. The reality is the other extreme. There is no glamour, no beauty, in such a quest. Even now, as I look back at our deteriorated condition, I marvel at the sordidness of it all. We were riddled with worms and shaking with fever, and all of us, even me, were suffering from terrible diarrhoea, but our physical state was irrelevant. It was a mere discomfort. Far more grave was the hostility between one man and another.

Over several days a sense of utter hatred infected us all. At first we fought against it, struggling to apologize to those we had wronged. But the hatred, and that is what it was, took root and overwhelmed each of us. I knew then that if we could not redeem the situation the expedition would flounder in the most spectacular way.

I did not understand how the team had lost hope, and why they blamed their misery on me. I might have felt pity for them, but I did not. Instead, their gloom fuelled my heartlessness. Even now, with the facility of hindsight, compassion does not come easily. We were in the cloud-forest for a reason and, the way I saw it, anything or anyone who was not working flat out to reach that goal was my opponent.

A day passed, perhaps two. We rounded a sharp bend and caught sight of a colossal *pongo*, breakers cascading over rocks. Some of the men crossed themselves, and kissed their knuckles. Oscar broke down and wept. I did not allow anyone to stop, to ponder the danger or the size of the obstacle. Instead I commanded them to charge up through the rapids. The forlorn procession moved on, like a column of spent soldiers on a suicide run. I knew that if they paused for a single moment there would be no hope in making an advance.

So we struggled up through the wall of water, the chaos of stones and waves, the slime and dissipating fog. In the middle of it, sucked down by the current, I was overcome with a sense of futility. It lasted for a full minute and almost caused my death. My eyes poured with tears, which were washed from my face and swept downstream by the unrelenting rage of water. The forest did not tolerate frailty of body or mind. Show your weakness, and it would consume you without hesitation.

Beyond the great rapids I permitted the men to rest. They huffed at the command and would certainly have mutinied right there if my order had been any different. They sprawled on a patch of gravel, panting. A flock of small black birds flew over, beating the air with miniature wings. Pancho pointed to them. "They are going to the lake," he said.

"What lake?"

The tribesman motioned upriver, where the eastern ridge swept down to the forest floor. "It is there, up there," he said.

"Is it the lake at the ruins?"

Pancho grinned. I didn't wait for a reply, but clapped my hands. "¡Vamos! Let's go!"

The porters did not respond to the order. They were too fatigued. I feared they would revolt if pressed, but without coaxing they would have given up. The ever-enthusiastic Swedes pointed out that I was losing the support of the men. "They might kill us," they warned earnestly.

After consideration, I agreed that the best solution was to camp there overnight. It would give the film crew a chance to mediate a truce. The extent of the gulf dividing the porters and myself became apparent after the evening meal. Leon went to speak to the men, who were huddled round a fire, the glow of the embers illuminating their faces. Twenty minutes of talking passed and then Leon came over to me. "The situation is bad," he said. "They are threatening to go back. They want double wages."

"But they are already on double wages!"

"They want them doubled again," he said.

I would rather have let them run off. I was sick of them all, and felt I could do much better on my own. But Leon made me see reason. "If we don't pay up," he said, "the expedition is over. We will never find Paititi."

He was right, of course, but I resented what I regarded as outright blackmail.

Next morning hostilities with the porters reached new heights. They had decided to take the day off, and wanted to be paid for resting. I am sure they dreamed up the plan to pique my anger; if they did, it worked. I lined them up and berated them for making a mockery of the quest.

To my surprise, they backed down, gathered up their loads and followed me into the river. We walked up through a smaller set of rapids, and covered a considerable distance. No one spoke. The only sound was that of the water surging round our waists as we pressed forward. I asked Pancho time and time again if we were closing in on the lake, but he would merely point ahead and say, "*Arriba.*"

We trudged on all that day and all the next. It was obvious now that we had reached the furthest limit of our resources. There was still some food, but the men were broken. They had lost the will to carry on. I felt a pang of satisfaction easing through me. It is terrible to admit it, but I took pleasure in the knowledge that I had subjugated my team.

They had started to follow my orders without dispute. None of them had the energy to contest the plan, none except Julio. He was still strong, his mind still sharp. I sensed that he was waiting, biding his time. Perhaps unwisely, I made the most of the team's co-operation, driving them on hard before they bit back.

In the early afternoon the mist returned, ebbing through the jungle like steam off piping hot bisque. It gave a ghostly aspect to the place, and compounded the sense of fear. I found myself wishing that Hector was still there. He was a madman, but he possessed an unwavering confidence, the ability to remain composed. The cloud-forest had an energy about it, a cold, calculating presence, as if it was waiting too — waiting for our dismal parade to surrender.

The men reached a slender scrap of beach, and crouched on their haunches, pack straps cutting into their shoulders. They were waiting for my signal to move on. I was about to give it, but it was then that Pancho nudged a finger at the ridge and emitted the reviled word: "*Arriba*."

Twenty-four hours later I was alone, deserted by the film crew, the porters and Pancho. The willowy warrior had led the way up the granite rockface to the top of the ridge. He climbed nimbly, a sharp contrast to my display of wheezing and puffing. I envied him, and hated him at the same time.

At the top, we parted ways. He wasn't going on. He left as quickly as he had come. The message I got from his silence was that he wanted *me* to go on. But I would have to take the last steps by myself.

I felt sure that Pancho had brought me to the brink, but he had sworn to the tribe never to reveal the actual location of the ruins. Without him and the porters the expedition was crippled, but I knew Paititi was close. If need be, I was prepared to go on alone for days. The Swedes had begged me to turn back. They had said there was no hope. I was adamant that we were on the verge of victory.

I had all I needed to survive in a kit-bag: some plastic sheeting, matches, a machete, sleeping-bag and flashlight, a change of clothes, plenty of food and some water. Once Pancho was gone, I took stock of the situation, and made a small camp at the foot of a rubber tree. I erected a canopy, tied the corners down tight, and set about gathering wood for a fire. My only fear was of *Tremarctos ornatus*, the so-called spectacled bear, but I hoped the fire would keep them away.

To be there alone in that wilderness was the most daunting yet elevating experience. I felt *alive*, truly alive. I was almost lame, my feet severely damaged by weeks in the river, and I was ground down by the recurring fever. But at the same time I felt stronger than I ever had before.

284

I passed the night quite peacefully, protected by my ingenuousness. The fog lingered until first light, shrouding my camp like a muslin veil. I slept on and off, and talked to myself a great deal. When the sun was up and the air was touched by its heat, I marched on, searching for the Inca stone road or the lake. Words cannot describe the sensation. It was as if I was on top of the world, looking down across an unending carpet of trees, millions and millions of trees. I was small, and getting smaller. The jungle was massive and, with every step, it doubled in size and magnificence.

I took great care to stay in radio contact with the film crew who, along with the men, had made their way back down to the river. Every few hundred feet I put a marker in the GPS, the limit of my skill. I was wearing gloves for the first time: without them the bamboo lacerated my hands. I staggered ahead, hoping, praying, bleeding.

The highlight of the first day was the meal. I cooked two Pot Noodles and gorged myself on them. Pancho had shown me how to take water from bamboo, but still I rationed it, using the bare minimum, and became dehydrated as a result.

The lack of water probably added to my mental infirmity. By the second day my mind was raging with a ferocious anger, a madness that called for revenge. I was against the world, against humanity, against my men. I didn't give a damn about them. I wanted Paititi. I deserved it. To Hell with the rest of them. I hoped they would rot in their horrible contortion of life. I pushed on.

The trees teemed with termites and soldier ants, and monkeys howled high in the branches, baiting me, boosting my rage. There were so many monkeys, no doubt kin of the one Julio had shot and cooked. I cursed them all. The wildlife coveted by package tourists on peaceful safaris is not the same odious life-taking fauna as exists in deep jungle. *Real* wildlife is an executioner, a barbaric devourer of the dead. It was waiting for me to expire, longing to carve me up. I could sense the jungle placing bets on how long I would survive. Every ant, termite, tapir and macaw was guilty, each vying for a piece of my flesh.

As for the others, they were cowards. I cursed them, slandering their names, even those of the Swedes. Their film had destroyed my expedition. They had stifled the search, the quest, with their ludicrous luggage. In a cruel, deranged moment, I prayed that they would all lose their way home, and pass from this world to the next in the most appalling agony.

The hunt for Paititi brings out the best and the worst. But in some people, like myself, it only brought out the worst. The fuel that energized me was a blend of anger, bitterness and bile. I spat insults, cursed, begged for retribution.

On the third night alone on that mountain ridge, I squatted on the ground in misery. The fire had not caught, the wood was far too wet. The nocturnal sounds pressed close. Pancho, no doubt, would have found them comforting. To me, they were the choir of the devil. I removed my boots and unwound the bandages from my feet, anointed the skin with rubbing alcohol, and allowed the sores to touch the breeze. The sensation was soothing. One lives for such moments in times of hardship.

Crouching there, I pondered our own world, and the notion that one only knows a place by going far from it. We live in an illusion of comfort and invented luxury. We dwell on aspects of life that are framed in absolute insignificance. Such hollowness consumes us and we forget *how* to live. The jungle was at the other extreme: a seething, accursed champion of vitality, uncontrollable and untamed.

Next morning I cut a path north-west down the ridge, charting the slow progress on the GPS. A machete is a clumsy tool in inexperienced, blistered hands. Pancho and the others had an inbuilt dexterity; most had used the long, unwieldy blades since infancy. They would have choked with laughter to see me thrashing forward in search of the great stone road.

But the road never came.

The enormity of the cloud-forest was overpowering. I was a speck moving through it like any insect marching across the jungle floor. The only difference between us was that I thought I had a vague comprehension of the scale.

I climbed a tree to gain vantage over the panorama, and stared out, my eyes streaming. I was overcome with shame at my wretched state.

A man who embarks on a journey must know when to end it. The ending had come. Perhaps it had come long before and I had not had the bravery to face it. Sitting in the tree, gazing out at the emerald mantle before me, I considered my expedition to locate Paititi. I had encountered good men, madmen and dreamers, and had descended into the *real* world to be with them.

The golden city of Paititi, last outpost of the Incas, has stood the test of time astonishingly well. Constructed as a secret haven from European greed, it has remained undefiled for five centuries: that is, if it exists at all.

I have no idea whether the House of the Tiger King is legend or fact. To the natives fact and fantasy were blurred, two inseparable elements. To them, the search for ruins was empty of any meaning. As one who had spent months in *their* world, I too now realized how meaningless it would be to find a lost city.

Epilogue

On Concluding the Journey
When your journey draws near its close, resist restless feelings; make every effort before it is too late to supplement deficiencies in your various collections; take stock of what you have gathered together and think how the things will serve in England to illustrate your journey or your book.

The Art of Travel

The last night I slept alone on the ridge I had a powerful dream that Pancho had come back up the granite rockface, found me nestled in my sleeping-bag and led me by the arm on a night journey. I had moved with the sleekness of a Machiguenga, almost as if I were floating through the forest. I had asked where we were going, but the warrior only smiled.

We drifted along for some time. I was oblivious to the sounds, to the danger, breathing easily like a man who is at peace in a hostile world. Pancho pointed upwards. I followed the line of his arm and saw a jaguar asleep in the fork of a cacao tree. Beyond it, the ridge fell away to the east. We moved past it, drifting like the souls of dead men, down through a curtain of tall trees. Down further and further until we came to a mirrored surface of silent water, glinting in the moon's light, lustrous and calm.

Pancho did not look at me and did not speak. He led me along the edge of the water, until we came to a wall built from massive stone blocks. It was overgrown, shrouded with vines, secret, vast. I asked him how we would ever scale such a thing. The warrior smiled again and motioned for me to climb on to his back. I did so and he carried me effortlessly up and over the barrier. We found ourselves in another realm, in the sacred city of Paititi.

Pancho didn't utter a word. If I had not known better, I might have thought he was smug. He led me through the remnants of what must have been a great city, the outpost of an empire. There were walls everywhere, all built with the same massive stone blocks, the roofs long fallen in, ravaged with creepers and vines. There was a central heap of stones, a sacrificial place, a site of execution, perhaps. I asked Pancho, but he led me away, taking my arm again. We crossed the city, a diameter of about half a mile, gliding over the tumbled ruins like birds in flight.

"*Te mostraré*, I will show you," the warrior said earnestly.

"What?"

"Come, follow me."

Pancho took me to a place where three high walls met at an angle like the spokes of a wheel. He started to dig down with his hands. I watched as his fingers pushed into the soft earth beneath the ferns.

"What are you searching for?"

The warrior burst out laughing: uproarious, wild laughter. In his hands was a hatchet, its blade clearly adorned with gold.

Pancho had not taken me to Paititi, but then again he had. He might not have shown me tangible stone ruins, but he had led me to the lost city, the one that lived in his mind. His world was the bridge between fact and fantasy, two realms blurred into one. It may sound like foolish reasoning, but I felt it right now to uphold my side of our pact.

A month later, after a truly horrifying return through the jungle, I arrived with Pancho in Cusco. I was unsure whether it was correct to take him there, whether I was crossing a line of what is considered acceptable. But he begged me to take him and, at the time, I saw I had little choice.

The week we spent together in Cusco was one of the most evocative, rewarding experiences of my life. And I can hope that the Machiguenga warrior gained from it as I did. The days were spent in experimentation, interacting with things that we take for granted: sitting on a chair, looking at a television, walking upstairs, eating ice-cream, driving in a car. One morning we walked down a side-street where the walls were made of new concrete. Pancho ran his hands over them in wonder, searching for a break, a cleft of some kind.

"It is stone," he said, in a puzzled voice, "but it is *not* stone."

As we walked around the town, Pancho observed everything I showed him with interest, but he remained remote, almost if he was not there at all.

I took him shopping for clothes and he selected a voluminous yellow and blue anorak, bright red sweatpants and a billowing pink fluorescent shirt. He slipped them on over the ubiquitous football strip that forms the second skin of all Machiguengas. In the next shop he chose Nike running shoes for his bare feet, and an American baseball cap embroidered with the words "No Fear". He peered into a full-length mirror for the first time in his life and giggled.

"You look like a rap-star," I said.

The warrior stared at himself, crossed his arms, grimaced and giggled some more.

One problem was that Pancho lived according to jungle time. He rose with the birds. At about four a.m. he would sit in his room in the hotel, staring out of the window as the darkness became dawn. The city might have been quiet but it was too dangerous for him to go out unescorted. Just as the jungle all looked the same to me, the streets all looked the same to him. Then there was the traffic. On his first day Pancho was nearly knocked down twice. In the jungle man has few predators, and almost everything yields to him. In the city the danger is all around, all of it caused by other men.

He murmured constantly of his dream to visit a brothel, to mix with painted girls in high-heeled shoes. He had heard that white women had large cleavages, and he wanted one of them naked, sprawled out on a

292

bed, ready and willing to service his needs. It was an obsession of which he spoke often, sometimes in the lewdest detail.

I was against this craving and wore Pancho down. I suggested instead that we visit a disco and he could find a nice girl, dance with her and invite her out. Pancho was happy because his other ambition was to dance in a room with coloured flashing lights and music that no one was making.

The warrior's internal clock struck again. He could not stay awake after seven p.m., and none of the discos opened until ten. I would ply him with coffee, and make him walk up and down. But by six thirty he had invariably fallen into a deep stupor-like sleep.

He liked his room in the hotel. It was furnished simply: a bed, a table, a chair and an electric bedside lamp. He switched it on and off incessantly, intrigued that he could control the darkness so easily. He shunned the bed, preferring to sleep on the floor furled up in a sheet, his new possessions nestled around him. His favourite mod con by far was the lavatory. I showed him how it was used on the first morning, and he was delighted with it, although he disapproved strongly of using loo paper. He thought it a waste to wipe his bottom on it, and took to winding it round his neck as a scarf. As for the lavatory itself, he was so delighted that he found another use for it — washing his head. He would bend down, knees on the tiled floor, stuff his head into the bowl and pull the handle sharply. The result was an immediate, impressive head flush. The warrior's enthusiasm did not extend to the shower, of which he was suspicious. The only time he used it as it was designed, he kept on his second skin, the blue and green football strip.

On the last day, we spent the morning trawling through Cusco's shops. I bought virtually anything Pancho pointed to. By noon we were laden with gifts for his entire family: blankets and beads, fishing tackle and extra clothes, machetes and rope, acres of plastic and a wind-up radio. I hoped that the warrior's status would now rise in the estimation of the tribe.

"*Ellos dirán, '¡Pancho estuvo en* Cusco!'. They will say, 'Pancho has been to Cusco!' " he said solemnly. "Maybe now my wife will come back." He paused to think for a moment. He folded his arms again and smiled. "Maybe," he said, "I will meet a girl in the disco and she will come with me to the jungle. Then if my wife comes back, I will beat her with a sharp stick."

We passed the afternoon drinking espresso to keep the warrior awake. I longed to ask him about the ruins again, to quiz him now that we were out of the jungle. But I knew the answers would be ambiguous, couched in mystery, just as the expedition itself had been.

By six p.m. Pancho was falling asleep. He begged me to let him go for a quick head flush and then to bed. "I'm taking you back to the jungle tomorrow," I said. "This is your last chance for disco-dancing and kissing high-heeled girls."

Pancho glared at me. A single tear formed in the corner of his eye and rolled silently down his cheek. "The women in the city are beautiful," he said. "Why will they want to dance with me?"

294

"Because you are a warrior," I said grandly.

A little later Pancho gave himself a long head flush, put on his rap-star clothes and followed me on to Cusco's cobbled streets. His hair was wet and slicked back, his eyelids heavy. He walked with a swagger, like a cowboy with a six-shooter on his hip. The air was cold, and we could see our breath. The night was filled with expectation, as if it were Christmas Eve. We went into the first disco we came to, a hole in the wall called El Cerebro, The Brain.

I paid the entrance fee, and we were frisked for concealed weapons, as one often is in Peru. A bouncer pulled apart the swing doors and we were thrust into a bedlam of bright lights and blaring techno music. The room was heaving with local youths, overfed and underdressed, the floor a skating rink of warm beer. I tried to apologize to Pancho, but he could not hear me. He swaggered past a line of striking girls, licking his lips like a hunting dog on the prowl.

"*¡Chinani!*" he said boisterously. "*Chicas*, girls."

Without another word Pancho grabbed the prettiest girl and dragged her on to the dance-floor by the hair. She struggled at first, but soon understood that the warrior was giving her no choice. I was expecting a fight to ensue, but Pancho danced like I have never before seen a man dance. He spun the girl round and round, sliding her between his open legs, caressing her with his coarse fingers, his body gyrating, his face dripping with sweat. The other dancers stopped, hustled to the edge of the floor, and watched. Pancho's routine gathered speed and sleekness. He moved faster and faster, tossing his partner around like a rag doll. He may have been dressed like a rap-star of the techno age, but his moves were pure Disco 1975.

At the end of it, the warrior was left on his knees, panting, his arms out and the girl laid across them. The applause was tremendous, as was the line of other women longing to dance with the master.

"Vamos, let's go," Pancho said.

"What about the other women? They love you!"

The warrior blew into his cupped hands. "The jungle is waiting," he said.

Glossary

Achiote: plant whose oily red seeds are used as facial paints by Shuar and other Upper Amazonian peoples.

Agouti: medium-sized tropical rodent, popular as food.

Aguaje: hard-shelled fruit, high in vitamin C, with yellow-orange flesh, popular in Upper Amazon.

Alpaca: domesticated llama, prized for its wool.

Altiplano: high plateau of southern Peru and northern Bolivia.

Arriflex: brand of cinematic film camera, celebrated for its durability.

Atlantis: legendary island said to have existed in the Atlantic, only to have sunk below the ocean.

Ayahuasca (Banisteriopsis caapi): complex hallucinogen prepared in the Upper Amazon, based on the juice of a vine that allows the body to absorb alkaloids which it would normally filter out.

Banisteriopsis caapi: vine containing harmaline, used in preparing *ayahuasca*.

Birdmen: Term for a member of the Shuar tribe who takes a hallucinogen — generally *ayahuasca* — with the intention to "fly" into another spiritual plane.

Boutou: indigenous name for pink river dolphins found in the Amazon basin.

Breadfruit: tall, tropical tree of the mulberry family that produces a large starchy fruit.

Brujería: Spanish for "witchcraft."

Campesino: Spanish for "country person".

Cassava: long, starchy tubular root popular with tribal communities in the Madre de Dios area, especially for making *masato*.

Cecropia: leafy jungle plant which induces drowsiness when eaten by sloths.

Chacapa: ritualistic rattle used by Amazonian shamans.

Chamaga: Machiguenga word for "syphilis".

Chica: Spanish for "girl".

Chigger fly: six-legged fly that burrows beneath the skin to lay its eggs; known to the Machiguenga as *uta*.

Chinani: Machiguenga word for "girl".

Chonta: jungle palm, the heart of whose inner stem is regarded as a delicacy.

Conquistadores: Spanish conquering army that subdued the Inca empire in the sixteenth century.

Curassow: various species of large tree-dwelling birds, native to Peru, prized for their meat.

Curse Lines: invisible malevolent lines supposed by shamans to run through the jungle.

Datura (*Brugmansia arbori*): member of the potato family, native to the Americas, with long alluring yellow or white flowers, known as the Trumpet of the Devil. The plant is regarded highly for its strong hallucinogenic properties.

Dengue fever: infectious viral illness transmitted by mosquitoes, whose symptoms are acute aching, extreme perspiration and headaches.

El Dorado: mythical land thought to be made of gold.

El Escorial: site of a famous monastic complex in the Guadarrama mountains, north-west of Madrid, associated with several generations of Spanish royalty.

GPS: Global Positioning System, device that uses multiple satellites to locate one's position.

Green Hell: "El Infierno Verde", name used by Spanish *conquistadores* to describe the Amazon and surrounding region.

Guinea worm: long parasitic worm, indigenous to tropical regions.

Howler monkey: indigenous monkey found in Central and South America, noted for its prehensile tail and loud cry.

Huaquero: Spanish for "grave-robber".

Inca: Quechua-speaking people of Peru, whose empire was destroyed by the invading *conquistadores* in the sixteenth century; also the title name of the reigning emperor.

INRENA: acronym for Peru's National Institute of Natural Resources, responsible for giving permission for entering restricted areas.

Intihuatana: stone post at Machu Picchu to which the Incas ceremoniously tied the sun.

Kapok: tropical tree whose seed pods contain a silky fluff traditionally used for mattress stuffing, etc.

Leatherman: brand of folding knife tool, regarded as the most durable of its type.

Lifta: Quechua term for slaked lime, which is used to help absorb the cocaine in coca leaves.

Machetero: man who cuts a passage through the jungle with a machete.

Machiguenga: tribe native to the Madre de Dios jungle region of Peru.

Maestro: master; a traditional healer or shaman.

Maloca: traditional thatched hut or long-house.

Mapacho: strong jungle tobacco used in shamanic ceremonies.

Masato: masticated cassava beverage.

Matamata (*Chelus fimbriatus*): species of "prehistoric" turtle found in the Upper Amazon.

Mirador: vantage-point from which one can see a landscape.

Motorista: man in charge of driving a boat.

Mu: lost landmass said by some to have existed in the Pacific Ocean; possibly connected with the Mayan civilization.

Nazca: desert town on the Peruvian coast, famous for the mysterious symbols etched on the surface of the desert that are known as the "Nazca Lines".

Paca: solitary nocturnal rodent.

Pacamama: species of rat found in the Peruvian jungle, known for its loud, dog-like bark.

Paititi: city to which the fleeing Incas are thought to have retreated, commonly believed to be in the Madre de Dios jungle in Peru.

Paka: thorny bamboo.

Palicio de Gallos: place where cock-fighting bouts are held for public entertainment.

Pampa: extensive flatlands of western Peru, as at Nazca.

Paracas: town on the Peruvian coast, and the community that flourished there fifteen centuries ago.

Peekhwayo: fibrous savoury fruit with a hard exterior, which is boiled and eaten in the Madre de Dios jungle.

Peki-peki: local name in the Peruvian Amazon for a dugout canoe driven by a crude motor.

Pemmican: a concentrated meal used on expeditions until the early twentieth century; made from fat melted over dried meat.

Petroglyph: rock carving, inscribed in ancient times.

Piri-piri: indigenous root found in the Madre de Dios jungle, believed to be a strong antidote for snake-bite.

Pisco: grape brandy made in the coastal town of Pisco.

Pollería: restaurant in which grilled chicken is prepared.

Pongo: indigenous word for rapids.

Pont-neuf potatoes: fried, chipped potato in the shape of a wedge.

Psilocybe (*Psilocybe mexicana*): mushroom from which is derived a hallucinogen called psilocybin.

Quechua: ancient Andean language, supposedly predating the Incas.

Quellca: fabulous embroidered patterns made at the time of the Incas, used for recording or passing on information.

Sachavaca: local name for tapir — nocturnal tropical animal with a short snout, prized for its meat.

Sachsayhuaman: massive Inca fortress on the edge of Cusco, which was never completed.

Selva: Spanish for "jungle".

Sendero Luminoso: Shining Path, Marxist organization that terrorized Peru from about 1980 until 1992.

Seventh Day Adventist: millennialist Christian sect that believes in the second coming of Christ, and keeps the Sabbath sacred.

Shuar: native tribe residing in the Pastaza region, near the Peruvian — Ecuadorian border. Formerly known as Jivaro, which means "savage". Until the arrival of missionaries in the 1950s, they shrank the heads of their enemies.

Sinicuichi (*Heimia salicifolia*): an auditory hallucinogen, from a shrub, usually found in Mexico.

Sol (pl., *soles*): currency of Peru.

Spider monkey: agile South American monkey with slender limbs and long prehensile tail.

Tapir: *see Sachavaca*.

Tarapa: tropical flowering plant found in the Peruvian jungle, sight of which is believed by indigenous peoples to blind a man.

Tia: Spanish for "aunt".

Tigre: literally "tiger", used to describe jungle cats, as well as the idea of the malicious spirit of the jungle.

Tsantsa: trophy head taken in a Shuar raid and shrunk to the size of an orange.

Uta: Machiguenga word for the wound caused by the chigger fly.

Vicuñna: wild member of the llama family, prized for the softness of its wool.

Warango: species of tree that grows in the desert of the Peruvian coast; its hard wood was favoured in ancient times for the construction of tombs.

Yuka: *see* **Cassava**.

Zodiac: French brand of inflatable dinghy.

Also available in ISIS Large Print:

In Search of King Solomon's Mines

Tahir Shah

King Solomon, the Bible's wisest king, also possessed extraordinary wealth. He built a temple at Jerusalem that was said to be more fabulous than any other landmark in the ancient world and heavily adorned with gold from Ophir. The precise location of this legendary land has been one of history's great unsolved mysteries. Explorers, scientists and theologians have scoured the world for the source of the King's astonishing wealth.

While in Jerusalem, Tahir Shah bought a map showing the location of King Solomon's fabled gold mines. It persuaded him to take up the quest to find the lost mines, leading him to Ethiopia. Shah's trails take him to a remote monastery, to the ruined castles of Gondar, and to the churches of Lalibela. In the south he discovers an enormous illegal gold mine, itself like something out of the Old Testament, where thousands of men, women and children dig with their hands.

ISBN 0-7531-6867-7 (hb)
ISBN 0-7531-6868-5 (pb)

ISIS publish a wide range of books in large print, from fiction to biography. Any suggestions for books you would like to see in large print or audio are always welcome. Please send to the Editorial Department at:

ISIS Publishing Limited
7 Centremead
Osney Mead
Oxford OX2 0ES

A full list of titles is available free of charge from:

Ulverscroft Large Print Books Limited

(UK)
The Green
Bradgate Road, Anstey
Leicester LE7 7FU
Tel: (0116) 236 4325

(Australia)
P.O. Box 314
St Leonards
NSW 1590
Tel: (02) 9436 2622

(USA)
P.O. Box 1230
West Seneca
N.Y. 14224-1230
Tel: (716) 674 4270

(Canada)
P.O. Box 80038
Burlington
Ontario L7L 6B1
Tel: (905) 637 8734

(New Zealand)
P.O. Box 456
Feilding
Tel: (06) 323 6828

Details of **ISIS** complete and unabridged audio books are also available from these offices. Alternatively, contact your local library for details of their collection of **ISIS** large print and unabridged audio books.